Look Me
in the Eye

John Elder Robison

Look Me in the Eye

My Life with Asperger's

EBURY
PRESS

1 3 5 7 9 10 8 6 4 2

Published in 2008 by Ebury Press, an imprint of Ebury Publishing
A Random House Group Company
First published in the USA by Crown Publishers in 2007

Copyright © John Elder Robison 2007

The Random House Group Limited Reg. No. 954009

Addresses for companies within the Random House Group can be found at
www.randomhouse.co.uk

A CIP catalogue record for this book is available from the British Library

The Random House Group Limited supports The Forest Stewardship Council
(FSC), the leading international forest certification organisation. All our titles that
are printed on Greenpeace approved FSC certified paper carry the FSC logo. Our
paper procurement policy can be found at www.rbooks.co.uk/environment

Mixed Sources
Product group from well-managed
forests and other controlled sources
www.fsc.org Cert no. TT-COC-2139
© 1996 Forest Stewardship Council
FSC

Printed in the UK by CPI Mackays, Chatham, ME5 8TD

Hardback ISBN 9780091924690
Export trade paperback ISBN 9780091924683

To buy books by your favourite authors and register for offers visit
www.rbooks.co.uk

For my brother, who encouraged me to write the story,
and most especially for Unit Two and Cubby

Contents

Contents

Author's Note

IN THIS BOOK, I have done my very best to express my thoughts and feelings as accurately as possible. I have tried to do the same when it comes to people, places, and events, although that is sometimes more challenging. When writing of my time as a small child, it is obvious that there is no way for me to remember the exact words of conversations. But I do have a lifetime of experience with how my parents talked and acted, how I talk, and how I have interacted with other people over the years. Armed with that, I have reconstructed scenes and conversations that accurately describe how I thought, felt, and behaved at key times.

Memory is imperfect, even for Aspergians, and there might well be passages in which I have mixed up people or chronologies. However, this isn't a story with time-sensitive components. In most cases, I've used people's real names, but in cases where I do not want to embarrass someone or where I can't remember someone's name, I have used a pseudonym. In the case of characters that appeared in my brother Augusten Burroughs's first memoir, *Running with Scissors,* I have used the same pseudonyms he used.

I hope all the people who appear in my book feel good about my treatment of them. There are a few who may not feel good, and I hope they at least feel I was fair. I thought very hard about my portrayals of everyone, and I tried to treat the tougher scenes with sensitivity and compassion.

Above all, I hope this book demonstrates once and for all that however robotic we Aspergians might seem, we do have deep emotions.

Foreword

by Augusten Burroughs

MY BIG BROTHER and I were essentially raised by two different sets of parents. His mother and father were an optimistic young couple in their twenties, just starting out in their marriage, building a new life together. He was a young professor, she was an artistically gifted homemaker. My brother called them Dad and Mamma.

I was born eight years later. I was an accident that occurred within the wreckage of their marriage. By the time I was born, our mother's mental illness had taken root and our father was a dangerous, hopeless alcoholic. My brother's parents were hopeful and excited about their future together. My parents despised each other and were miserable together.

But my brother and I had each other.

He shaped my young life. First, he taught me how to walk. Then, armed with sticks and dead snakes, he chased me and I learned how to run.

I loved him and I hated him, in equal measure.

When I was eight, he abandoned me. At sixteen, he was a young, undisciplined, unsupervised genius, loose in the world. Our parents didn't try to stop him from leaving. They knew they couldn't give him whatever it was he needed. But I was devastated.

He would be away from home for weeks, then suddenly appear. And he didn't just come home with dirty laundry, he came home with stories about his life out there in the world. Stories so shocking and outlandish, so unspeakable and dangerous, they just had to be true. Plus, he had the scars, broken nose, and stuffed wallet to prove it all.

When he returned from one of his adventures, the tension at home evaporated. Suddenly, everyone was laughing. "What happened next?" we had to know. He entertained us for days with tales of his fantastical life, and I always hated to see him leave, to let him slip back into the world.

He was a natural and gifted storyteller. But when he grew up, he became a businessman, not a writer. And this always felt somewhat *wrong* to me. He was successful, but none of his employees or customers knew, would even believe, the stories the man contained.

In my memoir, *Running with Scissors,* I devote only one section to my older brother, because I saw him even less frequently during the years in which those events are set. In the chapter "He Was Raised Without a Proper Diagnosis," I describe some of his fascinating behavior as a young man who would later be diagnosed with Asperger's syndrome, a mild form of autism. Much to my amazement, when I embarked on my first book tour, people with Asperger's showed up and introduced themselves. *Running with Scissors* contains (among many indignities) a crazy mother, a psychiatrist who dresses like Santa, toilet bowl readings, a woman I mistook for a wolf, and a Christmas tree that just would not go away. And yet without fail, at every event, somebody approached me and said, "I have Asperger's syndrome, just like your brother. Thank you for writing about it." Sometimes parents asked questions about their Asperger children. I was tempted to dispense medical advice while I had their attention, but I resisted.

Aren't there any proper *books for these people?* I wondered. To my amazement, I discovered there was not all that much out there on the subject. There were a few scholarly works, and some simpler though still clinical texts that made people feel the best they could do for their Asperger children would be to buy them a mainframe computer and not worry about teaching table manners. But there was nothing that could even begin to describe my brother.

I wrote about him again in an essay in my collection *Magical Thinking*. And more people came forward. I began toying with the idea of writing a book about him. It would be fascinating, he would love the process, and all I'd really have to do is start him talking and type really, really fast. I could keep the essay's heartwarming title ("Ass Burger") and add the subtitle "A Memoir of My Brother." Though I enjoyed designing the cover in my head, I wasn't going to be free to write the book that went inside it anytime soon.

IN 2005, our father became terminally ill and my brother became distraught, confused, and fully human. For the first time in my life, I saw him weep openly as he sat at our father's hospital bed and stroked his head.

It had the outward appearance of a touching moment between father and son. But I'd never seen my brother behave like this before. People with Asperger's don't access or show feelings, certainly not to this extent. I'd never seen such an unbridled display of raw emotion.

I felt conflicted. On the one hand, it was a breakthrough. On the other hand, it's a bit of an understatement to say there is a history of mental illness in our family, so I was worried that it might be less break*through* than break*down*.

After our father died, my normally animated and "tail up and activated" brother was depleted and sad. He started to worry about his health and consider, perhaps for the first time, his own mortality.

Not knowing what else to do, I sent him an e-mail about our father's death with the instruction "Write about it." He responded with a question. "What am I supposed to write?" I explained that it might release some of the sad feelings he was dealing with, and I gave him the oldest rule in writing: Show, don't tell.

A few days later, he sent me an essay about our father, about visiting him in the hospital as he lay dying, and the memories—most of them dark—that arose from the past. It was stunningly honest and undeniably beautifully written.

I knew he had a story to tell, I thought, *but where the hell did that come from?*

The essay went up on my website and quickly became the most popular feature. Gratifyingly yet humblingly, about as much mail started to come in about him as about me. Will you publish more of his work online? Has he written anything else? How is your brother doing now?

So, in March 2006, I said to him, "You should write a memoir. About Asperger's, about growing up not knowing what you had. A memoir where you tell all your stories. Tell everything."

About five minutes later, he e-mailed me a sample chapter. "Like this?" was the subject line of the e-mail.

Yes. Like that.

Once again, my brilliant brother had found a way to channel his unstoppable Asperger energy and talent. When he decided to research our family history and create a family tree, the document ended up being more than two thousand pages long. So once the idea of writing a memoir was in his head, he dove in with an intensity that would send most people straight into a psychiatric hospital.

In a very short period of time, he'd completed his manuscript. It goes without saying that I am swollen with pride over the result. Of course it's brilliant; my big brother wrote it. But even if it hadn't been created by my big, lumbering, swearing, unshaven "early man" sibling, this is as sweet and funny and sad and true and heartfelt a memoir as one could find—utterly unspoiled, uninfluenced, and original.

My brother, after thirty years of silence, is a storyteller again.

Prologue

"Look me in the eye, young man!"

I cannot tell you how many times I heard that shrill, whining refrain. It started about the time I got to first grade. I heard it from parents, relatives, teachers, principals, and all manner of other people. I heard it so often I began to expect to hear it.

Sometimes it would be punctuated by a jab from a ruler or one of those rubber-tipped pointers teachers used in those days. The teachers would say, "Look at me when I'm speaking to you!" I would squirm and continue looking at the floor, which would just make them madder. I would glance up at their hostile faces and feel squirmier and more uncomfortable and unable to form words, and I would quickly look away.

My father would say, "Look at me! What are you hiding?"

"Nothing."

If my father had been drinking, he might interpret "nothing" as a smart-aleck answer and come after me. By the time I was in grade school, my father was buying his Gallo wine by the gallon jug, and he had made a pretty big dent in a jug every evening before I went to bed. He kept drinking long into the night, too.

He would say, "Look at me," and I would stare at the abstract composition of empty wine bottles stacked behind the chair and under the table. I looked at anything but him. When I was little, I ran and hid from him, and sometimes he chased me while waving his belt. Sometimes my mother would save me, sometimes not. When I got bigger and stronger and amassed a formidable collection of knives (about age twelve), he realized I was becoming dangerous and quit before coming to a bad end over "Look me in the eye."

Everyone thought they understood my behavior. They thought it was simple: I was just no good.

"Nobody trusts a man who won't look them in the eye."

"You look like a criminal."

"You're up to something. I know it!"

Most of the time, I wasn't. I didn't know why they were getting agitated. I didn't even understand what looking someone in the eye meant. And yet I felt ashamed, because people expected me to do it, and I knew it, and yet I didn't. So what was wrong with me?

"Sociopath" and "psycho" were two of the most common field diagnoses for my look and expression. I heard it all the time: "I've read about people like you. They have no expression because they have no feeling. Some of the worst murderers in history were sociopaths."

I came to believe what people said about me, because so many said the same thing, and the realization that I was defective hurt. I became shyer, more withdrawn. I began to read about deviant personalities and wonder if I would one day "go bad." Would I grow up to be a killer? I had read that they were shifty and didn't look people in the eyes.

I pondered it endlessly. I didn't attack people. I didn't start fires. I didn't torture animals. I had no desire to kill anyone. Yet. Maybe that would come later, though. I spent a lot of time wondering whether I would end up in prison. I read about them and determined that the federal ones were nicer. If I were ever incarcerated, I hoped for a medium-security federal prison, not a vicious state prison like Attica.

I was well into my teenage years before I figured out that I wasn't a killer, or worse. By then, I knew I wasn't being shifty or evasive when I failed to meet someone's gaze, and I had started to wonder why so many adults equated that behavior with shiftiness and evasiveness. Also, by then I had met shifty and scummy people who *did* look me in the eye, making me think the people who complained about me were hypocrites.

To this day, when I speak, I find visual input to be distracting. When I was younger, if I saw something interesting I might begin to watch it and stop speaking entirely. As a grown-up, I don't usually come to a complete stop, but I may still pause if something catches my eye. That's why I usually look somewhere neutral—at the ground or off into the distance—when I'm talking to someone. Because speaking while watching things has always been difficult for me, learning to drive a car and talk at the same time was a tough one, but I mastered it.

And now I know it is perfectly natural for me not to look at someone when I talk. Those of us with Asperger's are just not comfortable doing it. In fact, I don't really understand why it's considered normal to stare at someone's eyeballs.

It was a great relief to finally understand why I don't look people in the eye. If I had known this when I was younger, I might have been spared a lot of hurt.

SIXTY YEARS AGO, the Austrian psychiatrist Hans Asperger wrote about children who were smart, with above average vocabulary, but who exhibited a number of behaviors common to people with autism, such as pronounced deficiencies in social and communication skills. The condition was named Asperger's syndrome in 1981. In 1984, it was added to the *Diagnostic and Statistical Manual of Mental Disorders* used by mental health professionals.

Asperger's has always been with us, but it's a condition that has flown under the radar until quite recently. When I was a child, mental heath workers incorrectly diagnosed most Asperger's as depression, schizophrenia, or a host of other disorders.

Asperger's syndrome isn't all bad. It can bestow rare gifts. Some Aspergians have truly extraordinary natural insight into complex problems. An Aspergian child may grow up to be a brilliant engineer or scientist. Some have perfect pitch and otherworldly musical abilities. Many have such exceptional verbal skills that some people refer to the condition as Little Professor Syndrome. But don't be misled—most Aspergian kids do not grow up to be college professors. Growing up can be rough.

Asperger's exists along a continuum—some people exhibit the symptoms to such a degree that their ability to function alone in society is seriously impaired. Others, like me, are affected mildly enough that they can make their own way, after a fashion. Some Aspergians have actually been remarkably successful by finding work that showcases their unique abilities.

And Asperger's is turning out to be surprisingly common: A February 2007 report from the federal Centers for Disease Control and Prevention says that 1 person in 150 has Asperger's or some other autistic spectrum disorder. That's almost two million people in the United States alone.

Asperger's is something you are born with—not something that happens later in life. It was evident in me at a very early age, but, unfortunately, no one knew what to look for. All my parents knew was that I was different from the other kids. Even as a toddler, an observer would have thought that I was not quite right. I walked with a mechanical, robotic gait. I moved clumsily. My facial expressions were rigid, and I seldom smiled. Often I failed to respond to other people at all. I acted as if they weren't even there. Most of the time, I stayed alone, in my own little world, apart from my peers. I could be completely oblivious to my surroundings, totally absorbed in a pile of Tinkertoys. When I did interact with other kids, the interactions were usually awkward. I seldom met anyone's gaze.

Also, I never sat still; I bobbed and weaved and bounced. But with all that movement, I could never catch a ball or do anything athletic. My grandfather was a track star in college, a runner-up for the United States Olympic Team. Not me!

If I were a child today, it is possible that an observer would pick up on these things and refer me for evaluation, thereby saving me from the worst of the experiences I describe in this book. I was, as my brother said, raised without a diagnosis.

It was a lonely and painful way to grow up.

Asperger's is not a disease. It's a way of being. There is no cure, nor is there a need for one. There is, however, a need for knowledge and adaptation on the part of Aspergian kids and their families and friends. I hope readers—especially those who are struggling to grow up or live with Asperger's—will see that the twists and turns and unconventional choices I made led to a pretty good life, and will learn from my story.

It took a long while for me to get to this place, to learn who I am. My days of hiding in the corner or crawling under a rock are over. I am proud to be an Aspergian.

1

A Little Misfit

It was inconceivable to me that there could be more than one way to play in the dirt, but there it was. Doug couldn't get it right. And that's why I whacked him. *Bang!* On both ears, just like I saw on *The Three Stooges.* Being three years old was no excuse for disorderly play habits.

For example, I would use my mother's kitchen spoon to scoop out a ditch. Then, I would carefully lay out a line of blue blocks. I never mixed my food, and I never mixed my blocks. Blue blocks went with blue blocks, and red blocks with red ones. But Doug would lean over and put a red block on top of the blue ones.

Couldn't he see how wrong that was?

After I had whacked him, I sat back down and played. Correctly.

Sometimes, when I got frustrated with Doug, my mother would walk over and yell at me. I don't think she ever saw the terrible things *he* did. She just saw me whack him. I could usually ignore her, but if my father was there, too, he would get really mad and shake me, and then I would cry.

Most of the time, I liked Doug. He was my first friend. But some of the things he did were just too much for me to handle. I would park my truck by a log, and he would kick dirt on it. Our moms would give us blocks, and he would heap his in a sloppy pile and then giggle about it. It drove me wild.

Our playdates came to an abrupt end the following spring. Doug's father graduated from medical school and they moved far, far away to an Indian reservation in Billings, Montana. I didn't really understand that he could leave despite my wishes to the contrary. Even if he didn't know how to play correctly, he was my only regular playmate. I was sad.

I asked my mother about him each time we went to the park, where I now played alone. "I'm sure he'll send you a postcard," my mother said, but she had a funny look on her face, and I didn't know what to make of it. It was troubling.

I did hear the mothers whispering, but I never knew what they meant.

". . . drowned in an irrigation ditch . . ."

". . . the water was only six inches deep . . ."

". . . must have fallen on his face . . ."

". . . his mother couldn't see him, so she went outside and found him there . . ."

What is an irrigation ditch? I wondered. All I could figure out was, they weren't talking about me. I had no idea Doug was dead until years later.

Looking back, maybe my friendship with Doug wasn't the best omen. But at least I stopped whacking other kids. Somehow I figured out that whacking does not foster lasting friendship.

That fall, my mother enrolled me at Philadelphia's Mulberry Tree Nursery School. It was a small building with kids' drawings on the walls and a dusty playground enclosed with a chain-link fence. It was the first place where I was thrown together with children I didn't know. It didn't go well.

At first, I was excited. As soon as I saw the other kids, I wanted to meet them. I wanted them to like me. But they didn't. I could not figure out why. What was wrong with me? I particularly wanted to make friends with a little girl named Chuckie. She seemed to like trucks and trains, just like me. I knew we must have a lot in common.

At recess, I walked over to Chuckie and patted her on the head. My mother had shown me how to pet my poodle on the head to make friends with him. And my mother petted me sometimes, too, especially when I couldn't sleep. So as far as I could tell, petting worked. All the dogs my mother told me to pet had wagged their tails. They liked it. I figured Chuckie would like it, too.

Smack! She hit me!

Startled, I ran away. *That didn't work,* I said to myself. *Maybe I have to pet her a little longer to make friends. I can pet her with a stick so she can't smack me.* But the teacher intervened.

"John, leave Chuckie alone. We don't hit people with sticks."

"I wasn't hitting her. I was trying to pet her."

"People aren't dogs. You don't pet them. And you don't use sticks."

Chuckie eyed me warily. She stayed away for the rest of the day. But I didn't give up. *Maybe she likes me and doesn't know it,* I thought. My mother often told me I would like things I thought I wouldn't, and sometimes she was right.

The next day, I saw Chuckie playing in the big sandbox with a wooden truck. I knew a lot about trucks. And I knew she wasn't playing with her truck correctly. I would show her the right way. *She will admire me and we will be friends,* I thought. I walked over to her and took the truck away and sat down.

"Miss Laird! John took my truck!"

That was fast!

"I did not! I was showing her how to play with it! She was doing it wrong!" But Miss Laird believed Chuckie, not me. She led me away and gave me a truck of my own. Chuckie didn't follow. But tomorrow was another day. Tomorrow, I would succeed in making friends.

When tomorrow came, I had a new plan. I would talk to Chuckie. I would tell her about dinosaurs. I knew a lot about dinosaurs, because my father took me to the museum and showed me. Sometimes I had scary dreams about them, but overall, dinosaurs were the most interesting thing I knew of.

I walked over to Chuckie and sat down.

"I like dinosaurs. My favorite is the brontosaurus. He's really big."

Chuckie did not respond.

"He's really big but he just eats plants. He eats grass and trees.

"He has a long neck and a long tail."

Silence.

"He's as big as a bus.

"But an allosaurus can eat him."

Chuckie still didn't say anything. She looked intently at the ground, where she was drawing in the sand.

"I went to see the dinosaurs at the museum with my dad.

"There were little dinosaurs, too.

"I really like dinosaurs. They're neat!"

Chuckie got up and went inside. She had completely ignored me!

I looked down at the ground where she had been staring. *What was she looking at that was so interesting?* There was nothing there.

All my attempts to make a friend had failed. I was a failure. I began to cry. Alone in the corner of the playground, I sobbed and smashed the toy truck into the ground again and again and again, until my hands hurt too much to do it anymore.

At the end of recess, I was still there, sitting by myself. Staring into the dirt. Too humiliated to face the other kids. *Why don't they like me? What's wrong with me?* That was where Miss Laird found me.

"It's time to go back inside." She grabbed my little paw and towed me in. I wanted to roll up in a ball and disappear.

RECENTLY, ONE OF my friends read the passage above and said, "Shit, John, you're still that way now." He's right. I am. The only real difference is that I have learned what people expect in common social situations. So I can act more normal and there's less chance I'll offend anyone. But the difference is still there, and it always will be.

People with Asperger's or autism often lack the feelings of empathy that naturally guide most people in their interactions with others. That's why it never occurred to me that Chuckie might not respond to petting in the same way a dog would. The difference between a small person and a medium-sized dog was not really clear to me. And it never occurred to me that there might be more than one way to play with a toy truck, so I could not understand why she objected to my showing her.

The worst of it was, my teachers and most other people saw my behavior as bad when I was actually trying to be kind. My good intentions made the rejection by Chuckie all the more painful. I'd watched my parents talk to other grown-ups and I figured I could talk to Chuckie. But I had overlooked one key thing: *Successful conversations require a give and take between both people.* Being Aspergian, I missed that. Totally.

I never interacted with Chuckie again.

I stopped trying with any of the kids. The more I was rejected, the more I hurt inside and the more I retreated.

I had better luck dealing with grown-ups. My disjointed replies didn't bring the conversation to an abrupt halt. And I tended to listen to them more than I listened to kids, because I assumed they knew more. Grown-ups did grown-up things. They didn't play with toys, so I didn't have to show them *how* to play. If I tried to pet a grown-up with a stick, he'd take it away. He wouldn't humiliate me by yelling and running to the teacher. Grown-ups explained things to me, so I learned from them. Kids weren't so good at that.

Most of the time, I played by myself, with my toys. I liked the more complex toys, especially blocks and Lincoln Logs. I still remember the taste of Lincoln Logs. When I wasn't chewing them, I made forts and houses and fences. When I got a little bigger, I got an Erector Set. I was very proud of that. I built my first machines with the Erector Set.

Machines were never mean to me. They challenged me when I tried to figure them out. They never tricked me, and they never hurt my feelings. I was in charge of the machines. I liked that. I felt safe around them. I also felt safe around animals, most of the time. I petted other people's dogs when we went to the park. When I got my poodle, I made friends with him, too.

"Look what your grandpa Jack sent you, John Elder!" (My parents named me John Elder Robison to honor my great-grandpa John Glenn Elder, who died before I was born.) My dad had brought home a wooly, ill-tempered, and probably genetically defective dog, most likely a reject from some dog pound. But I didn't know that. I was fascinated. He growled at me and wet the floor when my father put him down.

I wasn't scared of him, because he was considerably smaller than me. I had not yet learned that sharp teeth can come in small packages.

"Poodles are very smart dogs," my father told me.

Maybe he was smart, but he wasn't very friendly. I named him Poodle, beginning a long tradition of functional pet naming. I didn't really know what to do with a dog, and I was always squeezing him and grabbing his tail and yanking in an effort to figure that out. He bit me whenever I yanked too hard. Sometimes he bit hard enough to make my arms bleed, and I would cry. Years later, I told that story to my mother, who said, "John Elder, Poodle never bit you hard enough to make your arms bleed! If he had, that would have been the end of Poodle in our house." All I could say to that was "Little bites are a *big* deal to little people." And that's how I remember it.

Once, I locked him in my room and he got out. He chewed a dog-sized hole in the bedroom door. We found him lying in the sun in the backyard.

Seeing that, I tried chewing the door myself. My teeth barely made a dent in the paint. I didn't even manage to bite a splinter out of the wood. I realized that Poodle had very sharp teeth. I learned to put my toys away before I went to bed every night. If I forgot, Poodle would come in during the night and eat them.

My parents didn't like Poodle because he ate their furniture. Despite that, Poodle and I slowly became friends. I was always a little wary of him, though, because I never knew what he'd do.

Our home wasn't very happy. The dog ate my toys and snapped, and my parents always fought. One night, I awoke to them yelling at each other in the next room. They often fought at night when they thought I was asleep. It was always stressful and unsettling to me, but this time was different. My mother was crying in addition to yelling. She didn't usually cry.

"Momma!" I yelled loud to make sure she heard me.

"It's okay, John Elder, go to sleep." She came in and patted me on the head, but she went right back out.

I didn't like that at all. Usually, she sat with me, and petted me, and sang to me till I fell asleep. *Where did she go? What's going on?*

The loud fights were disturbing because I was sure they were fighting about me, and I knew if they got tired of me they could just leave me somewhere to fend for myself. I thought, *I have to be really good, so they won't get rid of me.*

So I tried to be very quiet and act asleep. I figured that's what they expected.

"He'll go back to sleep," my mother said, quietly. Hearing that, I was wide awake, and even more scared.

"No, he won't," my father cried. "He'll remember this night when he's forty." And then he started sobbing, too. Anything that made both of them cry must be very, very bad.

"Daddy! Don't make Momma cry!" I could not help myself. I wanted to hide under the bed but I knew they'd find me. I was terrified.

My mother came back in and sang softly to me, but she sounded funny. After a few minutes, though, I fell into a troubled sleep.

Much later, I learned that my father had been having an affair with a secretary from the German department at the university where he was studying. My mother told me she looked just like her. I guess the affair unraveled that night, and my parents' marriage unraveled some more, too. That was when my father started to turn mean.

When I woke up the next morning, he was still in bed. He wasn't at school. "Your father is tired," my mother said. "He's resting." I walked over to him. He smelled normal, and he was snoring. I left him alone and my mother walked me to school like she always did.

When I got home from school, my father was gone. And that night, he didn't come home.

"Where is my dad?"

"Your father is in the hospital," my mother said, in a strained voice.

"Like when he broke his arm?" I asked hopefully.

The year before, my father had fallen on the icy sidewalk in front of our house. Luckily for us, the University of Pennsylvania Hospital was just a few blocks from where we lived. I didn't like the smell of the place, though, and I was already suspicious of the doctors there because they gave me shots. It was bad that he was in there.

"Yes, it's like when he broke his arm. We'll go see him tomorrow. He's gotten exhausted by his schoolwork and he needs to rest."

That left me feeling anxious, since I got tired and took naps every day. *What if I wake up in the hospital?* I was almost too scared to take a nap again. I was scared to go to sleep that night, too.

When my mother took me to see him, a nurse with a key let us into his room. I had not realized they could lock people up in a hospital. I resolved to be even more careful whenever my mom took me to the doctor. The visit was unsettling, because he didn't smell right, and he didn't act quite right.

My father did smile when he saw me. He said, "Hey, son, come here!" He grabbed me and picked me up, which made me very anxious. He squeezed me and his face was all scratchy. "I'll be okay. I'll be home soon," he said. He put me down and I backed away.

He ended up "resting" for a whole month. He still looked tired when he came home.

Shortly after my father came back, my mother took me on a vacation to see her parents in Georgia. I didn't like it much down there. The house smelled like old wooden matches, and the water tasted funny.

"It's the sulfur in the water," they said, but no one could tell me *why* they put sulfur in the water down there.

When we got back from Georgia, my dog was gone.

"Where's Poodle?" I asked. I was alarmed.

"He ran away," my father said. But he didn't sound right. I wondered what had really happened.

"Did you do something to Poodle?" I asked him.

"No!" he shouted. "Your dog ran away!" His sudden yelling scared me.

I knew then that my father had done something bad to my dog, but I didn't know what, and I was afraid to ask. I was much more afraid of my father after that. That fear lasted until I became a teenager and was able to defend myself.

As my parents fought more, my father got meaner. Especially at night. He was nastiest then, because he had started drinking wine. If he got mad at me, he'd spank me. Really hard. Or else he'd pick me up and shake me. I thought my head might come off.

After my father graduated, it was time for him to find a job. The one he picked was all the way across the country, in Seattle, Washington. It took us a whole month to drive there, in our black VW Bug. I really liked that VW. I still have a picture of myself standing by the front bumper. I used to crawl into the well behind the backseat to hide. I'd look out the back window at the sky and imagine I was flying through space.

It's been many years since I could fit into a space that small.

I liked squeezing myself up tight in a tiny ball when I was little, hiding where no one could see me. I still like the feeling of lying under things and having them press on me. Today, when I lie on the bed I'll pile the pillows on top of me because it feels better than a sheet. I've heard that's common with autistic people. I was certainly happy back there in the VW, curled up in a little ball on that scratchy gray carpet.

It was a great time. There were no other kids to hurt my feelings. My mom and dad talked to me all day. Best of all, there was no fighting at night. And there were fun new things to see all the time, like Mount Rushmore. I was impressed by the presidents carved in the side of the mountain, but I was even more excited when I found there was an Indian reservation at the base.

"Can we see Doug?" I asked.

"This isn't the reservation his parents moved to." My mom had a sad look. "They moved to Montana, and this is South Dakota. They're a long way from here."

When we arrived in Seattle, we moved into an apartment complex that was full of more kids than I had ever seen. As soon as I saw them, I wanted to go outside and join in, to be part of the kid pack. But it didn't work out that way.

The leader of the kid pack was a six-year-old named Ronnie Ronson. He was almost two years older than me, a really big kid. Ronnie and his kid pack played cowboys and Indians. They would run back and forth across the grassy square in the middle of our apartment complex, shouting, "Gitty up, gitty up, Ronson's cowboys." They waved lariats and shot cap guns as they ran back and forth. It was very exciting. I wanted to be part of it.

I tried running back and forth with them.

"What are you doing? You aren't a cowboy!" *What?* I looked at him, and I looked at myself. *Why was he a cowboy and I wasn't?*

I said, "I am too a cowboy!"

"No, you're not! You're a monkey face!" And he ran off. As I stood there, Ronnie's cowboys ran back and forth past me, saying, "Monkey Face!" every time they went by.

They would never let me be a cowboy. I was angry, and sad, and humiliated. I would never fit in. Why was I alive? I ran back to our apartment, crying. My mother picked me up and sat me in her lap.

"What's wrong?"

"I just don't know how to make friends," I sobbed. "No one likes me."

My mother didn't know what to say, but she petted me, and I calmed down. I looked out the window at Ronson's cowboys, and then sat down to work on Chippy, my tractor. Chippy was never mean to me. I always got along with machines. Even back then.

Our time in Seattle was probably the best family time of my childhood, even though I didn't have much luck making friends. My father took us camping almost every weekend. He showed me how to be a woodsman. We looked at books together, especially the *Boy Scout Woodsman* manual. I can still remember the pictures that showed how to make a trap, and the correct way to step over a fallen log.

I dreamed about trapping wolves and bears, but garter snakes and frogs were as close as I got. And I've never forgotten the woodsman's log-crossing techniques that I learned at five.

I was happy to discover that there were woods behind our apartment in Seattle. I liked it in the woods. When I was sad, I would go there and sit and think, and I would do woodsman things. That always made me feel better.

The woods seemed vast to me, but they were really only a few hundred feet deep. I know they didn't seem so huge to my parents, because they always told me not to go all the way through them and get onto Aurora, the big highway on the other side. They told me the highway went all the way to Alaska.

"Don't you go out by the highway. Someone might steal my baby boy!" I didn't want to be stolen, so I stayed clear.

There were a few other kids that weren't part of Ronnie's pack, and I got to know them slowly. We were the runts of the litter, the misfits. One of the other misfits—mostly due to his small size— was Jeff Crane, who was a year and a half younger than me. Jeff's mother became friendly with my mother, and we used to go to their apartment and visit. Jeff had big brothers and a big sister, too, but they weren't interested in us. So we played together.

Since I was older, I knew more than he did. I showed him things, like frogs and plants and how to make forts—all the things a five-year-old knows and a three-year-old wants to learn. Some-times we caught small snakes and put them in glass jars. Jeff's older brother came out and helped with snake catching. We had to punch holes in the metal tops so they could breathe.

Doing things with Jeff showed me that littler kids would look up to me as a teacher. I felt good about that. Of course, kids always think they know the answers. The difference in my case was that most of the time, I actually did. Even at five, I was beginning to understand the world of things better than the world of people.

When we moved from Seattle to Pittsburgh the next year, I gave Chippy to Jeff. Chippy was the first valuable thing I owned, and the first thing I gave away, but it seemed right because Jeff was my first real friend. He was younger than me, but he was smart, and he looked up to me, and he didn't make fun of me like the bigger kids. Besides, I was almost too big to drive Chippy anymore, and my parents had said they'd get me a bike when we got to Pittsburgh. I knew that having a bike was a sign of being a Big Kid. And maybe when I was a Big Kid, the other kids would like me.

2

A Permanent Playmate

"John Elder, we're going to move back to Pennsylvania," my father announced one day when he came home from school. I was more interested in the pile of silver dollars I had just discovered in his drawer. They were old and heavy, and some were from the 1880s. But he insisted on telling me about moving. He took the silver dollar out of my hand and said it again.

"John Elder, we're moving soon!"

Taking the silver dollar away did get my attention. But as I think back on events like this, I realize my parents were not always very affectionate toward me. Did they even want a child? I'll never know.

With my attention now on my father, I asked, "Are we moving to the same place we lived before?"

"No, this time it's Pittsburgh," my father said. He thought he'd found a permanent job. I'd be starting first grade in the Pittsburgh schools, with a new pack of kids. I was sad to say good-bye to my friend Jeff, but I wasn't very happy in Seattle, so I didn't mind moving away.

I had learned something from my humiliations at the hands of Ronnie Ronson and Chuckie and all the other kids I'd tried and failed to make friends with. I was starting to figure out that I was different. But I had a positive outlook. I would make the best of my lot in life as a defective child.

In Pittsburgh, I finally started learning how to make friends. I knew now that kids and dogs were different. I didn't try to pet kids anymore, or poke them with sticks. And at nine years of age, I had a life-changing revelation.

I figured out how to talk to other children.

I suddenly realized that when a kid said, "Look at my Tonka truck," he expected an answer that made sense in the context of what he had said. Here were some things I might have said prior to this revelation in response to "Look at my Tonka truck":

a) "I have a helicopter."
b) "I want some cookies."
c) "My mom is mad at me today."
d) "I rode a horse at the fair."

I was so used to living inside my own world that I answered with whatever I had been thinking. If I was remembering riding a horse at the fair, it didn't matter if a kid came up to me and said, "Look at my truck!" or "My mom is in the hospital!" I was still going to answer, "I rode a horse at the fair." The other kid's words did not change the course of my thoughts. It was almost like I didn't hear him. But on some level, I did hear, because I responded. Even though the response didn't make any sense to the person speaking to me.

My new understanding changed that. All of a sudden, I realized that the response the kid was looking for, the correct answer, was:

e) "That's a neat truck! Can I hold it?"

Even more important, I realized that responses A, B, C, and D would annoy the other kid. With my newfound social brilliance, I understood why Ronnie's cowboys hadn't wanted to talk to me.

Maybe that was why Chuckie had ignored me, too. (Or maybe Chuckie was just another defective kid, like me. After all, she did like trucks, and she did look at the dirt when I talked.)

After I suddenly got it, my answers made sense—most of the time. I wasn't ready to be the life of the party, but I was able to participate. Conversations no longer came to a screeching halt. Things were getting better.

In some ways, the grown-ups around me had actually kept me from figuring this out sooner. Adults—almost all family members or friends of my parents—would approach me and say something to start a conversation. If my response made no sense, they never told me. They just played along. So I never learned how to carry on a conversation from talking to grown-ups, because they just adapted to whatever I said. Kids, on the other hand, got mad or frustrated.

How do normal kids figure this out? They learn it from seeing how other kids react to their words, something my brain is not wired to do. I have since learned that kids with Asperger's don't pick up on common social cues. They don't recognize a lot of body language or facial expressions. I know I didn't. I only recognized pretty extreme reactions, and by the time things were extreme, it was usually too late.

With my incredible new skills, I made friends right away. I met the Meyers girls across the street, Christine and Lisa. I made friends with Lenny Persichetti, five doors down. We formed a kid pack, playing hide-and-seek and building forts in the woods. We hung out in the garage behind our house, where some older kids had formed a band. My new friends and I roamed the neighborhood, exploring things without our parents for the first time. Lenny and I found abandoned castles and ruins and ancient machinery hidden in the woods of Frick Park. There were all sorts of things to explore.

That summer, we became Big Kids. We were free. No one was watching us. I loved it, because all of a sudden, I was no longer alone. Then I got another big surprise.

"John Elder, I'm going to have a baby!" my mother said.

I didn't know what to say. Would it be a sister, I wondered? I hoped not. What good would a little sister be? A brother would be better. Yes. A little brother! For me! I would have my own permanent playmate.

Mom got bigger and bigger and I was able to listen to the baby inside. I was excited.

On the day the baby was born, my mother's brother Mercer came and stayed with me while my parents went to the hospital. I couldn't wait to see my new brother. My uncle drove me to the hospital to see him for the first time. He was just a few hours old.

"Christopher Richter Robison. What a beautiful baby boy!"

"Do you want to hold him?" My mother was holding him against her. He was tiny, smaller than I'd imagined.

"Will he get bigger?" Maybe he was a dwarf.

"You were the same size when you were born," my mother said. It was hard to believe, but if I was that small once he would probably grow up, too.

He was all red and kept his eyes closed most of the time. My mother handed him to me. I expected him to struggle, like when I picked up a dog or a cat, but he didn't do anything. I couldn't really even feel him, all wrapped up in a blanket. It was very different from picking up the dog. My own little brother. I was very excited, but I was careful not to show it, so they wouldn't take him away from me.

He came home wrapped in a yellow blanket, and my mother put him in a crib across the hall from me. I went in and watched him, but he didn't do anything. I looked at him, and sometimes he looked back at me, but mostly he slept. He was neat.

"Be careful. You have to support his head." I squeezed him against me so he wouldn't fall. I was always afraid his neck would break like my mother had said it could. But it never did.

I looked down at him. "Can you say anything?"

He snorted.

"Is that it?" I poked him in the nose the way I'd seen my parents do. He yelled. Quickly, I picked him up and rocked him back and forth. He quieted down, and snorted some more.

"I'll call you Snort," I said. Now he had a name.

I built a tall crane with my Erector Set and I lifted blocks up to his crib. I began moving wooden blocks from floor to crib. I was hoping Snort would play with them, but he just stared.

"Look, Snort, I'm lifting blocks for you." Snort watched them rise and fall.

"Mom, look, I made Snort a crane!" I was jealous, because my mother spent all her time with Snort. She had never ignored me before.

"That's very nice, John Elder." My mother followed me to Snort's crib, and she admired my crane. I even lifted some blocks for her, and she took my picture. But she seemed fixated on his name. "Your brother's name isn't Snort. It's Christopher. Or Chris." She had not yet realized that I would never call him Christopher or Chris. I didn't know it myself at that time, but for some reason I had a hard time with names, unless I made them up.

I brought my friends over to see my new brother. "This is my little brother. His name is Snort." They were impressed. None of them had a baby brother. I couldn't make him do much yet, but I knew he'd get bigger and then he'd be able to do things. I was proud of him.

A year passed, and he did learn more tricks. I taught him some, and he learned others on his own. At one year of age, he wasn't really useful for anything yet, but I could see the potential. Meanwhile, our parents were fighting even more, and they were talking about moving. I wished Snort would get bigger so I could talk to him and have him answer back.

"Your father has been looking for a permanent teaching job. We're looking at two schools. One is in Austin, Texas. The other is in Amherst, Massachusetts." My father had been looking for that permanent job for a few years now. More and more, my mother was doing the talking. My father was silent.

He was getting meaner, too. He had started drinking something called sherry. I tried it but immediately spat it out. I could not imagine why he wanted to drink glass after glass of the stuff, but he did. He sat by himself at the kitchen table and drank, and got meaner as it got later. I was learning to stay away from him in the evening.

I had never been to Amherst or Austin. But from my reading, I knew Austin was home to poisonous snakes and Gila monsters. It was hot and dry. "Let's go to Amherst," I said. My parents agreed.

Once again we moved. This time we ended up in Hadley, Massachusetts, a farming community about six miles from the University of Massachusetts at Amherst. My parents had both grown up in the country, but all my life we'd lived in cities. Now we were in the country. I was excited. We moved into an old farmhouse.

"It was built in 1743. It's one of the oldest houses in town, John Elder." My mother seemed proud of that.

There were cows in the front and crops out back. My mother introduced me to the landlords, Mr. and Mrs. Barstow. They seemed nice. Mr. Barstow was the farmer who owned all the fields around us. And best of all, his brother owned the farm next door, and they had four kids I could play with. With my refined interpersonal skills, I actually made friends in Hadley right away. By the time school started, I even had buddies to sit with on the bus. I had never ridden a bus before, but I didn't tell them that. I had learned not to reveal anything that might subject me to more ridicule than I already got.

There was a mountain behind us, and the Connecticut River was visible through the trees across the road. It was the prettiest place we'd lived. After school, the Barstow kids and I climbed the mountain and looked for amethysts. "They're purple. They're precious stones, like rubies," Dave Barstow said.

Snort was getting bigger, too. He had learned how to sit up on his own, and he crawled around after me. He lived in a pen with rubber mesh sides. I took him out when he yelled and if he became a pest I put him back. Occasionally, I would flip his pen upside down so Snort was in a jail with a roof. He didn't like that.

I decided to teach Snort to walk, in the squash field alongside the house. The plowed dirt was soft, so it wouldn't hurt if he fell. Plus, he was small and didn't have far to fall anyway. I would hold his little paw and we'd walk down the rows to the end of the field. Then we'd turn and go back. When we started out, I had to lift him by his paws and drag his feet on the ground so he'd get the idea to walk. He had a hard time but eventually I was able to lower his arms and he'd stand on his own. That seemed like progress. I was pleased. Then I started letting go of him completely.

"Go, Snort! Walk!"

The first time I did that, he yelled and sat right down. I nudged him with my foot and lifted him by a paw. He really wanted to crawl.

"Come on, Snort, walk!" He tried sitting down when I let go of him, but I kept pulling him up. Finally, I got him taking steps while I held onto him. He seemed proud of himself, but it was hard to tell because he still just babbled. And I wasn't sure how much I could expect anyway, because I still thought he might be defective. He showed no interest at all in reading even though I showed him my books and I even read him stories.

Soon I had him walking on his own. He still liked being picked up, and he still resorted to crawling, but more and more he used his hind legs exclusively to get around. When I saw him following on four legs, I would step in the middle of his back and squash him on the floor. Or I would nudge him sideways with my foot, upending him the way you'd flip a turtle. He'd yell, but he got the idea to walk, not crawl.

"Two-wheel drive," I said. "Not four-wheel drive." Now that I was big, I read *Motor Trend* magazine, and I felt sure the analogy would be obvious to Snort.

By wintertime, he was toddling all over. He wasn't talking much yet, but my mother assured me he would. I had my doubts. I expected him to be doing more.

"Your brother is not defective! He's just a baby. He will be talking just like you in a few years." My mother continued to stick up for him, even when confronted with the evidence, which annoyed me. After all, he wasn't talking, and he wasn't reading.

I tried to show him things, but he didn't seem to study what I showed him. Usually, he put whatever I handed him in his mouth. He would try to eat anything. I fed him Tabasco sauce and he yelled. Having a little brother helped me learn to relate to other people. Being a little brother, Snort learned to watch what he put in his mouth.

For some reason, whatever I did to him, Snort still idolized me. I was bigger, and I knew more. I liked having a little brother. It made me feel more mature. "Watch out for your brother," my mother would say when we went outside to play. I would walk and he would toddle after me, like a pet. I liked feeling responsible and taking care of him. And I did a good job of it. Unlike some older brothers, I never set him on fire, or cut off an arm or a leg, or drowned him in the tub. I took really good care of Snort, and it showed. He got bigger every month, and he continued to follow me around. He was thriving.

Gradually, he stopped snorting and drooling. He began to take my toys and play with them himself. My little brother was becoming a nuisance. It was time for a new name.

"Snort, come here. You are getting bigger. So I've decided to give you a new name. From now on, you are going to be called Varmint. Got it?"

"Varmint?"

He said the word a few times and toddled off to tell his mother the news.

The crushing loneliness that I had felt as a five-year-old was mostly gone. Now I only felt lonely on special occasions, when I would be reminded of my inferiority. When I had a birthday, my parents would bake a cake and get me some presents and everyone ran around looking jolly. But every now and then I got invited to birthday parties for other kids, and at those parties there would be ten or twenty kids, all running around laughing. Those were the good parties, I thought. Mine were crummy.

I was seldom laughing and happy, and I was never surrounded by kids. I didn't fully understand the reasons why, but I knew their situation was better than mine, and it hurt to see what I was missing.

As I moved through school as another marginal kid, my dad and my teachers started forecasting my future. They told me I would never amount to anything. They said I was headed for a career pumping gas or jail or the Army—if they would take me. I was contrary and I would not apply myself.

But I'd show them.

3

Empathy

By the time I was twelve, I had progressed from "If he doesn't get better, he may have to be institutionalized" to "He's a weird, screwed-up kid." But although my communication abilities had developed by leaps and bounds, people had ever higher expectations for me, and I began having trouble with what the therapists called "inappropriate expressions."

One time, my mother had invited her friend Betsy over. I wandered in as they sat on the sofa, smoking cigarettes and talking.

Betsy said, "Did you hear about Eleanor Parker's son? Last Saturday he got hit by a train and killed. He was playing on the tracks."

I smiled at her words. She turned to me with a shocked expression on her face. "What! Do you think that's funny?"

I felt embarrassed and a little humiliated. "No, I guess not," I said as I slunk away. I didn't know what to say. I knew they thought it was bad for me to be smiling, but I didn't know why I was grinning, and I couldn't help it. I didn't feel joy or happiness. At the time, as I approached my teenage years, it was hard to figure out exactly what I did feel. And I felt powerless to react any differently.

As I left, I could hear Betsy. "What's the matter with that boy?"

My mother sent me to therapists, all of whom focused on the wrong things. Mostly, they made me feel worse than I already did, dwelling on my so-called evil and sociopathic thoughts. They were all full of shit. They didn't make me better. They just made me feel worse. None of them figured out why I grinned when I heard Eleanor's kid had been run over by a train.

But now I know. And I figured it out myself.

I didn't really know Eleanor. And I had never met her kid. So there was no reason for me to feel joy or sorrow on account of anything that might happen to them. Here is what went through my mind that summer day:

Someone got killed.

Damn! I'm glad I didn't get killed.

I'm glad Varmint or my parents didn't get killed.

I'm glad all my friends are okay.

He must have been a pretty dumb kid, playing on the train tracks.

I would never get run over by a train like that.

I'm glad I'm okay.

And at the end, I smiled with relief. Whatever killed that kid was not going to get me. I didn't even know him. It was all going to be okay, at least for me. Today my feelings would be exactly the same in that situation. The only difference is, now I have better control of my facial expressions.

The fact is, from an evolutionary standpoint, people have an inbred tendency to care about and protect themselves and their immediate family. We do not naturally care about people we don't know. If ten people get killed in a bus crash in Brazil, I don't feel anything at all. I understand intellectually that it's sad, but I don't feel sad. But then I see people making a big deal over it and it puzzles and troubles me because I don't seem to be reacting the same way. For much of my life, being different equated to being bad, even though I never thought of myself that way.

"That's terrible! Oh, I just feel awful!" Some people will cry and carry on, and I wonder . . . *Do they really feel that, or is it just a play for attention?* It is very hard for me to know. People die every minute, all over the world. If we tried to feel sorry for every death, our little hearts would explode.

As I've gotten older, I have taught myself to act "normal." I can do it well enough to fool the average person for a whole evening, maybe longer. But it all falls apart if I hear something that elicits a strong emotional reaction from me that is different from what people expect. In an instant, in their eyes, I turn into the sociopathic killer I was believed to be forty years ago.

Ten years ago, I got a call from the state police. "Your father's been in a car accident. He's being taken to the Greenfield hospital."

"Shit, that's terrible," I said.

I immediately felt anxious, almost nauseous. I was worried. I was frantic. Would he die? Within moments, I had dropped what I was doing and I was speeding toward the Greenfield hospital.

As it happened, my father didn't die. He and my stepmother both recovered from that accident. But the sick, anxious feeling did not leave me until I had reached the hospital, seen them, talked to the doctors, and satisfied myself that they were going to be all right.

I contrast that in my mind with hearing the news that a plane just crashed in Uzbekistan. Fifty-six people are dead.

"Shit, that's terrible," I say.

To an observer, my reaction to those two events was the same. But to me there is a night-and-day difference. Caring—or pretending to care—about other people is a learned behavior. It's one of several kinds of empathy, I suppose. I have true empathy for my family and close friends. If I hear of something bad happening to one of them, I feel tense, or nauseous, or anxious. My neck muscles cramp. I get jumpy. That, to me, is one kind of empathy that's "real."

When something sort of bad happens, I don't have the physical reaction but I still react to the news. When the bad news does not involve danger, my immediate thought is, *What can I do to fix things?*

When I was fourteen, my mother came home one day and said, "John Elder, the car's on fire!" I went downstairs and out to the car. The inside was full of smoke. *I have to fix this for her,* I thought. *And I have to do it before my father gets home.*

I opened the windows and disconnected the battery. When the smoke cleared, I crawled under the dash and found a wire from the cigarette lighter that was melted and burning. I cut it out and repaired it, and I removed the penny that my mother had dropped into the lighter socket. I did all that despite the fact that the car was filthy and full of cigarette butts and old paper matches, the most disgusting things in the world to me. I did it for my mother.

That's another kind of empathy. I didn't have to fix the car. I could have played dumb and she'd never have been any the wiser. I would not have fixed it for anyone besides my mother. But I felt a need to help because a family member was in trouble.

I have what you might call "logical empathy" for people I don't know. That is, I can understand that it's a shame that those people died in the plane crash. And I understand they have families, and they are sad. But I don't have any physical reaction to the news. And there's no reason I should. I don't know them and the news has no effect on my life. Yes, it's sad, but the same day thousands of other people died from murder, accident, disease, natural disaster, and all manner of other causes. I feel I must put things like this in perspective and save my worry for things that truly matter to me.

As a logical thinker, I cannot help thinking, based on the evidence, that many people who exhibit dramatic reactions to bad news involving strangers are hypocrites. That troubles me. People like that hear bad news from across the world, and they burst into wails and tears as though their own children have just been run over by a bus. To me, they don't seem very different from actors and actresses—they are able to burst into tears on command, but does it really mean anything?

Often those same people will turn to me and say things like, "What's wrong with you? You're not saying anything. Don't you care that all those people got killed? They had families, you know!"

As I got older, I found myself in trouble more and more for saying things that were true, but that people didn't want to hear. I did not understand tact. I developed some ability to avoid saying what I was thinking. But I still thought it. It's just that I didn't let on quite so often.

A Trickster's Tale

4

A Trickster Is Born

About this time, I figured out one way to capitalize on my differences from the mass of humanity. In school, I became the class clown. Out of school, I became a trickster. I made quite a few trips to the principal's office in those years. But it was worth it.

I was good at thinking up tricks. When I did, the other kids laughed with me, not at me. We all laughed at the teachers or whomever else I poked fun at. As long as my pranks lasted, I was popular. It felt great, having other kids admire me and like me.

I didn't even have to ask the other kids to join in. They did it on their own. And even if they didn't, they never made fun of me over my tricks.

Of course, once I figured that out, I kept doing it. And I got better with time.

I read all the time, and I was learning all sorts of new things. In fact, I kept the more interesting volumes of the *Encyclopaedia Britannica* next to my bed. I knew my tractors or dinosaurs or ships or astronomy or rocks or whatever else I was studying at that moment.

People began looking at me and listening to me as if I was a prodigy. This was especially true of my family, my few friends, and my parents' close friends. They were a good audience, because they always seemed to like me, even when other people didn't. They saw how intently I studied things. They saw how often I was right, and they heard the certainty in my voice when I said things. It seemed to be a case of "say it and it must be so."

I had an idea: Perhaps I could create my own reality. My first experiments were relatively simple. When I pointed out stars and constellations in the night sky to my grandparents, I added one.

"There's the Big Dipper," I said. "See, over there. And over there, that's Orion."

"You just know all your stars, John Elder!" My grandmother was impressed.

"And that bright star—that's Sirius, the Dog Star. And that one there, that's Bovinius, the Cow Star."

"Are you pulling my leg, John Elder? I never heard of the Cow Star." My grandparents were skeptical.

"I read about it in my book of mythology. The one you bought me. Cows are sacred in India, and that's their star. Wanna read about it?"

"No, son, I'm sure you're right."

The trick was weaving enough truth into the story to make it plausible. I pointed out stars and constellations they knew, and then I showed them a new one. All the elements of my explanation made sense. Maybe there was a Cow Star after all.

And so Bovinius began to shine over Georgia. My grandfather continued to spread the legend.

"Hey, Jeb, look up there. You see that star? That's the goddamn Cow Star. My grandson told me about it. Kid read about it in a book."

"Cow Star, huh?"

"Yeah. Goddamn Indians. Named a goddamn star for a cow," my grandfather said.

"Indians?"

"Yeah, real Indians. From India."

"Cow Star."

As I got older and smarter, my pranks became better, more pol-ished. More sophisticated. Sometimes my stories would acquire a life of their own.

I started out tricking my family. When my grandfather found out he was being tricked, he thought it was funny. He encouraged me. My father was mean, and he was dangerous to trick. But it worked with my mother and brother all the time. The vanishing kid trick became a staple. I worked endless variations for many years.

The first time was when our mother left Varmint and me together at the petting zoo at Look Park in Northampton. Look Park was a supposedly safe place close to home. She went off to the bathroom, and to get us some snacks. She was gone less than five minutes. Varmint was six, and I was fourteen. I had a sudden flash of inspiration.

"Quick, Varmint, hide in that shed before Mom gets back. We'll trick her."

I pointed to a small building where they stored maintenance tools and supplies. Varmint slipped in and pulled the door shut, but opened it a crack so he could see what would happen.

When our mother came back, I was leaning on the rail, reach-ing out to pet a deer.

"John Elder, where is your brother?"

Without even looking around, I said, "He went to find you."

She headed back the way she came, looking for Varmint. So far, so good. I glanced over to the shed and grinned at Varmint.

Soon she was back. "John Elder, I don't see your brother."

"Well, he'll turn up."

Looking unconcerned, I wandered off. My mother followed me. I continued to act indifferent, which got her even more agitated.

"John Elder, where is Chris?"

"He's fine. And anyway, he's just a Varmint."

"I wish you wouldn't talk about your brother like that."

Now ten minutes had passed with no sign of the Varmint. I was proud of him, staying quiet in the shed all that time. He was doing very well. Our mother was getting really upset. It was time to spring the trap.

"John Elder, I'm getting worried about your brother."

Yes, it was definitely time.

"Why are you worried? He's with your friend Paul. He's fine."

My mother did not have a friend Paul. She turned white.

"John Elder!! What are you talking about?"

"Varmint went with Paul. They went to find you and ride the train."

We had her now. She was panicked.

"I don't know any Paul. Who is he?"

"How should I know? He's your friend."

That was just the right thing to say. I was getting really good at thinking on my feet.

"Oh my God. Wait here."

She ran off.

I decided we might have trouble if she came back with the police and they went looking for Paul. I motioned Varmint out. He was grinning. Even though all he'd done was stand still, he was still proud of his part.

"Okay, Varmint, you have to keep a straight face now. Can you do it?"

"I think so," he said.

Our mother returned with two policemen. She saw the Varmint. She ran and grabbed him.

"Christopher Robison, where have you been?"

The police saw this, lost interest, and wandered away. Before Varmint could say anything, I said, "Paul brought him back, just like I told you."

Varmint rose to the challenge.

"We rode the train, and got an ice cream." He made that up all on his own. I could see it then. One day, he might be as good as me at telling stories.

Our mother was suspicious, but she wasn't sure what to say. She didn't want to scare him unnecessarily. She had no idea the whole thing was all a trick, and we were in on it together. She was afraid to say more about this mysterious Paul, since Varmint was, after all, seemingly back in one piece. It was time to distract her.

"Varmint, let's go get a paddleboat and ram the other boats and sink them."

She never figured out who Varmint had gone off with, but we were on to something else as we headed for the paddleboats.

I didn't stop there. I tricked the neighbors, too, and my teachers. I had a particularly disagreeable high school biology teacher. His ideas of the work I should do, and how and when I should do it, were far removed from my own. He tormented me during my weekly lab, holding up my "sloppily dissected frog" for everyone to ridicule. He also singled me out in class, asking questions he knew I couldn't answer.

"What's this?" he would ask, pointing to a spitball-sized bit of frog spoiling on my tray. *How should I know?* I thought, but I fumed and said nothing. I could not close my eyes for a moment in his class, because he'd pounce. It was exhausting and humiliating. I pondered how I might respond.

I decided he needed reading material to distract him. Something to take his mind off harassing nice kids like me.

So I went to Burtle's, the local newsstand. I headed for the magazine racks. They had by far the best selection of smut in town. They had magazines like *Playboy* and *Penthouse* on an upper shelf in back, but the serious stuff was under the counter, by the cash register. I needed those magazines, but I could not see any way to get my hands on them. I didn't need to take them from the store. After all, I only wanted the subscription forms. But how would I get them?

There was only one answer. I would have to buy them. That called for some groundwork, because I didn't have any money.

The next day was a Saturday. I went into town with a metal camping plate and a sign. I swiped two milk crates from behind

Eddie's, the town grocer. I set up across the street, in front of the Quicksilver Bar and Grill. In that location, everyone walking through town would see me and my sign. The sign, which I had made with my mother's art supplies, read:

CHILDREN'S AND ORPHANS' RELIEF
HELP US HELP THEM
YOUR DONATIONS COUNT
SAVE A CHILD

It was remarkably easy. Amherst was a great town for panhandling. In just a few hours, I had thirty dollars in change and sixteen dollar bills. My pockets were bulging. Many people just walked by and dropped money into my pan. Often they looked away from me while doing so. Surprisingly, no one questioned or challenged me. I was glad no one I knew walked by. That would have been embarrassing for me. Although, for them, it might have been inspirational. If some of my friends had seen my panhandling success, they'd have been out there the next day themselves.

By this time in my life, I had gotten to know many of the lowlifes that hung around downtown during the day. Rug, Stump, Fatso, and Freddie. And Willie the bookie and Charles the pimp. I found Rug sitting in a doorway next to a Miller High Life beer sign.

"Rug, can you go over to Burtle's and buy me some porn? The good stuff, from under the counter. Buy me five good ones and you can keep one for yourself."

He was still hesitant.

"Come on, I'll buy you a quart of Schlitz." That did it. I could have saved the cost of a magazine for a sixty-nine-cent quart of beer.

"Okay." Rug smirked, thinking I was buying material to satisfy my own base desires.

"Fuck you, Rug," I said. "It's not for me. It's for my teacher."

"Hey, you don't have to explain yourself to me," he said. He clearly did not believe the magazines were for my teacher. But he bought them anyway.

That evening, I looked up my teacher's address. I filled out the subscription cards in his name, checking the "bill me" boxes. Then I hid one of the leftover magazines in my father's chest of drawers and another in his part of the bookcase—places where my mother would find them and not associate them with me. I slipped one into the parents' waiting area in the school guidance office. And I left the last one in a pew in the church downtown.

Before distributing the magazines, I looked through them to verify the quality of my gift. In the back pages of one, I found the ideal product for a lonely high school teacher.

REVERSIBLE URSULA
THE ULTIMATE INFLATABLE DOLL
BOY OR GIRL
A FRIEND WHO WILL NEVER LET YOU DOWN

She was too good to let get away. I went to the post office with seventeen of my panhandled dollars and ordered her.

Nothing happened for a few weeks. Then, out of the blue, my biology teacher walked up to me one day in the hall.

"Say, John, what do you know about Ursula?"

"Ursula? I don't know her."

"I thought not." He sounded sarcastic. I knew then that I had won, and I smiled to myself. He gave me an F in the course, but I didn't care. I got Fs in all my courses by that time. Failing grades didn't scare me anymore. I don't know if he gave me the F because he didn't like my work, or because I stopped going to class, or because he suspected me of sending the lovely Ursula into his life.

But I had the last laugh. After school let out, I called Lane Quarry and ordered him two loads of crushed stone.

"Just drop it in the driveway, please," I said. "Leave the bill in the mailbox. The workmen will take care of it tomorrow."

More than 100,000 pounds of rock. And best of all, they were going to expect him to *pay* for it.

Maybe Ursula would help him shovel it out of his driveway.

5

I Find a Porsche

When I was eleven, my father got tenure, and my parents finally bought a house of their own. The one they chose was way out in the woods, in a small town called Shutesbury. I looked up Shutesbury in the Reader's Digest atlas my grandfather had given me. Population: 273. Small towns don't come much smaller than that.

Our house seemed very remote. There were five houses in a row where we lived, but they were all separated by trees so none of us could see our neighbors. After the row of houses, our dirt road went on forever with no houses at all. Just woods and hills. In fact, all the roads through the woods were named for hills. We lived on Market Hill Road. Nearby, I found Sand Hill Road, Pulpit Hill Road, January Hills Road, and even Flat Hills Road. And shortly after we moved in, they built a new road, High Point Hill Drive.

All the houses on our street were brand-new. And all the parents living in them taught at the university, except for a few who taught at other schools, like Amherst College or Smith or Mount Holyoke. I soon discovered that some of them had kids my age. We were a little neighborhood in the middle of the woods.

It was the spring of 1968 when we moved. My parents moved me from the big Hadley school to a two-room school in

Shutesbury right at the end of the school year. Once again, I made new friends. The couple in the house on our left had five kids. Their son, Ken, was my age, and we quickly became buddies. He had just moved into his house, too, so we spent that summer patroling the woods around our new homes.

After living in cities and then the open fields of Hadley, Shutesbury was a big change. We were only miles from a busy college town, where all sorts of interesting things were always happening, but there were also miles of woods and roads to explore, delineated with signs reading:

TOWN OF AMHERST
WATERSHED
NO TRESPASSING

Which every boy in the neighborhood understood as:

PRIVATE PRESERVE FOR KIDS

One day, I saw fresh tracks going down one of the abandoned roads into our private preserve. I walked those old roads every day, but I never saw cars driving on them. The roads were narrow, with trees and rocks in the middle and brush hanging over the sides. It had been many years since cars used those roads, many of which didn't even go anywhere anymore. Or if they did go somewhere, the somewhere was now a hole in the ground with a stone post out front where horses were once hitched.

Cautiously, I followed the tracks. A few hundred yards in, I reached a clearing. In the clearing sat a new Porsche. A blue one. With tan seats. And a chrome "90" on the back.

Someone had left it there. Just for me. I knew what it was. I read *Hot Rod* and *Road and Track,* and I knew every model of car there was. So I had read about Porsches, but up till now I had never seen one up close.

I approached it slowly. The hood was open. I looked inside, but I didn't see any engine. Had it broken down? Maybe someone had removed the engine to fix it. Then I had another thought. Maybe it was stolen. I remembered what I'd read about car thieves in my Hardy Boys stories. Maybe they were hiding nearby. Suddenly, I was scared. I didn't want to end up tied to a tree with tape over my mouth like the kids in the Hardy Boys stories.

I looked all around, but I didn't see anything. There were no sounds but the rustle of the wind and the chirping of birds. Quietly, I closed the hood and crept away.

I walked to Ken's house. He was a year older than me. He would know what we should do. Together we returned to the Porsche. Ken looked at it. Right away, he knew what was going on.

"The police parked it here. It's a stakeout. I've seen them on TV. They hide and watch until someone steals it. Then they jump out and arrest them. Maybe they're watching us now. Maybe they've staked out the road."

"But it doesn't have an engine," I said.

"That's so we can't get away. They must be watching us right now," he answered confidently. I looked around, imagining police in camouflage, hiding under bushes. Or maybe in foxholes, like the Green Berets I read about in *National Geographic*.

We ran off. When we crept back the next day, the car was still there. We circled it, but found no evidence of a stakeout. We entered the clearing.

"I'm getting in," I said to Ken.

"Maybe they'll fingerprint it. And arrest you at school."

I paused. Could they do that? Then I made up my mind. "They can't arrest me. I'm just a kid. I'm too young to steal it."

The car was still sitting just as we had left it. I opened the door and climbed inside. I can still remember the feel and the smell of the tan leather seats. I shut the door and looked around. The speedometer went to 120. But I knew it was faster. I had heard any Porsche could pin the speedometer needle. There was a tach, too, to show the speed of the engine. And a clock and some other gauges.

There was also a radio, with push buttons marked "AM" and "SW." It took a moment to figure that out. Shortwave. American cars didn't have shortwave radios. I was really impressed. My father had a shortwave radio at home, but I had never seen an SW button on a car radio. I imagined listening to the BBC from London, or HCJB from Quito, Ecuador. The Voice of the Andes. We listened to them at home some nights.

Seeing the SW on the radio reaffirmed how special Porsches were. My mother had just gotten a new car, but it was a Chrysler Newport. A brown one. Why didn't she have a car like this? I started it up, though there was no key. Suddenly, I was driving at Le Mans. I raced through the corners, sliding off the course at one point. I had read how Porsches had the engines in the back, and they spun out on corners. I had to be careful.

I sped down the straightaway. Over a hundred miles an hour. Or maybe it was 150. It got dark, and the headlamps cut tunnels through the night.

I drove for hours in that Porsche. Then I got out, shut the door, and walked home for dinner.

The next day, a truck appeared and took the Porsche away.

"I guess the stakeout didn't work. They'll probably plant it somewhere else," Ken said as we watched Amherst Towing carry it off. They did all the towing for the police in town. I realized Ken had probably been right all along about the stakeout. But I couldn't figure out how they were watching us.

When I got a little older, and walked a little farther, I realized people had been stealing cars and dumping them in the woods for years. I'd find them in the strangest places, with trees growing where windows used to be. A '37 Buick Roadmaster. A '56 Chevy Nomad. A '52 Studebaker Champion. And the occasional sports car or truck.

My next encounter with a Porsche was three years later. I could drive for real by then, and I was more worldly. I had friends with cars of their own, and I helped work on them. Sometimes I even test-drove them.

It was summer, and I was at my grandparents' house in Georgia. My grandfather called home from the road. He traveled all over the South, selling veterinary medicines. He knew everyone and every place in Georgia, Alabama, the Carolinas, and Tennessee. He even knew people in Mississippi and Louisiana.

"John Elder, we have to go to Birmingham. I just bought a car at an estate sale. It's a Porsche."

"What model is it?" I asked. I knew all the models. The 911. The 912. The new 914. The old 356s. I even knew about rare models like the 904 and the 550. I could identify every single Porsche on the streets of my town. I hoped he had bought a 911S. Maybe he would get tired of it and give it to me. He always drove Cadillacs, and I thought he might be too fat to fit in a Porsche.

My grandfather knew exactly what he had bought.

"It's an orange one, John Elder. I gave two thousand dollars for it. Let's go drive it back."

My grandfather was always buying stuff at auctions. The Porsche was his latest in a long string of diamonds, oriental rugs, fur coats, boat motors, china cabinets, and jade figurines. We headed out together to get the Porsche. In a few hours, we arrived at the car, which was parked in front of a nice-looking house whose contents were being dragged away, piece by piece, by movers and thugs in pickup trucks.

It was a 914. The more powerful model, with the two-liter engine. I opened the hood and proceeded to check it out. It looked like a VW Squareback motor. I was familiar with them, because my friend Mark had a Squareback, and I'd helped rebuild its engine that spring.

"Can I drive it?" I asked. I had never driven a Porsche before. I didn't have a driver's license yet, but Jack didn't know or didn't care. Licenses weren't as big a deal down South in those days.

I got in, and immediately I recognized the smell from that

long-ago day in the woods. I started it up and Jack stuffed himself in the passenger seat.

"Damn! These furrin cars sure are tight," he said. Jack gave me directions as we headed for the highway.

It was very tight, but I liked it. The only small cars I had driven before this were VWs. The Porsche was a lot quicker, and it handled like it was on rails compared to the Volkswagens. I pulled onto the interstate and, without noticing, my speed crept higher and higher.

"You're gonna get a mighty expensive ticket, boy." Jack was looking at the speedometer needle, which sat right near the one hundred mark. I hadn't realized I was going so fast. I slowed down till he looked away. But I knew they wouldn't give us a ticket anyway. Not in Alabama. My grandfather had a proclamation from the governor, George Wallace, appointing him a colonel in the state militia. And he had a little plate for his own car. It said GOVERNOR'S STAFF. And below that, STAND UP FOR ALABAMA.

When we got back to Lawrenceville, I carefully washed and waxed the Porsche. I tried to impress my grandparents by taking really good care of that car. I even polished and waxed the farm tractor to earn brownie points. With any luck, The Porsche would soon be My Porsche. My grandfather just had to lose interest in it, and what else could he do but give it to me?

But he didn't give it to me. He let my uncle Bob borrow it. And Bob ran it into a tree. Once again, my Porsche was lost.

I would not get another Porsche until I was twenty-five years old. That was when I saw a beige 912 for sale on a side street a few miles from where I lived. I bought that car and drove it home.

I spent countless hours restoring that old Porsche. I rebuilt the engine, and then rebuilt the body. I probably removed and repaired every single part of that car, one piece at a time. I stripped the old beige paint and refinished it in a nice aqua green. I got tired of that and repainted it metallic red. It looked flawless. Then one day, I realized that there was a fundamental problem with my Porsche:

There was nothing left to fix. So I sold it and found another Porsche to restore, a gray 911E.

Since that day, I've owned seventeen Porsches, and I've fixed up or restored every single one. Even when I had money, I never bought new cars. *Any fool with money can buy a new Porsche,* I thought. *It takes a craftsman to restore an old one.* And that's what I dreamed of being. A craftsman. An artist, working in automotive steel.

6

The Nightmare Years

A dark cloud slid over our family about the time we moved to Shutesbury. There were some bright spots—the woods and my Porsche, for example—but things were spiraling out of control with my parents. Life turned really ugly when we moved into the April House, to use the moronic jolly name my brother and mother gave our new home. They gave it that name because we moved there in April 1968.

My father had been drinking for quite a while, but now he picked up the pace. The empty bottles began accumulating under the kitchen table. They lined the wall, and when we went to the dump, they filled the back of the car. They were not little bottles, either; they were gallon jugs. S.S. Pierce and Gallo were his favorite wines. Sherry, actually. His smell changed, too. He began to reek of liquor.

He had always been quick to spank me, but as his drinking increased, he turned meaner and nastier. He became dangerous. Shortly before we moved from Hadley, my father was sitting at the dining table drinking. I walked by him, and I guess I was too noisy, because he grabbed me, shook me violently, and then slammed me into the wall so hard that I fractured the plaster. I was stunned, but my mother ran in, yelling, "John! Leave John Elder alone!"

As I sank to the floor, unable to move, he ran outside, got in his car, and sped off.

"I hope he crashes and dies!" I cried.

I didn't like living in Hadley after that. It was a good thing we moved a few months later. The caved-in spot in the wall was an ugly reminder whenever I passed it.

As an eleven-year-old, I was somewhat able to defend myself. But it's a miracle that three-year-old Snort grew up to become a Varmint and then an adult. He could easily have ended his days with a little squeal, in a furnace or an unmarked hole in the ground. I'm sure quite a few unwanted three-year-olds end up that way. After all, when you live way out in the woods, who's going to notice if a toddler's there one day and gone the next? And my father didn't like Snort too much, back in those days.

My father would sit each night at the kitchen table, across from the sink and the black-and-white TV. His hair was tousled, his eyes black and sunken. He slouched back in the chair, with his glass in front of him and a half-empty jug on the floor. His cigarette smoldered in the ashtray, and the pack sat next to it on the table. Sometimes his hand slipped, and cigarette butts scattered all over the table. Sometimes my mother would be there, too, and then their cigarette butts could be anywhere. In the dishes. In the glasses. Even in our food.

As the night wore on, my mother would wander off. Sometimes she returned to taunt him, which made him all the meaner. I learned to be very careful around him at those times.

Sometimes he would call me.

"John Elder, come here, son."

He would reach out toward me.

If I moved toward him, he would try and grab me. That was bad. He'd say, "I love you, son," and he'd scrape his bristly chin against me and make slobbering noises while holding me painfully tight.

I was usually able to escape after a few moments, when his grip slackened or he reached for another drink.

"Come back, son," he would blubber. But I'd run to my room.

Sometimes we'd argue, and sometimes he'd whip me with his belt. If my mother was there, she might try to save me from a beating. Maybe he would turn on her instead. I don't remember.

Other nights, I'd hide in my room, thinking I'd gotten away. And then he'd appear in the door.

I buried my face in the pillows, but I could see his shadow, blocking the light from the hall. And I could smell him when he came in. Then I could hear him taking off his belt, and I would hope I had a good pile of blankets on me.

Whack! The belt would come down.

He would hit me as hard as he could. He seemed incredibly strong then, but he was just a drunken, out-of-shape college professor. Otherwise, he might have killed me.

I might sob, or I might be quiet. It depended on how hard he hit me. I thought of the knife my grandfather had given me for Christmas. Solingen steel. Eight inches long. Sharp. I could roll over and jam it into him, right to the hilt. Right in the belly. But I was afraid. *What if I miss? What if it doesn't kill him?* I had seen the movies, where they just kept on coming. They didn't die like they were supposed to. He might kill me for real, then.

So I never did. But I thought about it. Many nights.

Eventually, he would put on his belt, cinch up his pants, and leave.

In the daylight, I would go out into the yard and smash my little brother's Tonka trucks with rocks. Big rocks. The biggest I could find. It was all I could do.

One night, he called my brother instead of me.

"Commere, little Chris," he said, slurring his words.

My brother was too small to mistrust him. Stupid kid. He went closer, and my father grabbed him. Set him on his knee.

It looked so harmless. Just a brainless, smiling toddler, sitting on daddy's lap. He sat there a few minutes and nothing happened. I relaxed a little. Snort was smiling. Then daddy reached down and mashed his cigarette out. In the middle of Snort's forehead. My little brother screamed. He struggled. As I write this, forty years later, I can't remember whether he got away.

Like dogs that had been kicked, we were wary of him after that. But we would never admit it to anyone else. Getting abused or beaten up or bullied is humiliating, even more so when it happens at home. It took many years for me to gather the strength to tell the stories in this book.

Still, for some inexplicable reason, I did well in school—better than I had ever done, or would ever do again. When I graduated from sixth grade, our class had seven achievement prizes. I won six of them. I was used to hearing my father predict that I would end up pumping gas. That night, though, he said, "Son, I am really proud of what you've done." But then we went home, where he returned to his bottle of sherry, alone in the kitchen. And by nine o'clock, his proud feelings were long gone.

None of my teachers knew or guessed that my parents fought every day in those years. Loud, ugly fights. And my father began to fall apart. First, he got psoriasis: nasty white scabs all over his body. I had thought the cigarettes were disgusting, but those scales were worse. They fell off constantly, clogging the drain in the tub. He left a trail of white flecks wherever he went. On the floor. On the rugs. On his clothes. The worst concentrations were in his bathroom and his bed. I kept well clear of those places.

My mother had to wash our clothes separately, because if any of mine got mixed up with his, they came out with little white bits of scale on them and I wouldn't wear them. It would take three or four washings to get them clean enough to wear again.

The way he acted, though, he didn't get much sympathy from me.

And then there was the arthritis. And his knees—fluid, and pain, and gold shots, and cortisone shots, and who knows what else. He was only thirty-five and yet he was falling apart. No one knew why then, or so they said. But now I know. He was miserable beyond belief. Both my parents had gone from bad childhoods to a bad marriage, and now I was living with the result.

Our father would have been enough for any family, but we had my mother, too. By this time, she had begun the slow slide into madness that would eventually send her to the Northampton State Hospital in restraints. She started seeing things overhead. Demons, people, ghosts . . . I never knew who or what she saw. They were in the light fixtures, in the corners, or on the ceiling. "Don't you see them?" she would ask. I never did.

Some of the things she said were so disturbing, I blocked them from my mind and can't repeat them today. My memories of that time are like blinding flashes of harsh, actinic light. They hurt to recall.

My parents drove each other crazy, and they almost drove me crazy. Luckily, the Asperger's isolated me from the worst of the insanity until I was old enough to escape.

My mother would say, "John Elder, your father is a very smart, very dangerous man. He's too smart for the doctors. He fools them into thinking he's normal. I'm afraid your father is going to try and kill us. We need to hide. We need to get away from him until the doctor can get him under control."

For a long time, I believed her. My brother was littler, and he believed her longer. Now I know. It was all madness, or meanness. On both of their parts.

By the time I turned thirteen and my brother was five, my mother had found the Dr. Finch that my brother wrote about in *Running with Scissors*. I remember going to see the doctor for the first time, with my whole family. I was dubious, because my mother had been sending me to therapists, playgroups, and counselors for a while, trying to find out what was wrong. Nothing had worked. But even back then, I could see one thing that was definitely wrong.

"We have the wrong parents, Varmint. I've watched my friends' parents. They aren't like ours." Varmint didn't really know. He was too little.

My parents often left me to watch the Varmint while they were out. But this time I was going, too. So I spoke to him before we left.

"Varmint, we're all going out to talk about you with a shrink. I can't stay with you because they want to ask me what to do. Come down here. We'll chain you to the heating oil tank so you'll be safe till we get back."

"John Elder! Don't you scare Chris like that. We have a babysitter for him."

We left Varmint and set out for the doctor's office, on the top floor of one of the old buildings that lined the main street of Northampton. We rode an antique elevator, the kind that looks like an open cage, to the third floor, exiting into a large waiting room filled with threadbare furniture, with a girl who turned out to be the doctor's daughter at a schoolteacher's desk against the wall.

The doctor's office was behind an old wooden door with his name stenciled on a frosted glass pane, just like the door to the private detective's office in the movies. Inside, the office was very hot and stuffy. The steam heat hissed all the time, and I smelled it in the air. The windows looked like they had never been opened. The office smelled of old carpets and tired people.

The doctor came out to meet us. Or maybe we went in to meet him.

"Good afternoon. I'm Doctor Finch!" he boomed at us.

He was old and chubby, with white hair and a vaguely foreign accent. Apparently, my mother and father had made a few visits already, and my father had told my grandfather about them.

"Watch out for that Doctor Finch," my grandfather said on the phone, when I told him we were going to see him. "I had him investigated."

Why he would investigate the doctor was a mystery to me.

"They ran him out of Kingsport, Tennessee, on a rail, I heard," he said.

I had read about running people out of town on rails in my history books.

"Did they tar and feather him, too?" I asked. Lots of times, angry mobs did that as part of the running on a rail ceremony. At least according to what I had read.

"I don't know. Just watch him."

So I watched him. Closely.

One at a time, my mother, my father, and I went in to talk to the doctor, and then at the end we went in together. I can't remember what we talked about in that first visit, but shortly after we started seeing him, Dr. Finch did two things that changed my life: He told me I could call my parents anything I wanted, and he told my father that he could not smack me around. And, unlike the suggestions of every shrink in the past, Dr. Finch's suggestions took hold. My father never hit me again. For this, I will always be grateful to Dr. Finch, despite his bizarre behavior later.

"John has decided on new names for both of you," he said, calling them in after meeting with me alone. "I have encouraged him in this, as a sign of his free expression. John . . . ?" He paused and turned to me.

"I have decided to name you Slave," I said, looking at my mother.

"And your name is Stupid," I told my father.

"Yes, John Elder," said my mother. Anything to humor me.

"I don't really like that," said my father.

"Well, you have to respect John's choices," the doctor said.

Dr. Finch may not have known about Asperger's, but he was the first person to support and encourage my naming of things on my own.

"And whatever he says, you can't hit him." This was repeated for my father's benefit. My mother never beat me up. And from that day on, my father didn't, either.

I began accompanying Slave and Stupid to regular sessions with Dr. Finch. And my parents went to more sessions by themselves. Varmint was too small to attend therapy with us at first, and my mother was reluctant to adopt my suggestion that we chain him up in the basement. Mrs. Stosz, the grandmother of one of my class-mates, volunteered to babysit the Varmint.

As we got to know the doctor's family, they kind of adopted us. I began hanging out with his daughter Hope and another patient, Neil Bookman. There was no denying that Dr. Finch was eccentric. He lived in a big old Victorian house near the center of town that was always swarming with friends and patients. They all seemed to worship him. I was a little dubious of that, but he'd gotten results for me, so I left it alone.

My grandfather never stopped telling me, "Watch out for that Finch . . . ," and I heard rumors about him from people in town, but he was the first shrink with whom I'd had a positive experience, and he did right by me in those early years. It was a shame things went so wrong a few years later.

7

Assembly Required

Until my thirteenth Christmas, I studied rocks and minerals, dinosaurs, the planets, ships, tanks, bulldozers, and airplanes. That Christmas, I got something new: an electronics kit!

My parents gave me a RadioShack computer kit with forty-two components, including three transistors, three dials, and a meter. In a black plastic case. Easy assembly. Batteries not included.

The word *computer* meant something very different in the late 1960s than it does today. My new computer was really an electronic slide rule, for those who remember slide rules. To use it, you turned the two left dials until their pointers were lined up over the two numbers you wanted to multiply. You then turned the third dial until the meter read zero. When that happened, you looked at that third dial and it showed the product of the two numbers.

Before I could turn the dials, though, I had to build the computer. I had a bag of resistors, transistors, potentiometers, a battery holder, and a meter.

"How do I build it?" I asked.

"I don't know, son. What do the directions say?"

"It says 'easy assembly,' whatever that means. We need pliers, wire cutters, a soldering iron, and rosin core solder."

"Well, we have solder here. To solder the plumbing." Sometimes my father imagined himself a handyman.

"The manual says we need *rosin core* solder. It says acid core plumber's solder will ruin it."

The nighttime version of my father could turn ugly in the blink of an eye, but the daytime version was actually pretty nice. He almost never said anything nasty about me before dark, and at times like this he actually worked with me on my projects.

How I struggled with that computer! It probably had no more than twenty parts inside, the rest of the "forty-two components" being the terminal strips those parts were mounted on, and the nuts, bolts, dials, scales, meter, and case that everything else lived in. Simple as it was, I arranged and rearranged pieces for two weeks before I got it working.

My parents bought me books they hoped would help: *Basic Electronics* and *101 Electronic Projects.* My favorite, *The Radio Amateur's Handbook,* was recommended by the salesman at RadioShack. By reading those books, I figured it out. On the way, I learned to solder, and I began to understand what the different electronic components were, and how they worked. Resistors, capacitors, transistors, and diodes all became real to me—not just words on a page. I was feeling proud of myself, and I was ready for more.

I decided to sign up for an electronics class at the high school. *Maybe I'll do well in that,* I thought. I had gotten straight As in sixth grade, but my grades had gone steadily downhill once I started junior high, and electronics sounded a lot more interesting than biology or German or gym.

Since electronics was a high school class and I was still in junior high, I had to see the teacher and take a quiz of sorts.

"What is ohm's law?" Mr. Gray began.

"E over I and R," I answered. "E is volts, I is amps, R is ohms."

Twenty more easy questions, and I was in. I already knew more than the basic textbooks had to offer. Mr. Gray had an office in a closet filled with vacuum tubes, resistors, capacitors, wire, connectors, and all manner of other parts. I was fascinated. He thought I had already learned enough to skip Electronics I and go directly to Electronics II, but I was so driven that I completed the course material for Electronics II in my first few weeks. Then I began nosing around the university and learning what I could on my own.

My mother suggested that I go see Professor Edwards, the husband of a friend. Dr. Edwards taught electrical engineering at UMass, and he opened the door for me to a whole new world. He got me into the labs in Engineering East, the university's engineering building, and introduced me to the brand-new Research Computing Center, where they had a Control Data 3800 computer system in a huge air-conditioned room.

They adopted me as a pet in the engineering labs. I studied there after school almost every day, continuing with an aggressive home study program at night.

I began eyeing the TVs and radios in the house. They were getting old anyway, and I was itching to take them apart so I could figure out how they worked. I decided that my parents should turn over all the household electronics to me, right then.

"Okay, you can have the old Zenith radio. But not the new one!"

My parents began handing over the radios. The old TV followed a few weeks later and I began to amass a considerable inventory of parts on top of the chest of drawers in my room, and on the dining table.

"Clean these parts off the kitchen table!"

"Ow! I just cut my foot on some old radio part!"

The complaints became more frequent, and my father decided to take matters into his own hands. Luckily for me, this happened in the afternoon. Later that night, drunk, he would have just thrown my things into the trash.

"Son, why don't we build you a work area in the basement?"

That sounded good to me. There just happened to be a big door leaning against the basement wall. My father got legs, attached them, and the door became my very own workbench.

Soon I was spending all my time in the basement, and I had moved from taking things apart to putting new things together. I began by building simple devices. Some, like my radios, were useful. Others were merely entertaining. For example, I discovered I could solder some stiff wires onto a capacitor and charge it up. For a few minutes, till the charge leaked away, I had a crude stun gun.

I tried it out on the dog, who ran and hid. That was no fun. So I decided to try it on my little brother. I charged the capacitor to a snappy but nonlethal level from a power supply I'd recently removed from our old Zenith television.

"Hey, let's play Jab a Varmint," I said. I tried to smile disarmingly, keeping the capacitor behind my back and making sure I didn't ruin the effect by jabbing myself or some other object.

"What's that?" he asked, suspiciously.

Before he could escape, I stepped across the room and jabbed him. He jumped. Pretty high, too. Sometimes he would fight back, but this time he ran. The jab was totally unexpected, and he didn't realize I only had the one jab in my capacitor. It would be several years before I had the skill to make a multishot Varmint Jabber.

He ran down the hall, yelling, "Momma, John Elder did Jab a Varmint!"

I soon moved on to more sophisticated experiments. But I ran into a roadblock: The college engineering textbooks used equations to describe how things worked, but I didn't understand the math. I could visualize the equations in my head, but the ones in my head seemed to have nothing in common with those on the page. It was as though I thought in an entirely different language. When I saw a wave in a book, it was printed next to an equation with symbols I didn't understand. When I saw a wave in my mind, I associated it with a particular sound. If I concentrated hard, I could almost hear the waves. There were no symbols at all. I could not figure out how to relate the two. Yet. Luckily, it was about then that my interests in electronics and music began to converge.

I had first become interested in music in the fifth grade. I tried playing the French horn with no success. A few years later, while I was in Georgia, I saw my cousin, Little Bob, taking guitar lessons, and I decided to try playing a bass guitar. My grandmother took me to Wallace Reed Music in Duluth, Georgia, outside Atlanta, where I looked at a git-tar with four strings.

Down South, they don't say guitar. They say *git-tar.* And they don't say violin. They say *fiddle.*

"That there's a bass, sonny," the salesman said.

My grandmother asked the salesman if he could play it. He plugged it in to an amplifier, played a few lines, and handed it to me. I had no idea how to play it, but I touched a string and it thrummed in my chest. I was entranced. Thirty minutes and a lot of wheedling later, we loaded the bass, a Fender Showman amplifier, a speaker cabinet, some cords, and some music books into the trunk of my grandmother's silver Cadillac and headed home.

I practiced all summer, playing along with the radio and studying my sheet music. I was a terrible bass player, though. I could hear the songs in my mind. I could read the music. But I could not translate the music in my head into movements of my fingers over the strings. The sounds that emanated from my bass were clumsy, just as I was clumsy.

I eyed my Fender Showman amp. Leo Fender had designed some of the most famous guitars and amplifiers in the world, but I still thought there was room for improvement. Could I take it apart and make it better? Maybe if I couldn't play the bass, I could make something out of the amp.

I found a book that might help, *Musical Instrument Amplifiers,* and whined and pleaded relentlessly until my parents bought it for me. I was full of ideas for integrating my stash of former television pieces into the Showman amplifier my grandmother had bought me.

My ideas worked. My Fender amp got louder, a lot louder, and it began to sound hotter. I took it to some local shows and had the musicians play it against their own amps. It ran circles around most of them.

"Man, this sound is hot!" Musicians were quick to praise my work. I had a winner.

"Hey, can you do that to mine?" became a common refrain after someone played my equipment, so I started modifying amplifiers for local musicians, and they told other musicians. I also started fixing broken equipment.

I began to understand the relationship between my design changes and how things sounded. Musicians saw that.

"Can you make the bass snappier?"

"Can you get more definition in the low notes?"

"Can you soften the overdrive sound?"

With a bit of practice, I became able to turn the words of a musician into technical descriptions that I used in my designs. For example, "This sound is fat" translated to "There's a lot of even-harmonic distortion." And I knew how to add even-harmonic distortion on command.

Soon the musicians and I moved from changing the sound of the amplifier to creating entirely new sound effects. In those days, reverb and tremolo were the only effects available to most musicians. I began to experiment, producing new effects, new sounds.

I also began experimenting with transistorized circuits. The Fender amps were tube technology—designs from the 1950s. Transistor circuitry was newer, and integrated circuits were state of the art. By studying the circuits, I figured out how to make little battery-powered special-effect boxes. I worked hard to imagine the results of my designs, and I refined my thought process as I visualized a circuit, then built it for real, and compared my imagined results with the real results. Gradually, I became able to visualize the results of my designs with a fair degree of accuracy. My earlier problems with math texts stopped holding me back as I developed the ability to visualize and even hear the flow of sounds through my circuits.

At that point, I had made several key breakthroughs. First, I had gained an understanding of the electronic components themselves. They were the building blocks of everything to follow. Next, I somehow figured out how to visualize the complex calculus functions that describe the behavior of electronic circuits in time. For example, I saw the pure tones of a guitar going into a circuit, and I saw the modified waves—immeasurably more complex— coming out. I understood how changes in the circuit topology or component values would alter the waves. And, most remarkably, I developed the ability to translate those waves I saw in my mind into sounds I imagined in my head, and those imagined sounds closely matched what emerged from the circuits when I built them.

No one knows why one person has a gift like this and another doesn't, but I've met other Aspergian people with savantlike abilities like mine. In my opinion, part of this ability—which I seem to have been born with—comes from my extraordinary powers of concentration. I have an extremely sharp focus.

I spent my free evenings at local concerts, and became part of the scene. Club owners, bouncers, and even bartenders began to recognize me; musicians talked to me and everyone seemed to respect me. I felt good about myself, and I felt even better when I discovered that many of them were misfits like me. Maybe I had finally found a place I'd fit in.

This was a relief, because the situation at home was deteriorating. We had been seeing Dr. Finch for a while now, and my father certainly treated me better, but my parents' fights with each other were still brutal. And both of them were going downhill fast. My father was drinking more than ever, and he was depressed and withdrawn. Sometimes he stayed in bed all day; often he was simply gone. We didn't have many family activities in those days. And my mother got more and more manic, until one day she vanished.

"Your mother has had a psychotic break," the doctor told me. My mother returned a few days later, drugged and subdued, but the handwriting was on the wall.

In search of distractions, I began hanging around the junior high's audiovisual center. Most of the kids hanging around the AV room were interested in the TV cameras and the school's state-of-the-art black-and-white TV studio. Not me. I wanted to learn how to take things apart, fix them, and make them better. And the two technicians, John Fuller and Fred Smead, taught me how to do it. The two of them really helped me on my way, and I owe them both a debt of gratitude.

"Did you ever fix a record player?" John gestured to a pile of Rheem Califone record players. The school had dozens of these players. The language departments played lessons on them. The music department played operas on them. Social studies teachers played records of old radio shows. They were fragile, and they were always breaking down. My new work-study job was to fix them.

Every item that I fixed in those days taught me something new. I learned how to solder the tiny wires to the phonograph needles, and how turntables and needles work. I learned what went wrong with the circuits and how to fix them. Soon I was banging out three and four repairs in an afternoon and, before long, the pile of broken record players was gone.

"Do you think we can start the kid on tape decks?" Fred said, in the same tone a mother might use to say, "Do you think we can start little Mikey on solid food?" With that, broken tape decks were added to my diet of record players. Within a week, I was fixing all the tape decks for the language lab. These machines had a hard life, going back and forth endlessly as students kept playing phrases and rewinding and playing them again. And it was all a waste: Five years after getting out of high school, I'll bet 90 percent of those kids couldn't have made a word of small talk on the streets of Paris or Berlin. But for me, the language lab's tape decks were a ticket to another world. Soon I was using what I had learned by working on them to make flangers and echo delays—a whole new generation of special effects. Local musicians loved them.

For the first time in my life, I was able to do something that grown-ups thought was valuable. I may have been rude. I may not have known what to say or do in social situations. But if I could fix five tape recorders in an afternoon, I was "great." No one except my grandparents had ever called me that before.

Another thing I found in the AV room was the girl who became my first wife. Mary Trompke was another shy kid with problems like me. Something about her fascinated me. She was very smart, but she didn't say much. Still, I was determined to get to know her. We began to talk. She would sit with me as I worked on record players and movie projectors. Soon she started to repair things, too, and we would work side by side on headsets and tape decks.

I began walking her home every day. She lived in South Amherst and I lived all the way over the North Amherst line in Shutesbury, so I got in a lot of walking in those years. Her parents were divorced, and she lived with her mother, her three brothers, and her sister in a small ranch house. Her father had been a violent drunk like mine. Her mother was overworked, absentminded, and very dubious of me. I was, after all, long-haired, dirty, loud, vulgar, and male. So she didn't think too much of me when I started walking her baby daughter home after school. But I persisted, because I felt Mary understood me, something I had never felt with anyone before.

I named her Little Bear. Her mother called her Mary Lee—Lee being her middle name—or Baby Daughter, but those names would never do for me. For some reason, I have always had a problem with names. For people that are close to me, for example, I must name them myself. Sometimes I would call her Baby Daughter to tease her, but she always got mad, and I eventually gave up. Little Bear was what she remained.

I thought she was cute—short and solid, with dark hair in pigtails. I was totally smitten. She was the first person I had met who could read as fast as me, maybe even faster. And she read exciting things: books by Asimov, Bradbury, and Heinlein. I immediately began reading them, too. But I was far too shy and insecure to ever tell her how I felt about her. So we just talked and read and fixed tape recorders and walked into town every day.

That was Aspergian dating, circa 1972.

8

The Dogs Begin to Fear Me

Any child will tell you that even the kindest and gentlest of dogs will bite if you yank its ears and pull its tail long enough. There is a dark side to Asperger's, and it comes from our childhood dealings with people who do not treat us the way they would like to be treated. As I grew older, it seemed as though there were very few people who made me feel loved. Little Bear was one of them. My father's parents also stuck by me. I used to visit them every summer in Georgia. They lived in Lawrenceville, a small town about an hour outside Atlanta.

In my thirteenth summer, my grandparents picked me up at the airport, the way they always did. My grandmother Carolyn was the first person I saw when I walked off the plane. She ran up and grabbed me and I squirmed away. I was getting a little big to be grabbed.

"Oooooooooh. John Elder! Look at you! You've grown so big! You are so handsome!"

I squirmed some more, but I really liked the way they were always so proud of me and so glad to see me. No one else was.

"Your uncle Bob is coming up this weekend and he said he was taking you driving! Ooooooooh lordy, my baby boy driving a car!"

She led me downstairs to baggage claim, and out to where my

grandfather Jack's Cadillac was idling in the no-parking zone at the curb. I climbed in and pointed the air conditioner vents at my face as we drove out of the airport.

It felt good to be back in Georgia.

That weekend, Bob and I got in my grandmother's new car. It was a Buick Electra 225, a burgundy two-door. I was a little nervous, but I moved the power seat forward until I could reach the pedals. I had been driving the farm equipment since I was twelve, but now I was about to drive a car. On a road.

"If you can drive a tractor, you can drive the Buick." That was easy for him to say. After all, the car belonged to my grandmother, not him. And as huge as it seemed, it was considerably smaller than my grandfather's Fleetwood.

"It's a lot easier to drive than the tractor. It's got an automatic transmission and power steering."

I drove the big tractor on the roads all the time, when I mowed or raked or did other work. It was a red Massey Ferguson. If my grandmother asked, "Can you get me some fertilizer and number six shotgun shells at the store, honey child?" I even drove the tractor all the way into town. Sometimes I drove to the Baskin-Robbins to get ice cream. I parked in the parking lot with the cars and went inside. I had to drive as fast as that tractor would go to get home before the ice cream melted.

I wasn't scared of tractors because they didn't go very fast. But the car was different. I put it in gear and touched the gas very carefully. The car leaped ahead, and I quickly slammed on the brakes. We skidded to a stop on the white sand driveway. Luckily, there was no one there to see us.

"Gentle, son," my uncle said.

Very carefully, I let off the brake. The car started rolling. Very gently, I pushed the brake. The car stopped. My uncle was right. It was easy to steer. And it had a lot of power.

We made it to the end of the driveway without a crash. I stopped where the dirt drive came out of the woods onto High-

way 27, right where I would turn the mower around if I was on
the tractor. The pavement shimmered in the heat, and every now
and then a car went speeding past. I looked across the street to
Matthews Pond, where I caught largemouth bass that my grandmother cleaned and cooked for dinner.

"It's okay. Look both ways, and pull out onto the road," Bob
reassured me from the passenger seat.

We pulled out onto the road. I gave the car a little gas, and all of
a sudden the speedometer showed 40.

"This car's got the four fifty-five engine and a four barrel. It's
fast," Bob said.

My grandfather always got the best of everything. I touched
the brakes to make sure I could stop, and the tires gave a little
chirp. We headed for my great-grandmother's house, a mile or so
up the road. My uncle and I called her Mamaw. She was ancient
and small and didn't go anywhere anymore. When I was little, I
thought she'd fought in the Civil War, which wasn't true, but she
was born only a little while after. She lived in a brick ranch house
about two miles up the road from my grandparents. She had snow-
balls made from aluminum foil in her cupboard, and she fed us
goulash and fried okra.

Mamaw had never seen me drive the tractor and was very
impressed that I could drive.

"Oh Lordy, John Elder, look at you! You've grown so big! And
now you're driving!"

Shit, I thought, *she's just as excited as my grandmother. They even
sound the same.* She just didn't show it as much because she was so
old. I was pleased and proud, but I was careful not to let on,
because I knew by this time that *real men* did not show emotions
over things like this.

She fussed around in the kitchen, looking for snacks. My relatives down South always fed me when I came around. My grandmother bought ice cream in five-gallon buckets just for me.

"You'll be a grown man soon, with your own car! Did you

know my daddy had the first car in Chickamauga? He had it shipped in from Chattanooga on the train."

I wiggled my ears. All these thousands of cars around me, and my great-great-grandfather had the first one in town. Of course, Chickamauga was a smaller town than Lawrenceville, but even so . . . Woof. I was impressed. I had a real motorcar pedigree.

Mamaw stood in the door to see me drive off. I backed out of the driveway and turned the wheel. I lined the car up, ready to shift into drive. I moved forward, but there was a problem. I got confused. The interactions were too much. The brakes. The gas pedal. The steering wheel. The shift lever.

I failed to properly coordinate the sequential operations of the various controls, and the Buick ended up in the ditch, on top of the mailbox. In Georgia, there was always a ditch at the edge of the road.

My uncle, who had gotten out of the car and was proudly watching me drive all by myself, quickly jumped back to avoid being flattened.

"Damn, John Elder! You wrecked the car! You ran over the mailbox!"

"Oooooooooooh, John Elder!" said Mamaw.

My uncle stepped over to the car and put it in park. I got out.

My uncle climbed in and backed the Buick into the street. We looked it over. The chrome didn't seem damaged. The mailbox seemed all right, too, just bent a little where it had been yanked out of the ground. I tried to put it back, but the hole was way too big and the mailbox just fell over. It seemed ruined. All of a sudden, I was frantic.

"It's gonna be okay," Bob said. "We'll go back and get the post-hole digger and fix it."

Bob drove us back home. Out behind the house, he had a shed filled with boxes of nuts and bolts, old tools, lawn mowers, and all sorts of nameless junk. Dandy—my great-grandfather—had filled the shed with all manner of wood-handled agricultural tools.

Uncle Bob chose a tool with two long handles coming up from a steel bucket.

I was fascinated. I had never noticed the posthole digger before. It looked like a metal clamshell with long handles. That was a tool that could do a lot more than dig postholes in a farmer's field.

I carried it out to the car. My uncle drove. I figured one trip was enough for me for a while.

"I can dig the hole," I said. I was anxious to try it out.

"I better do it, John Elder. We need to get finished before Mama gets home and finds out what we did to her car." Bob called my grandmother Mama. I called her Carolyn.

Bob rammed the digger down into the ground and picked up a bite of dirt. In a few minutes, he had a hole almost two feet deep. We replanted the mailbox and packed the dirt around the pole.

When we got back, I took the posthole digger out of the trunk. I walked over beside the shed and banged it into the ground, just like my Uncle Bob had done. It was hard work!

Two days later, I had dug a hole as deep as the handles were tall. I had dug as far as I could. There were so many things I could do with my new hole.

Jump in with a machine gun, and it's a foxhole.

Put some paper on top, and it's a pit trap.

Drop the dog inside, and it's a dog jail.

For the rest of the summer, I dug holes. I wanted to take the posthole digger home, but my grandparents said they needed it there.

When I went back to Massachusetts, I went to the basement to see what my father had for farming tools. He had a posthole digger, too.

I went into the front yard and started going at it. Before the hole was knee deep, I was stopped by rock. I moved over a few feet and the same thing happened. Pretty soon I had filled the front yard with rock-bottomed holes.

I hadn't hit rock in Georgia. That was just one more reason it was nicer down there.

We had a large pile of wood mulch to the side of the house. My father had gotten a truckload of the stuff to spread around and make the yard look nice. But he never did it, so the mulch was still there, decomposing, where the truck had dumped it. I decided that would be a good place to dig a deeper hole. There should not be any rocks in the wood chip pile.

Sure enough, it was easy to dig in wood chips. I hit rock again, but this time the hole was at least five feet deep. I was ready to try it out.

"Varmint, come outside. We have a hole to test," I yelled in the window. He was sitting in his room, wrapped in aluminum foil, looking at the pictures in *People* magazine. Varmint would often go along with my experiments because he had fun sometimes and didn't usually get damaged.

Varmint blinked as he emerged from the house into the light. He always stayed inside, in the dark, unless I lured him out. I motioned him over to where I was standing, by one of the smaller holes. I had to be careful not to make him suspicious or scare him off.

"I want to see how easy it is to get out of these hole traps. Lay down on the ground, and I'll drop you in. You see how fast you can get out."

"Okay," he said.

I picked him up by his legs and lowered him into one of the little holes. I had to start him on something easy. He swung his legs around, and climbed right out.

"That was easy!" Of course it was easy. That's why I'd dropped him in that one first. But I didn't say anything.

"Okay, let's try this hole."

We went over to the wood chip hole. I picked him up by the legs again and dropped him in. This hole was deeper than he was tall. He vanished from sight. He kicked and squirmed, but all he succeeded in doing was kicking wood chips from his feet down to bury his head. He was stuck good.

I was pleased. This was a fine hole, able to trap a big kid. I went inside for ten or fifteen minutes to get something to eat. When I came out, Varmint was nowhere to be seen. I had expected he would have gotten out in the time I was gone, but he was still in there. I kicked some wood chips in to see if filling the hole would cause him to emerge. He just yelled. I pulled him out before the neighbors heard him.

When he emerged, he was quite angry, despite the fact that I'd just rescued him. "You put me in a hole!" he shouted. His face was almost purple, and he waved his arms and jumped and yelled. I watched with interest, being sure to stay at a safe distance. He might have been red-faced because he was mad. Then again, he might have been red-faced because he'd been upside down for the previous fifteen minutes.

"Of course I put you in a hole, Varmint. That's what you came out here for. To test holes."

He looked puzzled for a minute, pondering the obvious truth of what I just said.

"Real Varmints live in holes. And a real Varmint wouldn't have gotten stuck like you did. You must be a retarded Varmint."

That was too much for him.

"I'm *not* a retarded Varmint!" And at that, Varmint started banging on me with little fists. I tried to jam him back in the hole but he ran off and started throwing sticks and rocks at me. I went in the house and locked the doors. I let him in when he calmed down.

The next day, I covered my holes with brown paper bags, which I then covered with dirt. I checked them daily to see if I had caught anything. I encouraged Varmint to try to trap some of his friends in the wood chip hole, but we never succeeded.

As summer turned into fall, my holes just sat there. Varmint had taken to driving his toy trucks in and out of the little holes, but he stayed clear of the big one. Halloween was coming, and I had an idea. Back then, explosive flash powder was available for pennies from theatrical supply places. I would fill the holes with flash powder wired to detonators in my room. I would make my own war movie for trick-or-treaters, one in which they would be the stars. I needed more holes. It was time to put Varmint to work.

We were ready by the time Halloween rolled around.

That Halloween, Varmint stood in the doorway like a sweet child, luring trick-or-treaters in with his innocent smile. He enjoyed being the bait. As they walked up the path, they passed my flash-powder-filled holes. Each hole was wired to an extension cord that led to my room, from which I watched the whole spectacle. When the kids got close, I would plug in a cord, detonating the powder in one of my holes. There would be a hell of a flash and a roar. A fireball would rise into the sky, and dirt would fly everywhere. The kids would scream and scatter.

That year was one of our most economical candy years. Very few trick-or-treaters braved the blasts for a second run. We ate the candy ourselves the next day.

As I got older, my practical jokes grew more sophisticated. When I was fourteen, my guidance counselor said, "John, some of your tricks are sick. They are evil. They indicate deep-seated emotional problems." It was true that some of my pranks had taken on a nasty edge. My sadness at how other kids had treated me all my life had turned to anger. If I had not found electronics and music, I might well have come to a bad end. It was around this time that I came up with one prank that trumped all the others.

It was one hot summer night in the Shutesbury woods when the rural quiet ended abruptly. Everyone in my house was asleep as I opened my bedroom window and dropped to the ground. I carried a knife and a flashlight, though I didn't expect I'd need either one unless something went very wrong. I knew my way and I was prepared. I walked up the dirt road, ducking into the bushes any time the lights of a car approached. It was about a mile from my house to my destination—the power lines on Sand Hill Road.

Underneath the steel high-tension tower, a hundred yards back from the road, five one-gallon cans of paint were arranged in a pentagram. I'd carefully swept the area clear of leaves and debris, and I'd cut straight pieces of wood from the trees nearby for the lines of the pentagram. The cans marked the points. There was a five-gallon pail of roofing tar in the middle with a circle of stones around it. I had set them out that afternoon, and now I lit them. With all of them burning, thick and poisonous black smoke rose in a cloud that blotted out the stars above.

I had hoped the paints—oil-based stains, actually—would burn in different colors, but they all burned with the same dull yellow flames. I had stolen the paint cans from a construction site down the road and I hadn't had time to test-burn them. I wished I had some kerosene, too, to liven things up. Maybe even some gasoline. But it was too late for that. The paint would have to do.

It was a moonless night and the rising smoke made it even darker up in the tower. But the fires would be burning brighter soon, and then I knew my guests would be able to see. My guests, of course, had not yet arrived.

I had set up the whole scene in the dark. It had been hard work, especially climbing the tower. It was scary, being up there with seventy-five thousand volts only a few feet above my head. A quick move up there might have been fatal. I felt the electricity crackle once when I raised my arm and I slowly and carefully lowered it back down. Rigging the rope was the hardest part. It was a heavy pull for a fourteen-year-old. But I did it. No one saw me.

By eleven o'clock, there was no traffic at all. I hadn't seen a car pass in over an hour. I was ready.

The fires were brighter, and anyone approaching would be sure to see what I'd done. About ten feet above the pentagram, a body was hanging. It was dressed in old clothes, and the rope around its neck was tied to the crosstree of the electric tower, thirty feet above. I had practiced making hangman's nooses until I got it right. The one up on the tower was perfect, as anyone with a flashlight could see. The feet had already turned black and greasy from the smoke and the blackness was trailing up the legs. Soon the whole body would be covered in disgusting oily black soot. The tar in the middle was bubbling now. The edges of the pots glowed dull red.

I'd adjusted the body's height carefully. Too high to recover from the ground, but low enough to see in the light of the fires. Overall, I was pleased.

Out at the road, a few hundred yards away, the fires were visible as a dim glow through the brush—not bright enough to attract attention. College students had campfires and all-night parties up there every weekend when school was in session.

But school wasn't in session, and this was no college party.

It was time to call the authorities.

I walked out to the road. It was pitch-black. There were no houses for half a mile in either direction, and no street lights. Just a lonely dirt road. The only people within shouting distance were the dead ones in the cemetery down near the stream. I climbed the telephone pole on the street and clipped on the wires from my linesman's telephone, which I had looted along with some other supplies from a visiting phone truck a few months earlier.

I clipped onto the phone circuit for Mr. Ellis, one of my least favorite neighbors. Out there, the phone circuits ran on individual pieces of copper wire, strung from pole to pole. Our town had 273 residents as of the last census, and they didn't all have phones. If you're going to climb poles and clip onto wires in the dark, you need to know which ones carry phone signals and which carry electrical power. Otherwise, you can get fried.

I had a dial tone. Hanging from the pole by a strap made from two belts I'd stolen from my father, I dialed the state police, whose number I had memorized.

"StatePoliceThisLineIsBeingRecorded," the trooper said.

"I'd like to report a hanging," I said, in my lowest and toughest voice.

"What?" That slowed him down.

"A ritual hanging. A person. On Sand Hill Road. From the power lines. Come see."

I unclipped the phone, climbed down, and retreated into the woods. *If they can trace the call,* I said to myself, *that jerk Ellis will get a visit tonight.* He had a kid, too, a snotty little shit. *Maybe they'll wake him up and ask him about this,* I thought. *Maybe they'll even arrest him.* I snickered at the thought.

I circled back through the stream, in case the visiting police had dogs. I felt at home in the woods after dark. My night vision was excellent, my hearing superb. I worked my way into a perch in a pine tree. From there, I had a panoramic view of the whole scene but I was far enough back in the trees that I was invisible, even if they shined lights. I could climb down silently, and I was high enough that casual searchers would pass under me if I needed to hide. I waited in the dark.

I used to be afraid of the dark, but I wasn't anymore. I used to fear barking dogs. I would cringe and say to myself, "Nice doggie please don't bite me I'll just go away," but by that night I could look at them and think, *I am your worst nightmare. Come closer and I will impale you upon my stick.* The more firmly I visualized it, the more the dogs believed it.

Now the tables had turned. Now the dogs feared me.

Fifteen minutes passed. Perhaps the police were far away. Perhaps they were napping. Finally, I saw headlights approaching. They had arrived. The wait was over.

The police car stopped in the road. The door opened and closed. There was only one trooper in the car. State troopers usually patrolled alone back then. I knew my fire would draw him in, like a moth to a flame. There was nothing else for him to see. There was only one power line, and my fire was the only light. It was burning even brighter now. The flickering light illuminated him as he walked on the path to the tower. He had his light in his hand. He aimed it up a bit. Above the fire, the body twisted gently in the smoke. The trooper stopped dead in his tracks.

"Holy shit!" I heard him say.

He looked around, swinging his flashlight back and forth, searching for an attacker in the brush. He drew his gun, but there was nothing to shoot. In the movies, this was the moment when something big and black grabbed the trooper and dragged him screaming into the swamp. From the look of him, I was sure he'd seen those movies, too. I was very still, not wanting to be shot. There was no sound other than the chirps and creaks of the night-time, and the occasional rustle of wind in the trees. He jumped and spun every time the trees rustled. There was no light except the flicker of the fires and the headlamps of the cruiser, up on the road. Suddenly, he holstered his gun, turned, and ran back to his cruiser. I heard the door open and shut.

I heard the click as he locked the doors. The blue light started flashing. He remained in his vehicle. I wasn't surprised. If I were him, all alone out there, I'd stay in my car, too, after seeing that. Police are supposed to be brave, but there are limits.

I heard the chatter on his radio but I could not make it out. I figured reinforcements were being called. Ten minutes passed. The fire got brighter. Two more cruisers arrived. They all got out of their cars. They talked. Everyone knows there is safety in numbers. Now they were brave.

"Where is he?"

The first trooper led the way. They walked down the power line road to the tower. They looked up.

"Sonofabitch!" one of the new troopers said.

"Wadda we do?"

"You climb up and cut him down."

"I'm not getting fuckin' electrocuted."

"He ain't goin' nowhere. He's dead."

"Call the fire department."

"Call the electric company."

They shined lights around, looking for perpetrators. One trooper returned to his cruiser, presumably to call the fire department and the power company. When he returned, he had the pump shotgun from his trunk. I'm sure it was loaded. But there was nothing to shoot. *There's no ambush tonight.* It was still quiet. More time passed. I was getting bored up in my tree.

They did not interfere with my burning pentagram. I wondered what they made of it. Was it devil worship? A lynching? An elaborate suicide? By now, the body was jet black from the soot, and it was starting to drip from the heat of the burning tar, which was bubbling in the pail. I was glad I had used tar. The drips and the foul black smoke kept the people back.

The fire department arrived. First came a single fire truck, then individual firemen in a ragtag collection of vehicles. Soon half a dozen cars and pickups clustered in the road, with red lights flashing.

The electric company crew arrived next, with a big yellow cherry picker truck. It had only taken one of me to hang my friend up in the tower, but it was going to take twenty of these people to get him down.

Now we had blue, red, and yellow lights all flashing. The road was blocked. Radios were cackling. If we had been in the city, there would have been a crowd gathered by now. They finally decided to put the fire out, but they acted as though it might be booby-trapped. The firemen seemed afraid to go near the paint cans. I guess the scene was unusual enough to be unsettling.

People continued shining flashlights into the grass around the tower, but there was no evidence to be found. I had made sure of that. I'd worn gloves, and all the materials had been scavenged or stolen. I hadn't bought anything that was up in the tower, and nothing was traceable to me. They couldn't get fingerprints off a tree. And they weren't going to catch me.

There were no fire hydrants on Sand Hill Road, but the fire truck had a water tank on board. They unrolled a hose and walked in the direction of the tower. I wondered why they didn't just drive there. Perhaps they'd blocked themselves in with all the cars up at the road. From fifty feet back, the firemen turned the water on my fire. The hose jumped, and a blast of water hit the burning pots and scattered them. All of a sudden there was a big cloud of steam and a flash; burning paint and tar went flying. Now the grass was on fire, too. All those firemen standing around suddenly had something to do. For a moment, the body was forgotten. More hoses came out, and shovels, and foam, and soon the whole area was wet and dark. Firemen walked around in the dark, stomping out embers. It was hard to see the body now that the light had gone. One of the cops shined a light on it.

"Turn the fucking light off! Don't you have any respect!"

The power line had been turned off. I could tell, because the faint crackle from the wires had stopped. There was no sound but the crickets. The power company truck bumped down the road to the tower. The driver stopped at its base, and put out his wheel chocks, just like he was on a highway. The ambulance followed him down, and they backed up to face the tower. Another power company truck lit the ground at the base of the tower with its headlights. The cherry picker on the first electric company truck started rising. The medics gathered at the base of the tower with a stretcher. It was time to recover the body.

"Ready down there?"

"Ready."

The lineman reached over and cut the rope. The body fell. The medics moved gingerly to pick it up. Suddenly, there was a shout, and the reverent mood changed.

"Fuck!!!"

A few seconds later, I heard the disgusted yell, "It's a fucking mannequin!"

"A department store dummy!"

"It's a fucking joke!"

Smiling, I slipped out of my tree and into the woods. I headed for home quickly, in case anyone came to check on me. I hid my lineman's phone and dark clothes in the cemetery on the way home. I climbed the board I had left leaning against the side of the house and crawled in through my bedroom window. Before I dropped inside, I kicked the board away and it fell among the high grass, car parts, and junk on the ground in front of the house. I slipped into bed and pretended to be asleep. Soon I was.

I had always known that someday I would find a use for that mannequin I saw in the Dumpster behind Mr. Walsh's clothing store. It had been hard getting him home and hiding him, but it had proved worth it.

The next day, I returned to the power line to get the mannequin. He was gone. I figured the police had taken him. There was no sign of the previous night's excitement except a burned spot in the grass near the tower and some empty charred paint cans on the ground. The tar had soaked into the dirt in the middle of the stones, and my sticks were scattered about. I wished I could tell someone about my adventure. I had few friends, and I couldn't tell my brother, because he was only six and had no sense. He would probably rat me out to some other little animal's mother. I didn't say anything about the incident to anyone for a long time.

A few days later my mother took me to the airport for my annual trip to visit my grandparents in Georgia. It was just as well that I'd be in Georgia in case the cops came around, asking about the mannequin.

9

I Drop Out of High School

As my sixteenth birthday approached, I found myself spending less time in school and more time hanging around bars with local bands. I was failing every subject. Working with John and Fred in the AV department was the only activity that interested me. That and walking Little Bear home. My graduation date seemed to recede two days into the future with every day that passed.

My parents seemed oblivious to my struggles. After all, they were starring in their own epic, and I was just a supporting player. At this point in their marriage, my parents largely left Varmint and me alone. That allowed them to focus all their energies on attacking each other. Their fights would increase in intensity until something blew. On several occasions, that meant a quick departure for my mother, my brother, and me.

"Your father has snapped," my mother declared on one of those occasions. "He's homicidal. He's planning to kill us all. We have to hide until the doctor can have him committed."

I had heard my mother say that before, and indeed I would hear it several more times in the year to come, but I still wasn't sure who was telling the truth. She might have been right, I figured, given my previous experience with my father. In retrospect, though, I suspect it was merely my mother's paranoia, fueled by her mental illness and Dr. Finch's increasingly bizarre behavior. He renamed his office the Institute of Maturation, and on sunny days, he paraded around town with an umbrella, towing a passel of balloons. He said he was drawing attention to his causes.

At times, when my mother posed a difficult question, he would use a technique called "Bible dipping" to arrive at an answer. He'd say, "Margaret, open the Bible and put your finger on a passage." She would do that, and he would read the passage and we'd discuss what to do. I don't mean to disparage the Bible, but, frankly, it does not strike me as the place to look for answers to questions like "Should we leave home and go stay in Gloucester for a while?" *I want a professional to tell me what to do,* I thought. *I can go home and read the Bible some other time.*

It was hard to object to even his most dubious techniques, though, because he and his family were always really nice to me, and he made me feel better.

After a few days' "vacation," we returned home. While we were gone, the police had arrested my father and locked him in the Northampton State Hospital for observation. When they let him out a week or so later, he was subdued and seemed to have less potential for violence. I watched him carefully because of his prior history, but I had always judged the probability of his murdering us to be low. When he got drunk, he was mostly just belligerent, and I doubted he would actually hunt us down and kill us while sober. Also, thanks to his talks with the doctor, he no longer attacked me, no matter how much he might have wanted to.

Dr. Finch was in some ways the least predictable variable in the whole equation. Sometimes it seemed like he calmed things down and other times it seemed like he fired my parents up.

Looking back, I can see that my father was seriously depressed. At the same time, my mother was becoming genuinely crazy. She would tell me about the demons that were watching her, interrupting herself periodically to howl like a wild animal. My brother has described it very well: She would get a glint in her eye, and she would become manic. She would talk nonstop and smoke nonstop and go faster and faster and faster and then surprise you by doing something totally outlandish, like eating cigarette butts in the middle of a conversation. *Is it hereditary?* I wondered. *Will it happen to me?* The terrifying threat of mental collapse followed me long into adulthood.

My brother and I lurched from one parent to another, with my parents' friends and the doctor's daughter Hope popping in to take care of us when both parents were down for the count. My mother's friend Pat Schneider sticks in my mind as helping more than most in that time, but many other people whose names I have forgotten pitched in. I don't know what would have happened if they had not been around. I guess we'd have ended up in foster homes or something even worse.

When the ambulance arrived to take my mother to the state hospital a few months after our "vacation," I agreed with Dr. Finch that she needed to be there. I dimly remember going to visit her. We had to go through several locked doors, as in a prison, and my mother looked like an inmate. She seemed to be in a zombielike state from whatever medication they had put her on. I wondered if she would ever get out.

That was a very hard time for Varmint and me, because we didn't know whom to believe. It seemed like everyone told us a different story.

"Your mother has temporarily lost her mind," our father would say when she wasn't around. "It runs in her family." This was said in a perfectly calm voice. And when she was gone, he didn't get drunk. *Why can't he be that way all the time?* I thought. Our mother, mean-while, prepared us for the idea that our father was planning to hunt us down and kill us someday. At least until she herself was locked up.

One of the toughest things about living with my parents was the way they changed at the drop of a hat. Some days, my father would just lie in bed, mumbling nonsense like "The bats are flying all around . . . I have to go get the sink." "He's just acting out," my mother would rage. Was he? I could never tell. The next day, it would be as if nothing had happened.

To my grandfather Jack, it seemed pretty black and white. "Your mother's family is just no damn good! All those Richters are crazy! Look at them!" I did look at them, and they seemed okay to me. Jack's comments really worried me, though. For a long time, I wished I could move down to Georgia and live with Jack, but I never did.

"Your parents are really good people, and they mean well. They're just having a hard time." Pat Schneider and Dr. Finch's daughter Hope would try to reassure us, but they were not the ones whose parents were raving or locked in cages.

I tried to look out for the Varmint, but it was hard.

With all the chaos, there wasn't much chance of my being an A student ever again, or even passing my courses. I had too many family problems and too many defects. I have already mentioned my problems looking people in the eye. There were other issues, too. Apparently, I was also guilty of bobbing and bouncing and weaving. And the stress was making it worse.

"Why are you bobbing your head like that?"

I heard that line a lot from teachers and other grown-ups when I was little. I still hear a variation of it today.

"Dad, stop being autistic!"

That's what my teenage son says when I rock back and forth in a restaurant.

Both comments—snivels, I would call them, since no harm is being done—refer to my tendency to move in some kind of regular pattern without knowing it. I might be lying on the sofa, moving my foot back and forth. Or I might be reading a menu, gently rocking from side to side. Or I might just be bobbing my head up and down. Whatever I am doing, it feels perfectly normal to me. But I guess "normal" people don't do it. I don't know what causes me to start; in fact, I seldom notice when I do start. It just happens.

Then someone says, "Stop bobbing!" and I come to a halt.

"What's the matter with you! I told you about that head bob-bing five minutes ago and now you're doing it again! Are you try-ing to make me mad?"

Reactions like that would just reinforce the feeling that I did not belong in school.

Along with bobbing and weaving, I was also frequently criti-cized or ridiculed for inappropriate expressions. These attacks seemed to me to come out of the blue, and they usually made me want to run off and hide.

"Why are you staring at me like that?"

"Wipe that stupid expression off your face! Right now!"

"You're scary! You're staring at me like a specimen in a jar!"

When I was in tenth grade, I heard the increasingly unwelcome "specimen in a jar" crack one time too often from my English teacher, Mrs. Crowley. "What *are* you staring at?" she would say. It was not a polite question but a rude demand. So one day I answered her rudeness with sweetness and light.

"Oh, Mrs. Crowley," I answered, in my nicest voice, "I was just imagining you chained up, in a deep hole, with a heavy steel grate on top. And rats. Lots of rats. Crawling all over you." Then I made a smile, baring my teeth the way dogs do when they're ready to bite.

That got me a trip to the principal, and then the guidance office, and then the school psychologist. But it was worth it. Mrs. Crowley never once made a crack to me again.

I don't recall any grown-up ever trying to figure out *why* I was staring. I might have been able to tell them if they had asked. Sometimes I was thinking of other things and just gazing their way absentmindedly. Other times I was watching them intently, trying to interpret their behavior.

My parents decided on a last-ditch effort to keep me in school. They enrolled me in a group for troubled kids. We would meet each week in an old farmhouse owned by the university and talk about our problems getting along. There were six of us, and a facilitator, who was a psychology major. They didn't teach me to get along, but I did learn that there were plenty of other kids who couldn't get along any better than me. That in itself was encouraging. I realized that I was not the bottom of the barrel. Or if I was, the bottom was roomy because there were a lot of us down there.

In the first sixteen years of my life, my parents took me to at least a dozen so-called mental health professionals. Not one of them ever came close to figuring out what was wrong with me. In their defense, I will concede that Asperger's did not yet exist as a diagnosis, but autism did, and no one ever mentioned I might have any kind of autistic spectrum disorder. Autism was viewed by many as a much more extreme condition—one where kids never talked and could not take care of themselves. Rather than take a close and sympathetic look at me, it proved easier and less controversial for the professionals to say I was just lazy, or angry, or defiant. But none of those words led to a solution for my problems.

It would take more than a discussion group to fix my school troubles. So when my next report card showed straight Fs, I realized it was time to go. There hadn't been much keeping me there anyway beyond the vague idea that being a legitimate high school graduate was better than being a dropout. There was only one problem. I was just fifteen, and it was against the law to quit school before the age of sixteen.

The school had such a strong desire to be rid of me that they stepped up to the plate with a solution. "If you take the GED and score at least seventy-five percent, we'll treat you as a graduate and you can leave." My guidance counselor presented this to me in the same tone of voice he'd use to sell some punk a two-hundred-dollar Cadillac in his second job as a used car salesman. I took the test and got a 96 percent. They offered me a diploma, "for a small recording fee."

"Only twenty dollars," the clerk said with a smile.

I smiled back. "No thanks," I said. "I don't need your diploma." And I never looked back. My parents hardly seemed to notice.

It was time to figure out what to do, now that I was a fifteen-year-old grown-up. It was a little scary. I retreated to the woods to think, just as I'd done as a little boy in Seattle.

I had always loved the outdoors, and once I wasn't in school it felt as though I had all the time in the world. It was spring, and I spent a lot of time alone, thinking about what I should do next. I would venture out from home for days at a time, living under trees and in falling-down cabins that I found in the forest.

One day I was walking through a glade of young pine trees, several miles from home, when a voice boomed out of nowhere.

"Stop right there!"

I ducked under some pine branches. There shouldn't have been anyone for miles in any direction.

But there was. Twenty feet in front of me, a shaggy-haired guy in army camouflage sat tending a coffeepot over a small fire.

What the fuck!

I stopped.

The guy was camped in the middle of a small clearing. I saw a green tent behind him. There were no guns in sight. There didn't seem to be anyone else around.

"You're just a kid. What are you doing out here?"

I didn't think of myself as "just a kid," but he was older and bigger and appeared to be living in the woods. I considered running away, but there didn't seem to be any threat. I decided to answer.

"I live here," I said. "About two miles away. What are *you* doing here?"

"I live here, too," he said. "Right here."

"Here in the woods?" Grown-ups were not supposed to live in tents.

"For now. I've lived in worse places," he said. "Have a seat." I sat down and he began to talk.

Paul told me he was a disabled Vietnam veteran. He had been shot, and his leg didn't work very well anymore. After getting out of the service, he'd been hitchhiking around the country, living off the land. I was fascinated.

"Want a drink?" he asked. I wasn't exactly sure what he was offering, but I nodded. He opened a small glass bottle filled with what looked like fizzy water. *Canada Dry* was all the label said. I took a sip and would have spit it out if I weren't on my best behavior.

"What is it?" I asked. I knew whiskey was nasty to swallow, but that drinking it was a sign of being grown up. Maybe this stuff would be the same.

"Quinine water!" He said it brightly, as though anyone should know what it was, and know it was good. By that point in my life, I had heard of all the most common types of liquor. Vodka. Whiskey. Rum. Tequila. Bourbon. None of them sounded anything like quinine water.

"I acquired a taste for it in 'Nam," he said. "It keeps you from getting malaria."

I had never heard of anyone in New England coming down with malaria. *Maybe it's one of those rare diseases, like meningitis,* I thought. *So it's like medicine water.* I took another drink. I had read about how they had to conquer malaria in order to build the Panama Canal. I looked around as I sipped my quinine water, comparing the Shutesbury woods to the Central American jungle.

Paul was living in a glade, far from roads, with nothing more than an army tent and a duffel bag. He had made a seat from a log, and he had a small ring of stones with a fire that warmed an old coffeepot. Where was his food?

"I live off the land, and I forage in town," he told me. Whatever he was doing must work, I figured, because he looked healthy.

"Why don't you build a shelter?" I asked.

"I don't want to settle down," he said. "I need to be able to move out on a moment's notice." In fact, he never did build a shelter. He seemed impervious to weather.

I had always thought I knew my way around the woods, but Paul showed me how much I still needed to learn. Paul could snare rabbits for a stew. He caught trout for breakfast. And to round it out, he knew how to forage in dumpsters for fresh baked goods and vegetables. Until I met him, I never knew the bounty that could be fished from a dumpster in a town like ours.

It was from Paul that I learned how to catch fish with a BB gun. It's surprisingly simple, provided you're a good shot. You sit at the edge of the pool, gun at the ready. Ideally, you sit in a tree branch so that you are eight to ten feet off the ground, looking down into the pool. Then you throw bread crumbs onto the pond's surface. When the fish swim up to eat them, you shoot them. It's a lot easier than fishing, but it does take a steady hand.

"I use a shotgun with slugs," Paul said. "That way, you don't have to hit the fish. They get stunned when the slug hits the water, and you just scoop 'em up. The only easier way to get fish is to toss a grenade in the pond and go in with a big net," he told me. I soon heard he'd done that, over at Smith College. The shore was lined with dead fish when I walked over to check it out.

Thanks to Paul, I learned to walk silently through the woods. I learned to flow around and under the brush, so as to pass without a sound and without a trace. I learned to live in the woods, not just visit.

I also learned to watch where I stepped.

"Watch that wire!"

Wire? Paul had rigged a perimeter of trip wires around his camp to prevent someone walking in and surprising him. They were virtually invisible.

"If that was rigged to a claymore mine, you'd be dead now!"

As a kid in the Shutesbury woods, it never would have occurred to me to watch for trip wires and land mines. Thirty years later, though, I still remember what he showed me, and I watch where I step.

He told me stories of his time in the Army. I expected a Vietnam vet to tell me of combat in faraway places, but that wasn't what I heard. He told me about being ambushed by tigers in the jungle. He told me about loading bales of drugs and contraband aboard DC-3 airplanes. He told me of setting booby traps for the

enemy, and impaling them with sharpened sticks. His stories bore
no resemblance to my previous notions of war, which were formed
watching Vic Morrow in the TV series *Combat*.

Paul stayed in his camp all through that summer. I walked up to
visit him almost every day, and I stayed several days on many occasions. It was a nice place to pass the time. There was no family
trouble, no pressure to get a job, and no one to give me a hard
time. The skills that had enabled Paul to hide in the Asian jungle
allowed him to remain perfectly hidden in Shutesbury. Whenever I
was there, I was invisible, too.

It was nice living in the Shutesbury woods with my friend
Paul, but anytime I wanted to go to town I faced a six-mile walk. I
never wanted to be a hermit. I always imagined myself being
around other people, even though I had a hard time interacting
with them. I realized that I needed some unique talent that would
make people interact with me. That way, I wouldn't have to initi-
ate any interactions—I'd just have to respond, which was easier for
me. Luckily, I was going somewhere with my talent for fixing and
improving and innovating musical equipment. I seemed to be able
to make it sing in a way that few others could. More and more,
musicians began seeking me out.

With every passing week, I was growing up. I had learned to avoid
land mines and had started imagining a future for myself in music.

That September, when the nights began getting cooler, Paul
began talking about going south to Florida. One fall morning, I
walked up to see him and he was gone. No trace of him. The camp
had been swept clear. I could have walked through a few days later
and I would never have known that someone had lived there for two
months. No trash, no disturbed ground, no evidence of any kind.

I never knew where he went, and I never told anyone about
him or what he taught me. Years later, I saw a news story about
Paul testifying at a Boston antiwar hearing and discovered that he
was a war hero, a highly decorated Green Beret.

It was time to come out of the woods and join society.

10

Collecting the Trash

For a long time, I had been considering how to escape my parents' house. When I was fifteen, my father had bought a motorcycle to commute to school. He wouldn't let me ride it, but it got me thinking about a bike of my own. I asked everyone I knew about motorcycles for sale. I scanned the classified ads for a cheap motorcycle. Finally, I found one. I bought a 1966 Honda Dream for twenty-five dollars. Once I made it run, I was able to get away, at least temporarily. It was with the possibility of escape in mind that I followed my parents to their friend Walter Henderson's fortieth birthday party. My parents were always on their best behavior when they were out in public, so I knew they would not turn on me. And I would be downtown, where it would be easy to get away if things got strange.

Slave and Stupid seldom did anything together. However, they both liked the Hendersons, so they headed to Walter's birthday party together. I liked Walter, too—at least what I knew of him. He taught English at Amherst College and wore a brown corduroy jacket. He was always an interesting fellow to talk to, and he seemed moderately interested in me. For some reason, my parents really wanted me to go to his party.

I had never gone to a faculty party before. They were for

grown-ups—usually my parents' friends. Some of their friends were okay, but others seemed to me arrogant and conceited, and it was starting to make me angry. I knew I was some kind of misfit, but it was becoming apparent that some of the grown-ups who smiled sweetly and told me how terrible and fucked-up I was were complete fuckups themselves. And my experience in the music scene had shown me that there were places in the world where misfits were welcome.

Slave said, "John Elder, Walter and Annette really like you. They really hope you'll come to their party." *Maybe they like me,* I thought. *Or maybe they think I'll be entertaining because I'm weird.* Yes, that was more likely. They thought I was weird.

Stupid said, "It's up to you, son, but they did invite you. If you ignore invitations, pretty soon they stop coming in."

As if I ever got invited to parties.

I decided to go, but I didn't ride with them. I went on my motorcycle. When we arrived, a big crowd was milling around in Walter's yard. They had a tent set up, and a table with food, and what looked like a band. Everyone was dressed better than me. *They probably all have good educations, respectable jobs, and families,* I thought. But I figured, *I'm clean. I shower every day. I'll be okay here.*

Walter had had cards printed for the occasion. He gave me one when we arrived. It said:

WALTER HENDERSON, 40
Lecturer, 40 different topics
Traveler, 40 different countries
Chef, 40 different courses
Lover, 40 different women

This was going to be my kind of party, I could already tell.

I didn't know what to do, so I just stood there. Annette saw me and led me over to talk to one of her friends. I guess she meant well. After a brief introduction, she flitted off to take care of the next guest. Her friend George turned out to be a rather pompous professor who tried to engage me in conversation.

"We have a son about your age," he told me. "We're very proud of him. He's starting at Harvard in the fall." Just then, another couple walked over and the woman said, "Our daughter Janet has decided to go to Smith. So she'll be nearby for four more years! What are you doing?"

All three of them looked at me.

I wasn't doing anything in particular. I certainly wasn't going to Harvard. Somehow, I was in the improbable position of scoring in the ninety-ninth percentile on the intelligence tests and still flunking out of high school.

I was sure this crowd would just sneer at the idea of my growing reputation with local bands, so I decided not to mention it.

"I've actually started on a career," I said.

"Really? What are you doing?" This came from Thurston, another pompous friend of Annette's. Thurston, a department head at Amherst College, was far removed from making any career choices himself. He stood there, drink in hand, with a superior smile. Perhaps he was thinking of visiting his Thugwald, or whatever his son's name was, at Yale.

"I've gotten into the waste management business. Down in Springfield. They've started me right at the bottom so I can really learn the business. On a truck, in the North End."

"You mean you're a garbage collector?" someone asked, polite but incredulous. Garbage collectors were not usually seen at Amherst College faculty parties. Garbage collectors came in afterward and emptied the trash. They didn't participate in creating the trash with their intellectual betters.

I smiled back.

"We don't call ourselves garbage collectors. We are Sanitary Engineers."

By this time, another older fellow had stepped over to join the conversation. I didn't know him, but with his curly hair, tweed coat, and bow tie, he probably wasn't a Sanitary Engineer.

"I'm an engineer. I went to college for eight years for the privilege. I don't think a mere city garbage collector has the credentials to call himself an engineer."

I decided to change the subject.

"You know, we see all kinds of things. Just last week one of my buddies found a dead baby in the Dumpster behind one of the dorms at the college."

That was met with shocked silence.

"We heard the mother was a student there. No one knows why she threw the baby away. Her father was the president of some big company. But she's in jail now."

There were now six people gathered around. I had given them something to think about. Would their kids do anything like that? One of the moms forced a smile and said, "It must be hard being out there in all kinds of weather."

"The weather isn't the problem. We can take weather. It's the packs of wild dogs and the feral children you really have to worry about."

"Feral children?" That surprised them.

"We meet them in the rougher parts of town. Two of them hit one of our guys in the head with a beer bottle full of gravel. Cut him badly. Almost killed him. They're worst when they're in packs. And some of them carry knives."

My audience looked shocked. "Can you get a police escort?" one asked.

"No, the police don't care. They have their own problems. It's a city, you know. We've started carrying billy clubs. They won't let us carry guns. A few of the guys carry motorcycle chains. They wear 'em like necklaces. A punk with a knife is no match for one of us, swinging a motorcycle chain."

I let them digest that for a moment. They would see their local trashman in a whole new light after that. They looked horrified, but they couldn't help themselves. I was not your usual faculty party entertainment.

"What do your parents think of your new career?"

"They wanted me to go to medical school, but when I told them how much money my boss makes, they were impressed. He does a lot better than any doctor I know. So I guess they're proud of me."

"How does your boss do so well?" asked a bookish-looking fellow who had recently walked up.

"Tips. We get tips everywhere we go."

"I've never heard of that. Who gives a garbage man tips? I've never done that." The woman who was speaking sounded pretty sure of herself. No tips for her garbage man.

"Well, if you're in the city, and you don't want the dumpster to spill shit all over your steps when they pick it up, you tip the trashman. One of those dumpsters can do a lot of damage if it falls on a car. A well-tipped driver makes sure that doesn't happen. And if you've got a restaurant, you make sure you tip good, otherwise your trash overflows, you have trouble with rats, and the health inspector shuts you down."

Inspired by the appalled silence, I continued.

"Did you read about that burger joint on Boston Road? Whole kitchen was full of rats. Little girl went in the bathroom and got bit. It was savage; her arms were all chewed up. And just nine years old. That place probably won't ever reopen. They didn't pay their Sanitary Engineer, and look what happened."

"Excuse me, may I talk to you a second?" said Annette. She and my mother had caught me entertaining their friends. They steered me away from the group. I moved toward the food table, picked up the shrimp platter, which had only eleven shrimp remaining on it, and began to eat. I was having a fine time.

"John Elder, what are you going to do? You can't lead those people on like that! They believe you!"

"Well, you invited me." And they had. But they wouldn't do so again.

"Hey, Annette, I've got a question for you. Which is easier to load on a garbage truck? A pile of bowling balls, or a pile of dead babies?"

"I don't know," she said sullenly.

"Dead babies. You can use a pitchfork."

My mother and Annette looked sick. They were both sorry they had invited me. I wasn't worried. I was sure Walter would see the whole thing as humorous. I ate the last shrimp.

"I'll go apologize to your friends. You wait here."

I walked back to the group of garbage aficionados I had collected.

"Folks, I'm sorry but I've got to go. They just called from work. Emergency. One of the other garbage companies firebombed one of our trucks. They're calling all of us in. See you later."

And with that, I walked quickly to my motorcycle, put on my helmet and leather jacket, and kicked over the engine. The back wheel spun up little clumps of grass as I rode away, my crazy parents and their friends receding in the rearview mirror.

11

The Flaming Washtub

Visiting my friend Jim Boughton's house was another of my escapes. We had similar interests, Jim and I. Rocketry. High-powered electricity. Explosives. Motorcycles. Fast cars. Jim lived about five miles away, in South Amherst. He was two years older than me, blond and heavyset, with a slightly demented look. He lived in a big old Victorian home that was owned by Amherst College, where his parents taught theater. The house was ours to wreck.

"Don't worry," Jim would say, as debris spattered the outside of the house. "Amherst College will fix it."

The Amherst College maintenance staff mowed the lawn, repainted the interior, and fixed all of our destruction. My father taught at the university, which was low-rent compared to Amherst. We didn't get a free house, and no one fixed anything. The holes I smashed in the doors at thirteen were still there three years later.

"Come check out what I built," Jim called and said one day.

Jim had been working feverishly on a top secret project, and it seemed he had finally gotten it to work. When I arrived at his house, he led me out to the shed, which stood about fifty feet behind his parents' house. Sitting in the middle of the floor was a burned-looking concrete barrel with a steel frame above it, from which a chain dropped into the barrel. A hose connected the barrel to a huge silver tank of propane.

"That's my new furnace," he said proudly.

Another eighteen-year-old would have shown off his new car, or his new guitar, or his new camera. Jim showed off his new blast furnace. He had built the whole thing himself, right there in the shed. He had made the pliers and tongs and equipment to handle molten metal. He had made the frames to hold the ceramic furnace body. And he had made the burner. Amazingly, almost everything was constructed from scrap. I was sure there was nothing else like it in Amherst.

"You've got your very own steel mill," I said.

"No. It's not a steel mill. You need oxygen injection to get the higher temperatures needed for steel. This is a nonferrous foundry for casting aluminum and bronze." I was a good audience. The average layperson would not have appreciated the distinction.

"Wanna see it work?" he asked. Without waiting for my agreement, he walked over and turned a switch. I heard the sound of a fan picking up speed.

"I've got two high-capacity vacuum cleaner blowers forcing air into the furnace. It's not as good as oxygen injection but it's free."

The sound of the fans got louder as they sped up. "I'm using the most powerful fans I could find at Grainger's, down in Springfield," Jim said. Those fans could move air. Inside the garage, my hair was starting to blow.

"Now we turn on the propane and light it off."

Jim turned what looked like a water faucet down low on the side of the machine. The smell of propane filled the garage.

"Ignition!"

He grinned, lit a ball of paper trash, and tossed it in the barrel.

There was a loud bang, and I was stunned for a second. A bright flash and the propane odor had vanished. If the shed had had windows, they would have blown out. But it didn't have windows, at least not since the first time the furnace had been fired up.

Once lit, it sounded like a jet engine at idle. I looked over the top of the barrel and saw flames swirling in the chamber.

"Let's crank it up," he said, as if it wasn't cranked already. He turned a big rheostat and the fans sped up as he turned the faucet to let more propane into the burner.

"We have to keep the propane mixture right," he said. "A yellow flame means carbon monoxide. We want an almost colorless blue flame."

The roar was increasing to the point where I needed earplugs. Blue flames came out the top of the barrel. The roar was incredible, unbearable. So was the heat.

"Let's melt some metal," he grinned. We tossed chunks of scrap aluminum into a bucket, which I quickly discovered was not a bucket when Jim corrected me.

"It's a number forty silicon carbide crucible. It holds forty pounds of aluminum or a hundred and twenty pounds of bronze. Molten, that is."

The aluminum chunks, former automobile transmissions, were about to liquefy.

Wearing heavy gloves, Jim hooked the crucible to the chains and used a pole to move it over the furnace. Then he lowered the crucible inside. The sound of the furnace changed slightly as it swallowed the metal. After a few seconds, the chain that dropped down into the barrel was glowing dull red, just like the barrel top. I was afraid to step over and look inside, but I did anyway. It had only been a few moments and already the hard edges of the broken metal were softening in the intense heat. His furnace looked like a jet engine running in a gardener's shed in South Amherst.

I opened the door to get some air, but Jim motioned me to close it.

"The roar antagonizes the neighbors. They might call the police." The police had visited Jim and his inventions in the past. We certainly didn't need them there again.

Jim pulled the chain and the crucible came up out of the furnace, glowing hot. He pulled it on the track and gripped it with long metal tongs. He handed me some gloves and another pair of tongs.

"You can help me pour."

I held the pouring shank—a long pole with a hoop in the middle that Jim had welded up in his garage workshop. Jim carefully set the crucible in the shank. He scooped the slag off the top, then slowly and smoothly poured the molten metal into a gray box on the floor. Steam jetted from the corners of the box as he poured. The box contained tightly packed damp sand. The object he wanted to mold in aluminum had been inserted into the damp sand, and then carefully withdrawn. The process was surprisingly delicate.

"It'll take a few minutes for the metal to harden, and we can crack the mold open."

He shut off the furnace. The fan spooled down, and the heat gradually diminished. Now that the noise was gone, he signaled that I could open the doors.

We cracked the mold halves apart. There, inside, lay a perfectly formed pair of human arms cast in gray aluminum. I was impressed.

"They're Andy's," Jim said proudly. Andy was his little brother. He had posed, if you can call it that, in Jim's sandbox while the arm molds were being made.

Jim sprayed the arms with water, and steam filled the garage. He lifted an arm.

"Look at the detail! Fingernails! Hair! Even fingerprints!" He was right. The casting was remarkably detailed.

A few months later, Jim was working in the garage attached to his parents' house. It was a big house with a big garage, which Jim had turned into his private auto repair shop. Jim had taken a huge soapstone washtub from the basement and made it into a parts-cleaning tank. He filled it with gasoline, which was flammable but very good for cleaning grease off old car parts.

That night, Jim and I were helping our friend John and his girl-friend, Carol, rebuild their VW engine. The engine block and a pile of other parts were soaking in the tank as we stood around, tinkering and drinking beer. Jim had installed a pump in the wash-tub to circulate the gasoline. It cleaned better if it was moving, but we couldn't run the pump all the time because the vapors were dangerous, and cleaning is a slow process. The gas was getting dirty, I guess. We'd already gone through a whole case of Old Mil-waukee, and less than half the parts were clean. It was after eleven, too late for more beer. We'd have to make do with what we had.

Jim walked over to plug the pump in, and a spark jumped clean across the garage. In an instant, the tub of gasoline was on fire. It seemed like the whole place was on fire. With all the fumes, it probably was.

"Fuck!"

"Fire!"

"Get out!"

"Now! Run!"

I was close to the door, so I jumped out, leaving my beer behind. All of a sudden, the seventy-five-degree night air felt cold. I didn't seem to be on fire, and I didn't feel damaged. I was lucky, I guess.

Everyone scattered through the open door, into the safety of the yard. Everyone but Jim. We could see him in the flame-filled garage. His arm was on fire. He took off his glove and swatted it, and the fire went out.

In only a matter of seconds, flames from the tub were hitting the garage ceiling. Yet Jim was still in there. He moved to the flaming tub, crouched low. With a mighty shove, he pushed the tub of burning gas and car parts out the door and into the drive-way. It came to rest about twenty feet away.

Jim was hardly burned at all. He was grinning, proud. He had saved the house. He took off his gloves, looked at each arm, and nodded approvingly.

"No damage!" He grinned.

In the heat of the burning garage, he had actually thought clearly enough to put on heavy gloves so that he could push the tub without destroying his hands. Remarkable.

"Good thing that tub was on wheels," Jim said.

It *was* good. Otherwise, the whole huge house would have burned to the ground.

Carol emerged from the house. I hadn't seen her go in, but then, a lot was happening. "I called the fire department," she said. "They're on the way."

Jim wasn't too happy to hear that. "Why did you call them?" he asked, as flames from the burning tub reached twenty feet into the sky. Truthfully, at that point it was harmless. It would have burned itself out in an hour or so, and provided entertainment. Jim, John, and I preferred not to involve the authorities in anything, for any reason. Two of us ran alongside the house and unreeled the garden hoses. There were two, more than enough, we figured, to wet down the surrounding area till the gas burned out.

The flames went out in the garage as Jim trained one of the hoses on the ceiling and on a few burning scraps on the floor. Out-side, however, the flames were roaring. The gasoline was burning fiercely, making a pyre higher than the roof of the house. Paint had started to bubble on the wall nearest the flames.

"I wish I'd pushed it a little farther away," Jim said.

It was way too hot to approach by then.

I looked at the scene and concluded the house was not in any real danger. Nothing fresh paint wouldn't fix.

At that moment, Jim's parents emerged. They had been reading at the other end of the house. They appeared calm. Jim's mother was smoking a cigar, and his father had a drink in his hand. They looked at us, the fire, and each other. Without a word, they went back inside.

Moments later, the fire department arrived. We were all standing back at least twenty feet because of the intense heat. Jim and I were regretting the loss of our engines, which would surely be nothing but slag when the fire cooled.

The fire department was ready to show its prowess. Four men ran down the driveway dragging a fire hose. Jim attempted to stop them.

"I don't think you want to do that. That tub contains gasoline and magnesium. You need foam, not water."

"We know what we're doing, son. Step out of the way."

"No! I'm telling you, water is dangerous on a magnesium fire! You need foam!"

"Step aside." The voice of authority spoke.

And with that, two men held the hose and blasted the tub. There was a violent explosion, as the water hit the burning magnesium, and the water broke down into its component parts, hydrogen and oxygen. The magnesium and gasoline exploded and rained down over the yard. We ran for cover.

Balls of magnesium, burning with a brilliant blue-white flame, were everywhere. The firefighters looked stunned. For some of them, the Vietnam veterans, it must have been like being back in combat. Right in Jim's backyard.

"Goddamn it, I warned you guys! Now look what you've done!"

It was a scene from hell. Chunks of burning magnesium had scattered everywhere from the blast. Some were eating holes in the van parked in the driveway. Some were burning on the roof of the house. Several seemed to be eating flaming holes through the driveway itself. Multiple fires were burning, many with the distinct white-hot glow of burning metal. The firefighters retreated to their truck, where it turned out they did carry foam.

Now they had some real work to do. They had sneered at foam before, but not now. Jim politely reminded them it was their fault. "You should've listened to me. Look at the mess you assholes made!"

They mixed the foam and—much more cautiously this time—approached the fires. Even the foam was slow to extinguish them. They would spray a spot and it would seem to be out, then explode again a minute later. It was scary, this mess the fire department had made.

Jim realized the root of their problem was lack of knowledge. "In a university town, you guys should be trained on chemical fires!" They did not respond.

Two firemen approached the tub with pikes, the sort of tools they use to break down doors. They knocked the burning tub over, presumably to let their buddy spray foam inside. They seemed to have forgotten Jim's warning.

"Stupid assholes, it's still full of gas!"

Now the yard, which had so far escaped destruction, was on fire, too. At least the scene was well lit. Two more fire trucks showed, and the chief arrived by car. A crowd had gathered. Jim's parents had come back out, and now they stood off to the side, speaking softly to each other. His dad had finished his drink and his mom was enjoying the last of her cigar by firelight. Their calm was remarkable.

It took the fire department over an hour to extinguish the blaze. When everything was out, and the night was once again dark, the chief had a long talk with Jim. There were calls for his arrest from some of the firefighters, but, really, there were no grounds. The chief could only threaten to return for periodic inspections of the house.

LATER ON, that night would seem like the calm before the storm, as my family and my life fell completely to pieces.

Little Bear told me she never wanted to speak to me again, and she wouldn't even tell me why. I was crushed. She wouldn't come to the phone and wouldn't see me. I didn't know what to do. I was so lonely. Two years would pass before I learned why she'd left.

On top of that, my parents finally separated. Varmint stayed with my mother, who moved to an apartment in town. Then, a few months later, my father moved to an apartment and my mother and Varmint returned to the house. The dog and I remained at the house through all of that, except for periodic forays into the woods.

Now that my parents had split, my mother decided she was bisexual. She took up with a woman her own age for a while, but then she got involved with a woman a year younger than me. It was unsettling, the idea that my mother would leave my father for a girl, but when her great love turned out to be even younger than me, that was just too weird.

Meanwhile, my father was struggling in his apartment in town, at one point eating sleeping pills in a drunken suicide attempt that left him drying out in the hospital. We were lucky his colleagues liked him and the university was tolerant. And I guess it's hard to fire a professor with tenure. He had stopped going to Dr. Finch, saying, "He has crazy ideas, son. I don't know what will happen with the doctor and your mother."

Despite the good things the doctor had accomplished for me, I, too, was troubled. Things just didn't seem right over there. I had gone to see doctors of one sort or another all my life. Their waiting rooms were places where other people actually waited. Patients flowed in and out. Their offices were always nice and clean. They looked, well, "professional."

Dr. Finch's office was nothing of the sort. It was old, and the furniture was run-down and threadbare. I never saw new faces there, just the same hangers-on—patients, he said—that I'd seen for years. Most of the time, the office was deserted except for Hope, the doctor, and us. It didn't look like any other medical office I'd ever seen.

"The doctor is unique," my mother would say.

"The doctor is crazy" was my grandfather's response.

Friends from town would say things like "I hear that Finch is a nutcase!" Even though the doctor had done good things for me, it was hard to maintain my confidence in the face of those remarks, especially when I began hearing them everywhere. Dr. Finch grew a long white beard, and wore a Santa hat in the middle of summer, which was not exactly reassuring. I learned he'd been fired from the state hospital before we'd met him. Hearing that, I thought of my grandfather's "run out of Kingsport, Tennessee" comment a few years back. Then I heard he was not even allowed in the local hospital. *Can that be true? What did he do?* I wondered.

Dr. Finch's strange behavior proved to be too much for my father and me. Both of us stopped going to see him. Not my mother, though. She believed in the doctor for six more years, right up until the day she escaped. And she dragged the Varmint along for a ride that got wilder and wilder as the doctor loaded her up on medications. Luckily for me, most of the shocking scenes that played out in front of my brother (described in his memoir *Running with Scissors*) were still a few years in the future, and by the time they occurred, I was well out of the doctor's orbit.

It was not until 1983 that my mother finally broke free. When she did, all the vague worries I had ever felt about Dr. Finch became concrete. My mother went to the DA, saying the doctor had medicated her and then sexually assaulted her at a motel. At the same time, DA investigators discovered that Dr. Finch had billed my father's health insurance for many nonexistent office visits. My mother was too upset to follow through with a sexual assault prosecution. She just wanted to escape.

So the DA filed larceny charges over the bogus billing. That allowed them to get a restraining order against Dr. Finch and protect my mother as a state witness. Even then, Dr. Finch tried to silence my mother by having her committed against her will. Knowing all this, I was not surprised when the doctor's medical license was revoked in 1986.

By then, I was long gone. It was music that took me from that insanity to a much better place. I was building a reputation among local musicians, and they welcomed me with open arms. Friday nights, I stepped from the madhouse that my family had become into the Rusty Nail, a local nightspot. Now that I was an insider, I didn't have to worry about sneaking in or getting carded. I'd even grown a beard, to look older. The bouncer and the cop actually greeted me at the door as they waved me inside.

As I walked into the room, the lead singer of a local band named Fat stepped up to the microphone. "This is rock 'n' roll, people!" He shouted it so loud, I saw the lights dim and felt my ears bleed. A palpable wave of energy rolled over the crowd, packed shoulder to shoulder. "Nineteen seventy-five!" When they launched into "King of the Highway," I was transported into my own world. I was so lucky I had the music to take me there.

I wish I could have brought the Varmint along. But I was just a kid myself, in grown-up clothes. He would be on his own.

12

I'm in Prison with the Band

It was Fat that saved me. Ever since I had dropped out of high school, I had been keeping their sound equipment going, and I had become friends with Dickie Marsh, the sound man, and Steve Ross, his assistant. Dickie was impressed that I had developed the ability to listen to the sound and tell him what knobs to trim on the graphic equalizer. He thought it was a natural gift, but it was really something I'd worked very hard at for several years.

After one show, Peter Newland, the lead singer and flute player, came to talk to me.

"You could move in with us and do music all the time," he said. "We could even pay you. Eighty dollars a week." With that, I joined Fat and had a home. The band members lived together in an old farmhouse in Ashfield, up in the Berkshires.

Billy Perry, the drummer, was across the hall from me. His drum practice ensured I'd never sleep too late. The rooms at the top of the stairs housed Mike Benson and Chris Newland, the band's two guitar players. Peter, Chris's brother and the band's leader, lived in the master bedroom up front. Dickie and Steve were squeezed in on the top floor. I moved my stuff into an empty room in the back corner of the ground floor and parked my motorcycle in the backyard, right next to my window.

Outside of time spent living in the woods as a feral child, this was the first time I had actually lived away from my family. With my own motorcycle, a place to live, and a role in a top band, I felt I had it made. To celebrate, I bought a Tektronix 504 oscilloscope, which became my pride and joy.

I spent my days working on the sound equipment in a quest to squeeze every last watt of power out of the amps and get the very best possible sound from all the instruments. Fat became known for its sound as well as the quality of its music. Steve, Dickie, and I took turns driving the truck to shows and lugging the equipment in and out.

It was a great life.

Fat was one of a small number of bands that played its own music in clubs all over New England. Our manager also got us jobs opening for bigger bands at large concerts in Boston. That winter, we played with James Montgomery, James Cotton, Roxy Music, and Black Sabbath. The time I spent with them allowed me to meet other musicians, and I got more calls to design things—from more powerful amps to an electric flute.

Old friends like Jim Boughton would come to my shows, but for the most part I was on my own, with a new circle of people around me. I was getting pretty good at adapting to new people and places.

I was even starting to see the world. Every time I had a day off, I took a trip somewhere on my motorcycle. I rode into Vermont, New Hampshire—anywhere I could go in a day's ride. That April, while the ground in Ashfield was still covered with two feet of snow, the band decided to take a trip to a Caribbean island, and I was included. They had saved up for this vacation, setting aside a few hundred dollars from every show. Personally, my entire net worth was the eighty dollars in my wallet when I left home, but Peter told me this would be an all-expenses-paid vacation. We flew from a dreary winter in western Massachusetts to Montserrat, a tropical paradise, where I would realize that I was kind of different from the typical rock 'n' roll musician.

The fun started at six in the morning, Easter Sunday, 1976. I was asleep in a villa high on a mountainside, with a long winding road leading from our door to the town of Plymouth far below. According to Peter, the villa belonged to some rich Englishman who liked musicians. The sun was just coming up, the air was clear, and it was a comfortable seventy-one degrees. All around us, the island was quiet. Montserrat has no industry, no highways, and no loud noise. It's warm and peaceful and very pretty.

You'd think anyone would be delighted to be there. Not me. All the small things I'd come to expect in life were missing. There was no regular American food. No hamburgers. No iced tea. There was nothing to eat but eggs and conch meat. And they said we could have chicken, but only if we killed the chicken, and if we killed it, we wouldn't have any eggs. But there was plenty of conch. However, I'd never eaten conch meat before and I was suspicious. It's like a cross between a scallop and a soft, decayed fish.

The truth was, I had no idea how to vacation. This was my first trip far from home with anyone besides my family. I had no money and there was hardly anything for me to do. One thing I learned from that trip was: *Bring money!*

Everyone except Willie, our native friend and guide, was asleep. I had taken a liking to Willie as soon as I met him, perhaps because he had a pet iguana that he led around on a leash made from scrap aircraft cable. This morning, the iguana was home and Willie was wild. He burst in the door and ran through the house, yelling at the top of his lungs.

"Wake up! Wake up, mons! It's a bust! Wake up!"

He ran down the hall, opening the doors and shouting at all of us.

"Wake up, mon, the law is coming!"

I opened my eyes and sat up. I didn't have any drugs. *I'm not up to anything,* I thought. *Why would I be getting busted?* I walked out onto the porch and looked down the hillside. Four carloads of ragged-looking natives were climbing the steep road to the villa. Each car had two guys riding on its hood and who knew how many guys inside. The ones on the hood had clubs. It didn't look like a raid. It looked like the natives were attacking.

I ran back inside.

"Fucking natives with clubs!"

"It's a fucking attack! Wake up!"

A few of the guys began flushing dope, coke, pills, and whatever shit they had down the sink and the toilet. I hoped there was a septic tank. Half these native toilets emptied onto the hillside a hundred feet away. Fine surprise that would be.

It was the girls who had gotten us into this mess. I knew they would be trouble.

When we arrived, they were in the house. They greeted us at the door like they belonged there. Maybe they did.

"Hi, I'm Jen and this is my friend Barbara. Joe told us we could stay here till next weekend." None of us knew who Joe was, but after a moment's thought, the guys in the band decided the two girls could stay. Hearing that, the girls became more talkative.

"We ran away from home three weeks ago."

"My father's a New Jersey policeman. But he'll never find me here."

"You wanna smoke some pot?"

Oh, shit, I thought.

I didn't like finding extra people in our vacation home. Arriving to find it populated by two girls made me feel like an intruder. Who really belonged in the house? Us? Them? I found it unsettling. I was actually finding the whole trip unsettling, because I didn't like changes in my environment. I liked sleeping in the same place and having the same people around.

The other guys didn't see it that way. Mike turned to Peter and said, "Two free girls, Peter. It's an omen." Two of the guys moved right in with them.

I never understood how some guys did things like that. A girlfriend for a week, just like that. I was too shy even to talk to them.

Billy Perry, Chris, and I went into town the first morning. The people all spoke in a rapid musical lilt that I found hard to understand at first but soon became used to. We learned one thing quickly—everyone knew where we were staying.

"Yes, mon, you stay with the girls in the Maxwell place."

Everywhere we went, the girls had preceded us. I never did find out exactly what they had done, but it seemed those girls had been having quite a party since they came to town a week or two before. And now we were part of whatever scene they had created.

There was plenty of pot in the house, and coke and pills and liquor, too. I drank some beer, but the rest of the stuff just didn't appeal to me, so I ignored it. Until that morning, when the law arrived. *Jesus Christ,* I thought. *I'm gonna go to jail for someone else's drugs! It's not my shit!* I wanted to yell out. But I didn't say anything.

By the time the raiders made it to the door, we were all awake. I was dressed. Peter opened the door for the law as I stood back and watched. There were no guns in sight, but the two guys out front did have clubs. They seemed respectful, though, and one of them showed us a badge. He looked like a homeless person, but I figured that's how the law looked in third world countries.

I stepped aside and they swarmed in. Eight of them. Working in teams, they began searching the villa.

I stood in the foyer, watching and listening. Every now and then I heard a shout as though someone had scored a point on the pinball machine in the bar in Plymouth. *They must have found something,* I said to myself. I became concerned about corruption. *Are they planting drugs in my socks or underwear?*

Finally, they emerged from the back of the house holding several bags. I couldn't see inside, but I consoled myself with the thought that the bags weren't mine. Still, they were grinning. They had something. I couldn't understand everything they said, but it became clear that we were supposed to accompany them somewhere. I stepped outside, where two more cars had arrived.

Mike turned to me and said nonchalantly, "Well, John, this is it. This is where they take us to jail and throw away the key." I looked around, but there was no possibility of escape. *Mike doesn't know anything,* I told myself. *He must be high.*

The raiders motioned me into an old Austin station wagon. It was built with seating for five, but eight of us climbed aboard. A native sat in my lap. *If the brakes fail on the way down the hill, he'll absorb the crash for me,* I thought. He didn't say a word the whole way down. Another native rode on the hood. I waited for our driver to slam on the brakes a bit too hard and send him flying under the wheels, but it never happened. He must have had practice. He grinned like he was on a roller coaster.

We headed into the town of Plymouth and stopped in front of a stone structure. The jail. A tropical prison, really. It had rough stone walls three feet thick. The natives who raided us turned out to be the island's entire police force, with a few drinking buddies thrown in for good measure. They were excited. A big bust! Us.

"Stand up, mon! Say cheese for the camera. It's your mug shot, mon!"

After taking the pictures, they all stood around watching them develop. They were using an old Polaroid Land Camera. My grandfather had one in the 1960s.

The leader said, "I'm Inspector Vincent, okay, gimme your passport, mon!"

"I don't have a passport. I just have an ID," I responded.

"Okay, then, mon, gimme your ID!"

I handed Inspector Vincent my Top of the Campus card, which, back home, entitled the bearer to admission to the ninth-floor bar at the University of Massachusetts. I never did get that card back. He copied my name, address, and date of birth in painfully tiny script on an index card, which he carefully filed in a recipe box. Since the spelling of my name and my date of birth were wrong on the Top of the Campus card, the inspector's card ended up wrong, too. I was pleased.

No one searched me. I realized they had forgotten about that. It made me wish I had a knife or a gun. But the natives were so friendly, I would have hated to stab or shoot one. I tried to edge out the door. Politely but firmly, Vincent's sidekick grabbed my arm and pointed back inside, to a seat.

"You have to stay inside, mon. This is jail." And he laughed. Asshole.

After we were all booked, Inspector Vincent led us to a cell. There were no windows, just rusty bars. At least it wasn't cold.

"Jesus Christ. I hope they don't have rats in here!" said Mike, the guitar player. Until he said it, I hadn't given any thought to rats.

"Do they have snakes here?" This was not the time for Mike's vivid imagination.

There was no way out through those stone walls, so I tugged at the bars. *I could break out,* I told myself, *but it's going to take some time and some work.* I hoped it didn't come to that. Besides us, the jail had one resident, an old run-down wife killer.

Our confinement didn't turn out to be very onerous. Inspector Vincent had some musicians on his crew, and once things calmed down, they unlocked our cell and brought out their guitars. We gave them money to buy food in town, and they served it with Coke in refillable glass bottles. I hadn't seen bottles like that since I was a child. When they were empty, one of the policemen filled them partway with water and played them like a musical instrument. I would have been impressed if I wasn't locked in fucking jail.

Peter had a friend who knew someone on the island, and he pledged some land for our bail, and we were released in time for dinner. The next morning, Peter's friend found us a lawyer, a wizened little specimen with a sharp disposition. He didn't seem especially enamored with us. *Perhaps he lives here and has daughters,* I thought. After all, he'd heard about those runaway girls.

When we were all together, he said, "Did you young men know certain kinds of drug possession are a hanging offense in a Crown colony?"

None of us said anything.

"Drug penalties in the colonies are, ahem, a bit draconian."

"Cops love busting musicians. I hope they don't lock us up forever."

"Fuck you," I said. Mike was full of happy thoughts that day.

Seeds seemed to be a big deal to Montserrat's finest. And that's what they had us on: some seeds in the bottom of a bag. Marijuana seeds meant *grower*. Dope smokers were okay, just prison time for them, but growers were executed. The coke, the mushrooms, the speed, the acid, all those things were still packed in the luggage in some quantity, despite everyone's best flushing efforts. They didn't care about any of it. Seeds were what they had come for, and seeds were what they got.

The trial was set for Wednesday. We all washed up and appeared in court as ordered that Wednesday morning. There didn't seem to be any other cases except ours, and the courtroom was empty except for us, the judge and court officers, the lawyers, and a few spectators. We had a brief appearance in front of the judge, who was wearing a wig that would have marked him as a transvestite back in New York. However, I felt sure he did not see himself as being in drag.

I couldn't actually hear most of what was said because the lawyer and the prosecutor and the judge were all huddled together up front, but the whole thing was over in half an hour. Two members of the band were fined five thousand BIWI dollars, which came to about twenty-five hundred U.S. dollars. The charges against me and the girls were dropped. We were free to go in time for lunch. I got the distinct impression that our arrest provided a considerable boost to the island government's economy.

One of the policemen drove me back to the villa, where I picked up our rental car. It was a Jeep-like rig called a Morris Moke. Mokes are a lot of fun, and a tropical island like Montserrat was the ideal place to have one. Prior to my arrest, I had even gotten a Montserrat driver's license for the thing. I was kind of proud of it.

It was actually a surprise that I would have any car to drive, given the fact that I was broke. As it happened, though, I hadn't needed any money when Billy Perry and I walked past the car rental place on our first day on the island. I had looked into their garage, where two mechanics seemed to be struggling to change the oil in an old Morris car.

"Need some help?" I was half-joking, but they took me seriously.

"He's a great mechanic. From the U.S." Billy pointed at me and they looked impressed. I ended up staying there two hours, helping them fix cars.

"You could make a great living if you wanna stay here, mon," they said.

They didn't have any money to pay me, but I didn't have a car. So we had the basis for a good trade. I fixed some Mokes and Austins, and I got wheels.

I drove my Moke back to the jail to ferry the crew home. When I got there, though, the plan had changed. It seemed we were now celebrities. Drinks were on the house at the local bar, and that's where we went.

When it came time to leave, we were all pretty drunk. I decided to go for a ride on the beach, which was only a short ride away. When I got there, I raced down the sandy straightaway, swerving around people as they lay on the sand. I headed to the end, into the little sand dunes. Mokes don't go very fast, but I had this one moving pretty good as I popped over a dune, and just like that, I was in the ocean.

The Moke sank, and I quickly discovered the tide was coming in. Soon the Moke was gone from sight.

Standing on the shore, I felt sick and drunk. My friends had wandered off. And I had lost my transportation. The only sign of my Moke was the little red flag that was on a pole sticking up from the back bumper. Every time there was a trough in the waves, the flag popped out of the sea.

Shit, I said to myself. *I'd better get it out of the water.*

There was no sign of the people I had been riding with. I trudged back to the bar to get help removing the car. When I went inside, a band had set up, and two guys were playing steel drums. It was magical, the way they played those trilling melodies on instruments made from old oil drums. One of the guys from the jail was there, too. He'd changed from a policeman to a musician. Looking at him, you'd never have guessed. I was tempted to stay at the bar all night, but I knew we had to get that Moke back. I couldn't afford to buy the rental agency another one.

I rounded up five guys and we walked back to the beach. The tide was still high, and we had to swim out to the Moke and stand on its hood and seats.

"All together, now, let's dive down, grab it, and drag it back. One . . . two . . . three . . . dive!" Shit, that was hard work! But we did it. Once the Moke was back on the sand, I removed all its filler caps and we flipped it on its head to drain. I got a ride home while it sat and dried out.

The next morning, I got up early and got a ride to the rental agency. As soon as I arrived, I heard, "Hey, I heard you sank our Moke in the ocean, mon!" It seemed news traveled fast on Montserrat.

"Don't worry," I said. "I'll have it running in a few hours." I got some gas, some oil, and a fresh battery, and then I trudged back to the beach with two guys from the rental place as assistants. We flipped the car back on its feet. I filled it with fresh fluids, changed the battery, and cleaned out the carburetor and the ignition. I pulled the plugs and shot oil into the cylinders. Amazingly, it ran. We drove back to the rental agency, where I rinsed it with a hose and pronounced it good as new.

The next day, our vacation came to an end. I said good-bye to Willie and his iguana, and we flew home on a World War II surplus DC-3 with no door and with chickens in cages stacked in the aisle. Skimming a thousand feet above the ocean, we headed back to the snow, the spring thaw, and the mud. And our next show, Friday night at the Rusty Nail. A few years later, most of Montserrat vanished when the volcano erupted. The villa, the jail, the roads . . . all gone.

I didn't end up staying with Fat very much longer. I had a hard time living with all the people in that house. I never knew what to say or do, and I often felt lost. But I had made a lot of contacts and become a lot more confident, at least with respect to engineering issues. Interacting about technical things had become comfortable, and the more I did it, the more I knew and the easier it got. I wouldn't hesitate at all to walk up to a sound man at a concert. But I was still terrified of walking up to a girl.

13

The Big Time

Good things started happening to me as the winter of '78 came to an end. That March, a long dark period of loneliness came to an end when I ran into Little Bear at the university one day. I was amazed to find that she was now a student there. We had not spoken in a very long time, but we reconnected right away. She told me that she'd left me when one of her friends made up an ugly story about me. She later learned it was all a lie, but by then it was too late. We both regretted the lost time.

We spent that spring walking the old railway lines around Amherst, collecting old railway spikes and glass telegraph insulators that had been abandoned in the grass. We talked about ourselves, our dreams, science fiction, electronics, cars, and motorcycles. I was in love.

I got another big break two months later: a job with a national sound company. One with big equipment. The kind used in stadiums, not barrooms.

The first to hire me was Britannia Row Audio, the sound company that Pink Floyd had formed to rent out their equipment when they were not on tour. Britro, as they were called in the United States, was headed by Mick Kluczynski, an English fellow who had been with Pink Floyd for years. I met Mick when he came to Amherst, doing sound for the university's spring concert. Sha Na Na was playing, and their amplifiers were breaking down. I could see they were having trouble as I wandered in during the sound check.

"Having troubles with those Phase Linears?" I asked. *Maybe this will be my chance,* I thought.

"Fookin' right we have trouble. I'm Mick, and this is Seth. Who are you?"

Mick was a short, chubby fellow with a strong English accent. "I run the main system," Mick continued, "and my mate Seth runs the monitors." The main sound system is the one that the audience hears—the system whose speakers flank the stage in huge piles. It's sometimes called the house system. The monitor system's speakers face the stage. Monitors allow the performers to hear themselves sing over the noise of the instrument amplifiers and everything else on stage.

"I'm John Robison. I'm an engineer. I know about Phase Linear troubles." That sounded impressive. At least, I hoped it did.

And it was true. At the time, Crown and Phase Linear were the two main companies making large amplifiers for big sound systems, and I had fixed several Phase Linears for local bands. They had an unfortunate tendency to explode when you played them too loud. But all I had ever seen till then were sound systems with one, or at most two, Phase Linears. These guys had a mountain of them, at least twenty that I could see at a glance. I had never seen anything like that before. I was very impressed.

"Well, come up look at these, Mister Engineer." Mick invited me up onto the stage and took me over to an area on the side that was filled with racks of auxiliary electronics. They had more equipment than I'd ever seen in one place, but I didn't let on.

I asked for a screwdriver, and they handed me a complete Xcelite tool kit. At the time, Xcelite was the Rolls-Royce of hand tools. I had one or two myself, but an entire kit was a luxury. I looked at the fuse panels. The DC fuses were blown, and the glass was black. The black coloring meant a dead short. The output transistors had fried. I could fix them, but not there. I needed a shop.

"Where do you guys come from?" I asked.

"We're from the U.K.," he said. "But we've just opened an office here in the States. In Long Island City." It took me a moment to figure out what "from the U.K." meant. For some reason, British musicians I spoke to were never "from England." They were always "from the U.K." "The Floyd sent me here to run the place," said Mick, "and Mr. Goldman here"—pointing to Seth—"is my number two."

"I could fix these amps for you, but I'd need bench space to take them apart. Do you have space down there?"

It turned out they had a big radio studio with all the room I would need. We made a date for the following week, and I loaded my tools into the car and headed for New York. I had never been to Long Island City before. I was a little scared. Could I really do this?

I arrived in front of a nondescript building on a side street, one of a hundred identical buildings. Had I made a mistake? There was nothing to give any clue what might be inside.

Seth opened the door when I rang. I stepped into a foyer that opened up into a huge studio. Sound and light gear covered the floor, and speaker cabinets were piled against a wall.

"You guys have a lot of gear," I said.

"We've got half the Floyd system here, with some stuff we've added," Seth answered. "The Floyd have the biggest sound system in the world, you know."

Just as they were "from the U.K.," they worked "for the Floyd." Only outsiders said "Pink Floyd." I caught on to that pretty fast even with my limited social skills. I also hadn't known that Floyd had the biggest sound system, but I nodded knowledgeably.

"Where are your broken amps?" I asked, anxious to prove myself.

Seth led me to a back room, where a long bench lined a wall and skylights provided illumination. There were probably fifty

Phase Linear amplifiers piled up against the wall. The mound of broken equipment was at least ten feet wide, and taller than me.

"Are *all* of those broken?" Surely that wasn't possible. I was expecting one or two broken amplifiers, not a truckload.

"Fookin' right," he said. "Have at it." And with that, he went back up front.

It took me three days, several trips to the parts store, and two overnight shipments from Phase Linear, but I fixed all but two of them. And those two I stripped for parts. When I was done, we hauled the repaired amplifiers onto the soundstage. One by one, we hooked them into the PA. Seth ran each one up to full power, playing tapes of Judas Priest and Roxy Music he'd made on the last tours.

All fifty-two of my amps passed the tests.

"Fookin' incredible," said Mick.

I was very proud of myself. It was the biggest and fastest repair job I had ever done. And they had more. Piles and piles of broken equipment. They had ideas, too.

"We've got a three-way system now, but we'd like to go five-way. No one has that on tour. Think you could build a five-way crossover?"

"Of course," I said, determined to sound confident. Then I headed home to think about it.

I told Little Bear about my plan.

"What's a five-way crossover?" she asked.

"It divides the sound into bands. So you have the low bass notes, your bass guitar sounds, going to the biggest speakers. Then you have upper bass, the low range on the guitars and piano, going to the next biggest speakers. You have your low mids, vocals mostly, going to their own speakers, Your high mids, the saxophones and horns, go to another set of speakers. And, finally, your highs, the high hats, the cymbals, go to special high-frequency speakers."

"Okay," she said. It wasn't clear if she understood or was merely humoring me.

I did the design and Little Bear made the circuit boards. We poured the acid to etch the boards into a Tupperware tray in the kitchen sink and assembled everything on the dining table in our apartment. Amazingly, it worked. I loaded it into the car to deliver it. On the ride to New Jersey, I pondered how far we had come from the two kids who'd fixed broken record players for the high school language lab just a few years before.

Seth was waiting when I arrived at the New Jersey Center for the Performing Arts.

"You're late. What took so fucking long?" he said.

"This crossover of yours better work. We don't have a spare." He was sure anxious.

There would be no rehearsal, I realized. We were going to plug it in and do a show. *Will it work?* I was tense and worried. *It worked when I did my last tests, five minutes before I put it in the car,* I told myself.

We hooked it up, and the first thing I heard through it was Gerry Rafferty's horns playing "Baker Street."

"Fucking clean." Seth was impressed. "Smooth. Listen to those horns."

It was like nothing I'd heard before. They *were* smooth. I was thrilled.

That night, I watched Meat Loaf play for a sellout crowd. During the show, his manager came over to me. "Fuckin' great sound you guys have tonight. So clear!" I smiled. The five-way idea had really worked.

Britro had plenty of work for me after that night. It seemed their sound systems were everywhere. Whenever I'd go to Long Island City, they'd be setting up a new tour, always using equipment I had designed or fixed or built or modified in some way. All different kinds of music—Judas Priest, Talking Heads, Blondie, Phoebe Snow.

And I was the sound engineer.

By the summer of 1978, Britro had several sound systems touring at any given time. That August, I got a call about a system we had put together for a band called April Wine. Apparently, they were having trouble with the bass cabinets. They had blown thirty bass drivers. Britro asked me to ride up with them the next day to sort it out.

"Okay, but I have to bring my girlfriend. I promised to go away with her this weekend."

"Okay," Seth said. "We'll pick you up tomorrow."

I called Little Bear and said, "Get ready, we're going on tour with April Wine tomorrow."

"Who's April Wine?" she asked.

"They've got an album called *First Glance*," I replied. People said that April Wine were the Rolling Stones of Canada, but they were unknown in the U.S.

The next day, a green station wagon pulled into my driveway with one of the crew from New York and a Brit I hadn't met before. There was just barely room to stuff ourselves, my tools, and all the speaker boxes into the car. It was packed to the gills. We hit the road with Nigel, the Brit, driving. And he drove hard. As we slid around the ramp onto I-91, Nigel turned to me and said, "I went to Rolls-Royce chauffeur school, I did. Taught me how to drive right proper. And we're in a bloody fookin' hurry here. They're waitin' on us for tomorrow's show, they are."

Once we left Massachusetts, I lost sight of the Buick's speedometer on the far side of 100. At the speed Nigel was going, curves on the interstate felt like hairpin turns. We made the border in record time. When we pulled in, the customs officer looked in the back. The back of the wagon was filled with cases stenciled PINK FLOYD—LONDON.

"Got Pink Floyd in the back of the car, do you?" he asked

"Righto, mate. We shrunk 'em and stuck 'em in fookin' boxes, we did," said Nigel.

Amazingly, the customs officer laughed and waved us through. We stopped for dinner at a little French restaurant outside Montreal, where I had one of the best meals I have ever eaten. With a change of drivers, we were off again, driving through the night. It must have been three in the morning when we caught up with the tour. April Wine was playing hockey rinks across eastern Canada, the only places big enough to hold the crowds. Nigel banged on the door for ten minutes before someone let us in.

Little Bear and I sat up, shook ourselves awake, and got to it. By dawn, we had changed out half the dead speakers—enough to do that night's show. We retreated to the motel.

We spent the next week pounding our way across Canada, fixing sound equipment as we went. Nigel took the wagon back to the city and returned with another load of speakers and parts so we could finish the job. By August 12, the day before my birthday, we had reached the Bay of Fundy on the eastern tip of Canada. That night, we took the ferry to St. John's, Newfoundland. It was an overnight trip, and Little Bear and I spent the night of my twenty-first birthday curled up on the top of the ferry, in the shelter of the smokestack. With an important job to do, the gentle roll of the ship, the stars, and the sea air, it seemed like magic.

I couldn't imagine a better life. I could almost forget my screwed-up family back home. I wished I could stay on the road forever.

14

The First Smoking Guitar

U sually, I worked almost alone in Britro's huge building, unless Little Bear was with me. I'd be in the back, and Seth and one or two of the crew would be fiddling with equipment out front on the soundstages. So I was surprised one day in 1978 to find a crowd milling around when I arrived with my cases of parts and tools. I could hear loud music playing, and as I walked in I recognized the song. KISS was there.

"They've rented a soundstage to get ready for their tour," Seth explained. "Just let them be and we'll do our work in back, right-o."

Right-o. I went to work on a fresh pile of dead Phase Linears.

I could see the stage from my bench in back, and I saw Ace Frehley, the guitar player, poking his fingers into a hole in the front of his Les Paul guitar. Being curious, I moved closer.

"What are you doing in there?" I asked.

"Hey, are you the engineer?" Without waiting for an answer, he continued, "I wanna put a smoke bomb in this guitar. I want it to catch fire at the end of my solo."

"I could do that. Can I see?"

Ace had carved a hole in the front of the guitar and embedded a smoke bomb. He had the idea that he'd set the bomb off and the

guitar would vanish in a cloud of smoke while he played his solo.
It was a good idea, but the implementation was less than optimal.

"This is a fucking mess," I said tactfully. I thought for a minute.
"We could build a metal box, embed it in the guitar, and put the
smoke bombs inside. That would work a lot better."

"Yeah, it would last longer, too, because we wouldn't be burning the wood."

"We could even insulate the box. And instead of fire, we could
put lights inside."

Ace was getting into the idea. And it turned out he had already
been thinking about lights.

"How about these?" He showed me a bulb. "They're for airplanes or movie projectors or something." Ace was never clear on
details like that. Regardless of where they came from, though,
they were supposed to be bright.

"Do you have a spare guitar?" I asked.

"Shit, if you can do that, I have all the guitars you need." He
called out to the crew member responsible for his equipment,
"Tex, have Gibson ship this guy a guitar tomorrow!" Then it hit
him. He turned to me. "Hey! What's your name?"

"John Robison," I said.

Ace clearly didn't think John summed me up. "We'll call you
Ampie!" he said, knowing that I built the amplifiers. I guess I
wasn't the only one who picked my own names. When I watched
John Belushi name the Flounder in *Animal House,* I knew just how
he felt.

Gibson's Les Paul model was the gold standard of the guitar
world. The version Ace played cost almost a thousand dollars. And
here he was, telling his roadie to call them and they'd ship me one,
overnight, just like that. In the music world, that's what power and
fame did.

That night, I headed home with a new job. I had never made
special effects before, but they didn't know that, and I wasn't going
to tell them. My experiments had so far been confined to child-

hood pranks—nothing on this scale. It was a little scary when I thought about it. What if I fucked it up?

You can do it, I said to myself as I drove home. And I knew just the person to help with this: my friend Jim Boughton, he of the foundry and the flaming washtub. I showed him the guitar the next day, as soon as FedEx delivered it to my house. It was a brand-new black Les Paul Custom. I had expected a factory second or something, not this. It was so perfect that I was almost afraid to touch it. But I did.

"He wants a guitar that explodes and blows fire and smoke? And plays? He's my kind of musician!" Jim grinned.

We laid the guitar on a blanket on the hood of his Fiat 124, and in short order we came up with a plan. For the first design iteration, Jim cast a firebox that we embedded in the back of the guitar. But it didn't work. It was crooked.

For our next effort, Jim welded a box from stainless steel. He used a router to carve a hole in the back of the guitar, then removed one of the pickups on the front. The box fit right behind where the pickup had been. The pickup location was now a hole leading into the box.

"Okay, we'll cut some steel in the shape of the pickup, and we'll use a spring and hinge to snap it open so the smoke can get out. We'll need to make an insulated pad so Ace doesn't get burned playing this thing. It's going to get hot!"

Tex, Ace's roadie, called me every few days to see how we were doing. At first, he was skeptical, along with the rest of the guys on the KISS crew.

"A metal box?? A fake pickup on a hinge???"

But after Tex came up to see what we were doing, he became a believer, and so did they. Overnight it became "Yeah!! A metal box!! A hinged pickup!!"

While Jim made the box and the rest of the mechanical parts, I worked on the electronics. KISS had just started using a brand-new technology—Shaffer Vega wireless radio systems—to send the signals from the guitars to the amplifiers. For a band like KISS, who moved around a lot, wireless was great because it meant there were no cords to trip over or yank out. It made my job harder, though, because it meant those huge lights Ace had found would have to run from batteries.

Tex helped solve that problem. He found a small company, Frezzolini Electronics, that made rechargeable battery packs for portable TV cameras. I went to see them in an industrial park in Hawthorne, New Jersey, and Jack Frezzolini and Jim Crawford came out and showed me around. It was exciting to be treated like a real visiting engineer and not a kid. We walked out back, into an area where a technician was welding individual rechargeable batteries the size of C cell batteries into packs of all shapes and sizes. Then the packs were shrink-wrapped in blue plastic.

There, on the bench, were the ones they had made for me. They were about five by six inches, not more than an inch thick, and weighed perhaps two pounds.

"This pack has all the power you need," Jack said.

"Really?" I was skeptical.

"Shit, you could start a car off this pack! Check this out." We walked over to a pair of lights, and he plugged in one of my packs. The lights blazed on, flooding the room, so bright that I had to look away. "We developed these packs so TV crews could run floodlights and get a good image anywhere," he explained. "How do you think they get TV coverage of car crashes, or mountain rescues, or animals in the woods? They use our batteries with light packs like these."

I was impressed. I left Frezzolini with two packs and two chargers.

"I'll send the bill to the band," Jim said. What a great deal, I thought. A whole office full of people who pay your bills and take care of you. Maybe I can have that someday.

When my creations came to life, I felt exhilarated. I loved to see and hear them run in a live performance. People would stare in amazement and roar with applause and cheers at the things I dreamed up. At times like that, it was fun being a misfit. When I looked around me, the creative people in the music scene all seemed to be misfits, so I blended right in. The only normal people were the managers, and I didn't deal too much with them. I liked the people in the bands, and they actually seemed to like me.

I had a girlfriend and I had a car. I had escaped my deranged parents. I was working for one of the hottest bands in the world. I was even making good money, when I worked. I'd gone from eighty dollars a week with Fat to eighty dollars every few hours. At long last, I was really making it.

At least, that was how I felt when things went well for me. When they didn't, I heard the little voices in my head.

You're just a fraud.

This shit will never work.

What will they say when they come to get it and it's in a million pieces on your bench?

Sometimes, working on the KISS guitars, I would get all tense and worried. But I would just work harder. There was only one thing to do. I had to make them work just as I had said they would.

There were countless details to be attended to. For example, there was the problem of the fake pickup—the metal piece that swung open to let the smoke and light out. It was stainless steel, cut in the shape of the pickup that had previously occupied that space. Should we paint it? If we did, I was afraid the soot from the smoke bombs would ruin the finish.

Tex had the perfect answer: decals. He even knew a guy who could make some. His buddy printed adhesive decals that looked like the front of a pickup, and we used them to cover the steel door. They could be changed every show, keeping them fresh. It was a great idea, and it worked. At the same time, the back of the guitar was hollowed out more to hold the Frezzolini batteries and the electronics I had put together.

This guitar project was my first experience doing something as part of a team. Between the batteries and the lights and the smoke bombs and Jim's welding and cutting, and Little Bear's tireless soldering, we were pulling it off!

Finally, we were done. We had transformed a stock Les Paul into a fire-breathing beast. The finished guitar looked just like any other Gibson Les Paul. But when you twisted the lower volume control, the bottom pickup swung back with a snap, the smoke bomb went off, and intense light blasted out of the hole. The effect of the light and the smoke was spectacular. It was time to bring it to New York.

I had never built anything for anyone famous before. KISS was one of the biggest bands in the world, and I was really proud that they had chosen me to make the guitar. I wondered what would happen next. Would I become famous? Would I get more work? When I arrived, Ace picked up my guitar and peered into the workings, visible through a clear plastic cover on the back.

"Far out! Let's see it run. Tex, let's wire up some smoke bombs!" When both smoke bombs lit off, the smoke poured out the front and filled the room. And it kept burning. In fact, it burned so hot that it popped two strings off the guitar. When I saw that, I just hoped our insulation held up.

"Son of a bitch!"

Ace was impressed. And the audience was, too, as soon as they saw it. Ace played the smoking guitar on the song "2000 Man." It was a huge hit with the crowds—they would roar when they saw the smoke and light pour out of it. After the first show, Ace came out to talk to me.

"Ampie, this is wild. I love it. What else can we do?"

That smoking guitar was the first of a long line of special guitars we would create over the next few years. Ace was full of ideas. I started designing when the tour opened and kept building and modifying my guitars as we traveled. The effects got better and better throughout the tour. I loved it and so did Ace.

After a lifetime of being unpopular, I found that the tables had suddenly turned for me. Relatives I hadn't seen since I was five showed up at the stage door, professing their fondness for me and requesting "two backstage passes, if you can spare them." I usually could.

Relatives weren't the only people I met. The sexual prowess of some of the guys on the tour was legendary, and I often bumped into their "friends." One night in Maryland, for example, we had reserved the whole top floor of the best hotel in the area, where we registered under assumed names. Despite our efforts, there were always groupies hanging around. I trudged past them after the show, headed for the elevators. As I stepped inside, two girls got in with me. They were quite pretty, and very provocatively dressed. The one I still remember had red hair and a red silk blouse, unbuttoned practically to her navel. With high heels. She wasn't dressed like a hooker. (By that time, I'd seen enough hookers to know the difference.) She was just, well, *aggressive.*

I pushed the button for the top floor, then turned to them and asked, "Which floor?"

"Top floor," said the girl with the bright red shirt.

"Do you have an invitation?" I asked. "Our security guys won't let you off otherwise."

"We're going to give Gene Simmons head. He's expecting us," she said with a dismissive tone.

"Okay," I said slowly. What else could I say? When we got to the top, I headed for my room and they headed for his. They were indeed expected.

I saw that kind of thing night after night, but the girl in the red shirt kind of stuck out. I guess it was her confidence—something I had never felt with anyone but Little Bear. That night, I closed the door of my room and went to work on my latest guitar modifications. Alone.

I was on my way to being a special-effects wizard for KISS. But that was in their world. When I went home, I stepped back into my own world, a much more ordinary place. The crowds, the noise, the stage—they were gone as if they had never existed. In fact, that's exactly what some people in the tiny town of Amherst thought—that I must have made them up.

Before we had gone on tour, we had set up the whole show and rehearsed on Long Island. On several occasions, I had brought Varmint with me. He loved it. One of his seventh-grade assignments that term was to write about what he did on vacation. So, of course, he wrote, "My brother works for KISS. He took me to rehearsal in Nassau, where I met Paul Stanley and Gene Simmons. I saw them without their makeup and they told me dirty jokes."

In those days, seeing the members of KISS at all, let alone without their heavy and wild makeup, was a very big deal. So they actually sent him to the school psychologist over this "crazy fantasy" that he insisted was true!

I accompanied him to school the following day and set them straight. "What the hell is the matter with you people, hassling my little brother?" I asked the psychologist. At twenty-one, I had not learned about tact, but I knew how to be clear and assertive. And the memory of my own bad experience in the Amherst schools was still fresh in my mind.

I don't know if it was my honest face, my size, or my vulgarity that did the trick. Or possibly the photos, which I carried in the gold briefcase Ace had given me, the inside of which was decorated with KISS backstage passes. Whatever it was, the school did not challenge Varmint's KISS tales ever again.

"What a bunch of assholes," I muttered to him on the way out.

"Yeah," he said. He followed my lead and quit school a few months later.

It always struck me as funny, the way people acted. It was so incredible to them, the idea that I worked with KISS. I just thought of it as a fun job. Someone had to do it. Why not me?

"I can't believe you know Ace Frehley! He's my absolute hero! What is he like?" Anna, the girl who worked behind the counter at Superior Pizzeria, gushed when I went in for my pepper and onion pies. I never knew how to respond to questions like that. *They're just musicians,* I thought. *What's the big deal?*

I tried to answer, once. "He's just a regular guy," I said. "Dark hair, a little shorter than me."

"Stop!" she said. "He's not a regular guy! And I know what he looks like!" And with that, she launched into five minutes of telling *me* what her hero was like. I slipped outside to polish my motorcycle. I had to escape, but I couldn't leave until I got my food. She followed me outside.

"What about Gene?"

"Gene who?" I asked distractedly, as I polished my chrome exhaust pipe.

"Gene Simmons!" she said. "Is it true, what they say? Can he really lick his own eyeballs?"

Jesus Christ, I thought. *This just doesn't end . . .*

"Well," I replied. "He does have a long tongue. And I know the girls really like him." I did not know what else to say. Luckily, at that moment, her boss carried my pizza out the door and gave me the excuse I needed to escape Anna and NuttyRockStarWorld.

I don't know if it's an Aspergian trait, or if it's just me, but I was never affected by celebrity. No matter how famous a musician was, he was just a guy with a broken guitar or an idea for a sound effect to me. But I could never explain that simple reality to other people.

"You're just modest," people said when they felt nice.

"What an arrogant asshole you are," they said when they felt nasty.

The truth was, all I really saw were my engineering creations. To me, the guitar player was like the driver of a race car, and I was the guy that built and tuned the engine. So we were on the same team, but I wasn't out there driving. I didn't even see the racetrack. The engine was my world.

15

The Ferry to Detroit

I called home every week when I was on the road with KISS that first season. There were no cell phones in those days, so calling home was harder than it is today. Motels had phones, but that was a real racket, with some sleazy innkeepers charging a dollar a minute for long distance. We carried our own telephones on the tour, in a big trunk with the other production office gear. As soon as we arrived at a new concert hall, we'd plug in to the switchboard and start dialing.

I always called Varmint. He seemed to miss me and I know he liked to hear from me. He was fourteen years old that summer.

Sometimes he had weird news of life in Northampton, where our mother had deposited him during her most recent bout of psychosis. That summer, he was living with Dr. Finch and his followers in a falling-down house near the center of town. The house had the atmosphere of a cult, and for that reason I seldom went there.

Sometimes his tone was urgent, as when I called from some civic center in the Midwest and he said, "John Elder, can I come see you? Maybe tomorrow?"

I realized something was up. *He must want me to buy him something,* I thought. With our father on the skids and an unemployed and nutty mom, I was shaping up as Varmint's cash drawer. In fact, it seemed like the Varmint's need for *things* was increasing even faster than my income. When he was little, he had dressed himself in aluminum foil. Now that he was older, he wanted designer clothes, and he figured I was the one to buy them. I looked forward to the day Varmint got a job.

"Okay," I said, "go to the AirKaman terminal at Bradley Field at six o'clock tomorrow. I'll fly you out to our show in Cleveland."

I picked him up in a Cadillac. I rented Cadillacs whenever I could, despite the business manager's whining about the expense. Varmint and I both liked them. They were always brand-new and they had a distinctive smell. Also, our grandmother had driven them when we were little, so we felt right at home.

I always treated my rented Caddies with respect, except for the time I loaned one to our pyrotechnics guy and he gave it to two stewardesses from Chattanooga. At least, they said they were stewardesses. They vanished with the car and Avis wanted to charge the whole thing—twenty thousand dollars—to my American Express card. Eventually, they found the car parked at the Charlotte airport. We never saw the stewardesses again. The band's business manager settled the bill.

I never loaned my Cadillacs to the crew after that.

The airport we flew into at Cleveland was way out of town. But as soon as we got there, my little brother started in on me.

"Where's the mall?" he asked. *He hasn't been here ten minutes and already he wants to shop!* I thought. Well, there were malls back home. He didn't need to be flown a thousand miles by jet to visit a mall.

"I need new clothes." He was trying to be reasonable.

Not wanting to let him loose on a buying spree, I turned off the highway into a residential neighborhood.

"There are no stores here." I gestured into the empty darkness.

Varmint looked around. We were in the middle of nowhere. Nothing but houses, and even those were increasingly far apart. It was a very dark night, and there were not many street lights. We had not even passed a 7-Eleven or a gas station.

Varmint *knew* there must be malls to serve the houses.

I had a sudden inspiration. Maybe I could pull it off. Varmint was a lot harder to trick now that he was older. But maybe . . .

"Varmint, there are no stores here. None at all. If you just came out here to shop, you're going to be disappointed. Cleveland is a religious community. That's what the name means. They're Clevites."

"What are Clevites?" he asked, skeptical. But I saw a hint of possibility.

"They are very religious people. They founded this city. They worship Saint Cleve, the patron saint of harvests. They're like the Shakers back home."

What could he say to that? He'd seen them worship the saints in Mexico. Slave had taken him there a few years back when she was looking for inspiration for her paintings. I continued. I had him now.

"Frankly, I was shocked to hear they allowed KISS to play here. Usually, they have gospel performers in places like this. You know, Varmint, there are other religious communities like this scattered around the country. The Mennonites. The Amish. The Moonies. They would never host a KISS concert. Not in a million years. But times are changing. We could be playing for the Mormons soon. In Salt Lake City."

But he couldn't get shopping out of his mind.

"I *really* need new clothes. Look, I brought pictures." He had Calvin Klein ads, and clippings from *People* and *US* magazines with nattily dressed stars and models. He had cut out his favorites and made a kind of collage. It would have been cute if he wasn't using it to shake five hundred dollars out of me.

"I can't look at that junk while I'm driving." *I should have put him in the trunk,* I thought. He was bouncing on the seat. The magazines were still in his hand. He wasn't letting go of this idea.

"Varmint, you don't get it. There are no retail stores in Cleveland. None. They just have churches, gas stations, and grocery stores. That's all."

"What do we do?" He said that as if it were *my* problem.

"I know what *I'm* doing. We have a show tomorrow, at Richfield Coliseum. I'm working. You can come along. You can see the new explosives we just rigged up for 'Rock and Roll All Night.'"

"But I need new clothes." He was whining now. I had a fresh inspiration. Varmint was lucky I could think on my feet. Most big brothers would have run out of ideas and smacked him silly. But I was just getting started.

"Look, if you really want to shop, you can take a taxi to the waterfront and catch the ferry to Detroit. It's ninety miles away, across Lake Erie. But I gotta warn you, it's a shameful scene, Varmint. I wouldn't do it, myself."

I could conjure an image of the ferry landing clearly in my mind. It was a scene straight from the Bible. Sodom and Gomorrah. Worship of Graven Images. Depraved, orgiastic sinners waiting to be smitten by a vengeful God. All that and more, right there at the Cleveland dockyards. My inspiration took wing.

"It's a sick scene, Varmint. All these greedy people, burning with lust to buy. Drinking, joking, jostling each other around. Gathered around the dock waiting for the ferry like junkies waiting for a heroin fix. I'm not going over there. And besides, I have clothes. I don't need new ones."

"Your clothes are disgusting," he said with a sneer. "They're dirty and they're not stylish at all."

"Well, I'm not spending the day on a ferry to go shopping. What if it sinks?"

"Do they sink?"

"Shit, Varmint, you'll be out of sight of land for hours while you're crossing Lake Erie. You heard that song about the *Edmund*

Fitzgerald, right? By Gordon Lightfoot? The *Edmund Fitzgerald* was a ship. Nine hundred feet long. It sank without a trace in a storm."

"Yes . . . " He was not sure how to respond to that.

"That was here, Varmint. On the Great Lakes."

The image of a nine-hundred-foot ship sinking, right there, did not seem to bother him at all. His need to buy was very, very strong.

"Twenty-nine people drowned. The whole crew."

"Well, if it's a nice day, I'm going anyway."

I tried to reassure him since he had made up his mind.

"When you get to the ferry terminal, if waves are breaking over the dock, don't go. Okay?"

"Okay," he agreed, but he hoped the weather would be nice. "You can drive me there in the morning and we'll check it out."

"I don't know how to get there. And I have to work. Take a taxi. I'll give you two hundred dollars for clothes and money for the taxi and the ferry. But you'll have to get yourself there."

"Thanks, John Elder." He figured he'd won.

We walked down the hall to our room. Our security staff had set up a roadblock to keep unwanted fans from our corner of the hotel. They knew Varmint.

We met Ace and one of the crew coming the other way.

"Heeeey! It's Baby Ampie!"

"And Big Ampie!"

Varmint did not really like being called Baby Ampie. He said, "I'm going to Detroit on the ferry. To get new clothes."

"Well far fucking out, Baby Ampie. Have a beer!"

Varmint backed away. We continued to our room, and I showed Varmint where he could sleep, on the floor by the window. There were two beds in the room, but I was using one for myself and the other as a workbench.

"I'm not sleeping on the floor. Clear that stuff off the bed!"

"Varmint, you should be grateful for what you've got. I used four thousand gallons of jet fuel to get you here. And now you want a bed, too?"

My little brother had no concept of the cost or trouble to bring him there. I didn't, either, but he didn't know that. I looked at the bed and considered the situation. If I put him on the floor, he'd whine all night. If I locked him in the hall, he'd make a scene. I decided to let him sleep on the workbench bed.

"Okay, help me move this stuff carefully onto the dresser. But first we have to remove the TV so we have some space. Get me the Phillips screwdriver from the tool kit."

Working together, we made a place for Varmint to sleep. Through it all, he did not show the least bit of interest in any of the electronic devices I was working on. I was disappointed.

It was clear that Varmint was not going to be able to sleep until he knew what was happening tomorrow with his shopping trip and the ferry ride. So he worked up his courage and headed for the front desk.

He got up on tiptoe to lean on the counter. Assuming a worldly expression, he said, "So where do I catch the ferry to Detroit?"

The clerk, a twenty-year-old farm girl with pimples, responded with a blank look.

"The ferry to Detroit," he said again, slowly, in case she was too dense to hear the first time.

"Uuuuuuuuuuuuuuuuuuuuuuuuuuuuuuuuh . . . I don't know," she mumbled, with a dazed look. The help at the motels we visited was not always of the highest caliber.

Varmint returned quickly and confronted me. "Is this a trick, John Elder?" But I was quick.

"Look around. Decide for yourself. Have you seen a single retail establishment since we got here?"

I had him there.

"I dunno." He was mumbling, too. He was confused. But he desperately wanted those clothes he'd seen in the magazines.

"The high point of the year in this community is the Festival of Saint Cleve," I told him. "Our concert is at the start of festival week. You didn't see them come out of church and go on a shopping spree in Mexico, did you?"

He realized I had a point.

I dismissed the whole thing. "Ask around. Find someone else."

Varmint headed down the hall and I snuck after him to eavesdrop. He asked the first people he met. They were a sweet-looking middle-aged couple.

"Excuse me. Do you know where I can catch the ferry to Detroit, please?" He was on his best behavior now.

"Sorry, we're from San Francisco." They smiled at the nice boy with the blond curls. Nice people like them buy children like him and raise them as pets. But he didn't want to be a pet today. He wanted clothes.

He realized he needed a local. Maybe someone else who worked there. Someone a little more on the ball than the clerk at the desk. So he found a janitor shuffling down the back corridor. Surely he lived around there. He'd know.

"Excuse me, where do I get the ferry to Detroit?" He was still polite.

The janitor just stared at him across his barrel of mops and brooms and rags.

"Whaaaaaaat?"

"I need to go shopping. How do I get to the ferry?"

"The ferry to Detroit? Waddaya, fuckin' nuts? Ya wanna go shoppin', ya go ta da fucking mall! Fuckin' half mile up the road!" He turned around and shuffled off. "Fuckin' idiot kid!" he muttered to himself as he rolled his barrel down the corridor. He coughed and spat on the carpet.

Varmint stood there with a sick smile, realizing he'd been had. He didn't say a thing.

I retreated to my room, feeling very proud of myself. Anyone can trick a four-year-old, but it takes a master to trick one ten years older. I realized Varmint was getting bigger, and smarter. I might never be able to trick him like that again.

Soon he would be too big to call Varmint. I would need to think of a new name for him. Chris, the name he came with, would never do.

I took him to the mall the next day. He went home after the Cleveland show with a bag of fresh clothes, mostly satisfied. The next time I heard from him, he wanted me to buy him a new bike.

16

One with the Machine

Many people with Asperger's have an affinity for machines. Sometimes I think I can relate better to a good machine than any kind of person. I've thought about why that is, and I've come up with a few ideas. One thought is that I control the machines. We don't interact as equals. No matter how big the machine, I am in charge. Machines don't talk back. They are predictable. They don't trick me, and they're never mean.

I have a lot of trouble reading other people. I am not very good at looking at people and knowing whether they like me, or they're mad, or they're just waiting for me to say something. I don't have problems like that with machines.

I feel an affinity with many different kinds of machines. I'll try to explain.

Imagine yourself at a sold-out concert. You're out on the floor—at what would be the fifty yard line if it were a football field—standing on a raised platform that holds the consoles that control the sound and lighting systems. You're looking over a sea of heads toward the stage. It's pitch-black, but you can see the NO SMOKING signs at the edges of the crowd. When the wind is right, you can smell the pot in the air. (Why is there wind in here, anyway?) The ceiling is so high, it seems like there might be clouds.

And all around you, the crowd is moving. Churning. Laser point-ers and cigarette lighters are flickering on and off like fireflies. The crowd is like a giant organism. It feels good to be standing above it, separate, with a little elbow room and a fence to keep people at bay.

Even with nothing going on, it's noisy. And you know the crowd can turn in the blink of an eye. You keep an ear open for gunshots. You worry about knives. You look down to see if the security guys are still in place in front of your platform. You are reassured to see them there, two weight lifters with black T-shirts that say "SECURITY" in big letters.

It's a Friday night in June, eighty-five degrees outside. Before the show, the road manager said there were ninety-two thousand people on the floor, and the line to get in looks half a mile long. Inside, it's supposed to be air-conditioned, but the air is hot. You're sweating, and you can smell the crowd. You'd like to take a walk, but wading five hundred feet through that crowd to get to the door is not an appealing prospect. You shudder to think what would happen if there was a fire.

The longer the lights stay off, the edgier the crowd gets. The only lights you can see are the exit signs and the work lights where you're standing. You're vulnerable. If they riot, you know they'll go for you first.

You think about that while you wait.

You, the lighting director, the sound guy, the road manager, and the fire chief are standing up there. The crowd is getting rest-less, and after a few minutes they begin to chant. It's almost time. The red LED flashes in front of you. The lighting director leans forward, keys the mike on the headset he's wearing, and says, "It's showtime, kiddies." You reach forward and fire the lights. The first time you hit the button, you feel it in your stomach . . . *What if nothing happens? What if they don't work?*

But then the light washes back from the stage and rolls over you. They do work. Your lights.

It's like magic, how it's all come together, though you don't think of it as magic because you understand how every single piece works and you know there's no magic involved. Just basic engineering principles. You've taken thousands of lifeless individual parts—lightbulbs, reflectors, circuit breakers, dimmer packs, power cables, clamps, and trusses—and turned them into a living thing. And you are its master.

You've designed it and built it, and now you've become a part of it. It's come alive. Electricity is its food, and you are its brain. You have become one with the machine. As long as you remain part of it, it's alive. Without you, it will revert to its component parts. But if it burns up while you're running it—maybe because you pushed too hard or made a mistake—that's death.

Becoming the brain of the lighting system takes intense focus and concentration. It's easy to say, "Push the button and the lights come on," but the reality is much more complex. The lights need to be brought up gently to keep them from burning out. To turn up all the lights, you must do a dance over the keyboard, bringing up first one, then another, because if you move too fast you could overload the system and blow a breaker, and you'd be left with nothing at all. Darkness. Your worst nightmare in the middle of a show. Darkness is when they riot, and you must never, never let that happen. You must develop a sixth sense for your system, to feel how it's doing, to be really great.

And now you're doing it. Cones of colored light are reaching down from the ceiling to the stage, washing over the scenery. The cones are moving and changing as you switch from light to light in a constant dance that follows the music. Fog machines behind the stage are generating clouds, and your lights are making patterns in the mist.

The faces of the crowd are visible, and they are all staring at the stage. There is action up there, and it's loud. And you're like the wizard of Oz. You're right there in the open, and no one sees you.

You feel a chill as the lights change in response to your commands. You've brought a million watts of lighting to life by leaning forward and moving two fingers. Just a gentle push and you've moved enough power to light a whole neighborhood. For now, all of your mental energy is focused on that lighting system. Once the show has started, there is no time for daydreaming. You know the color and focus and aiming point of every one of the three hundred lights that hang from your truss. Now you concentrate and pick out each one, one at a time, and you make small adjustments as you scan them.

Now that you're working, your concentration is so intense that you don't even hear the show. You don't see the crowd. Instead, you're seeing each of those hundreds of lights as individuals, and it's all you can do to keep them following the music. It's just like playing a huge musical instrument, and your hands never stop moving on the dimmers.

If you had been backstage, near the electrical panels, you'd have heard the hum as the power surge hit the panel when the lights came up. Fifty feet above the floor, three hundred lights came on and a wave of heat rolled off them like someone just opened the door to a furnace.

When the show started, everything happened at once. The lights came up, the cannons fired, and the band started playing. From up high in the back of the hall, the follow spots—ten-foot-long spotlights with powerful xenon lamps—came on and picked out the musicians with long fingers of white light. Next to you, the sound engineer watches his meters as they turn from green to red. The fire chief holds up his sound pressure meter and frowns and waves it in front of the road manager. It's too loud to talk. It shows 124 decibels, about the level of jets taking off at the Detroit airport. It's too loud to be legal, but no one hears the chief. The crowd roars and the music gets even louder.

And it's never enough. You can always have brighter lights, bigger amplifiers. These are machines that run at 100 percent, every show. One million watts of power, right there under your finger. There's nothing like it in the world.

17

Rock and Roll All Night

The Return of KISS tour hit the road in the summer of 1979. The first concert was scheduled for June 15 in Lakeland, Florida. I would be there.

I had been working since spring, building a new collection of special-effects guitars for Ace. Tex and I had worked with luthier Steve Carr to make my electronic creations playable. Carr had done the fretwork and final finishing, and Tex had test played the guitars. I had designed and built the electronics. The band had just released *Dynasty,* and their songs were once again climbing the charts.

For this tour, the band would be using all new equipment. The stage was new. The effects were new. The costumes were new. And all the special guitars we had created were new. All that new stuff would be very exciting except for the worry—would it really work?

A week before the first show, the rest of the crew had arrived in Florida to set up, and I was down to the wire. It seemed like I was working twenty-five hours a day. Tex and the road manager were calling me daily, asking what was taking so long, and I was in a state of high anxiety.

"We're all here waiting, Ampie," Tex would say. "The tour is starting!"

Back home, we were building and refining right up to the last minute. Would it really work? At a real concert? In front of an audience? I sure hoped so.

I finally arrived at the Orlando airport on a bright, hot Thursday morning two days before the show. With my cutoff blue jeans and long hair and beard, I looked more like a biker than a Florida tourist, but there I was. I had a bag of clothes, a box packed with explosives, tools, parts, and weapons, and two guitar cases. As I trooped off the plane, I found myself surrounded by hundreds of moms and kids headed for a big weekend at Disney World. They were loud, they were rude, they smelled funny, and most kept a respectful distance from me.

We all rode the monorail from the gate into the terminal building. Stray kids climbed over the luggage as I waited for my bags to emerge. I tried to remember what I'd read about the Florida gun laws and wondered which ones I was violating.

Outside the terminal, it was like a steam bath. I had flown first class, and now I rented a Lincoln, the most air-conditioned vehicle they had. I charged it all to the band. If those guitars worked, they would pay any bill I handed in. If they didn't work, a new life in the Caribbean was just a one-hour plane ride away.

I headed for the hotel, a sprawling two-story structure with peeling stucco, mold, and a faintly foul smell at the edge of a swamp. Everything in Florida was at the edge of a swamp. It was all swamp, except where people had drained it and paved it or built something. They gave me a room on the first floor in back with two beds and a TV.

The hotel was not what I expected in an upscale chain. Everything was run-down and cheap. The beds were hard, the chairs were flimsy, and there was a bottle opener bolted to the counter in the bathroom, within easy reach of the toilet. It was the sort of place where you didn't put your hands anywhere you couldn't see. The kind of place where even the grown-ups peed in the pool. But I figured it would do; I was only planning to be there two nights.

After I shut the door, I unpacked the guitars and laid them on one of the beds, carefully, so nothing would get scratched. They both used the Frezzolini rechargeable battery packs, so I plugged the guitars into their chargers and made sure the ready lights were lit. Nothing seemed to have broken on the ride down.

The guitars needed to charge for at least an hour before they could be used. While I was waiting, I retrieved my revolver and tour pass from the bottom of my suitcase. I got the bullets out of another bag—even then, it was against the law to carry a loaded gun on a plane—and filled the revolver's chamber, then stuck the gun under the false bottom of my Halliburton briefcase.

When the guitars were ready, I picked up the light one and gave the speed knob a quick twist. It came to life, with stripes of light moving over the face of the guitar. All 750 little lamps seemed to be working. I could feel the heat from the lamps on my hand, under the clear plastic face. I shut it off to save the battery.

I picked up the smoker and worked the mechanism. I hit the light switch and watched the lamp come on for a few seconds. I looked inside.

There was nothing left to do. I was as ready as I was going to get. I carried them to the car.

When I arrived at the arena, most of the setup work was done. Some of the guys were standing around a buffet, eating catered food. Another fellow was flying a model airplane over the seats, and two carpenters were behind the stage, doing line after line of coke. They asked if I wanted some. The coke could keep you moving, but I was zippy enough as it was. With all my worries about whether my stuff would work, I didn't need any drugs to keep me going.

I carried the guitar cases past the coke line and back into the dressing rooms where we'd set them up. Most of the people on the crew had never seen them before, and a crowd filled the room and spilled into the hall. Tex and Paul—the two crew members who handled the guitars—moved in close to check them out for the first time.

Everyone broke into grins when Tex turned on the light guitar and stripes of white light began running up and down the body. The light on the wall was like ripples swimming across a pond, but bright.

"That is incredibly cool, Ampie!"

A crowd gathered. No one had ever seen anything like that before.

"Damn, Ampie, that thing is bright!"

Someone shut off the ceiling lights and we all watched it for a moment. It was starting to feel like a winner.

Ace arrived. He picked the guitar up and turned it in his hands. Carefully, as though it were alive and might bite. I could understand that. When you held it, you could feel the heat from the lamps sweep up and down your skin as the patterns changed. It actually felt alive. With your hand on the face, it brushed your palm as it ran.

"Far out. Fuckin' Ampie. This is wild!"

We carried the guitars to the stage and plugged into Ace's stack of six Marshall amplifiers. The sounds filled the empty civic center. He loved them, and I was so proud and relieved. There was one more night before the show.

KISS played on custom-built staging, and I needed to have some stuff welded to the aluminum frames on Ace's side of the stage to hold pieces for one of the guitars. I told the head carpenter what I needed, and he said he'd have it done that night. "But that's a big favor. You owe me a full gallon of Tanqueray gin," he said. What could I do but agree? After all my anxiety about those guitars working, I was too cranked up to sleep, but eventually I went back to my room and passed out.

When I woke up, the sun was shining brightly through my windows. I had a ground floor room looking out onto a lawn that sloped down into tall marsh grasses. The view was kind of pretty, marred only by the sign on the lawn about ten feet from the door:

WARNING
REPTILES
DO NOT PROCEED BEYOND THIS POINT

I hadn't noticed the sign before, but I hadn't paid much attention to anything but those guitars when I arrived. Thinking I would take a picture of it, I opened the door and almost stepped on a large black water moccasin sunning himself on the concrete patio. *My* concrete patio.

He was three feet long, and fat. Almost as thick as my leg. Nasty looking. The snake saw me, and he quickly reared back and opened his mouth, ready to strike. The inside was all white with a little bit of pink. I had seen snakes like him before, on my grandparents' farm. Rattlesnakes would run away if you gave them the chance, but water moccasins would stand their ground or even attack. This one must have been thinking attack. I quickly closed the door and considered what to do next.

The first time I saw a poisonous snake I was probably eight years old. Even then, I knew just what to do. I went into the house. I went to the encyclopedia and turned to *snake*. I read all about them. Water moccasins were bad, and so were rattlers and copperheads, but I learned there were far more dangerous snakes elsewhere in the world. I decided then and there not to visit those places.

As a child, I had read that the risk of death from a snakebite was less than the risk of drowning in a swimming pool, or being killed in a car accident. But those statistics didn't apply today. Today I had an angry venomous snake two feet away, with just a flimsy steel motel door between me and him. I had to do something. If I went back to sleep, housekeeping would arrive to clean the room, and they'd let him in. I certainly didn't want him crawling in with me. If I wanted a chance to drown in the pool or die in a car accident, I would have to remove the snake or make it past him alive. The odds had turned.

People up North say, "Why do people kill them? Snakes are okay. They won't hurt you unless you provoke them." Down South they don't say things like that. They know better. On my grandparents' farm, Gerald—a hired hand—jabbed a water moccasin with a stick, thinking it would slither away. It didn't. Quick as lightning, it climbed the stick and bit him. His hand turned purple and he almost died.

When I was fifteen, one dropped off a branch into a rowboat I was paddling, and I shot it six times, clubbed it with an oar, and it still tried to bite me. The rowboat almost sank, too. My great-grandfather Dandy had long ago told me the best answer to any snake question.

"Number six shot."

That's what he loaded into the sawed-off shotgun that he carried in the high grass and swampland.

I didn't have a shotgun, but I had the next best thing. I went to my briefcase and took out my revolver. Dumping the hollow points onto the bed, I quickly loaded it with snake shot. Snake shot is like steel gravel, encased in a cartridge. Why would I have snake shot on a rock and roll tour, you ask? Don't. I was always armed, and I spent my summers in the South. I knew plenty about what lived in the Florida swamps.

I was ready. I opened the door, stepped out, lowered the gun, and shot that snake twice before he had a chance to collect his thoughts and bite me. The first shot knocked him down. The second shot blew him back about ten feet into the grass. I stepped out and shot him four more times, just to be safe. As the sound of the shots faded away, I looked around.

The cloud of gun smoke was dissipating. The snake was in two pieces. The tail was twitching. The bathers at the pool had all dived for cover. Some were in the water, some under the chairs. No one was moving.

"It's okay, folks. Just a snake!" I smiled and waved the gun reassuringly.

Still, nobody moved. I realized I was standing outside, next to a pool full of kids and sunbathing parents, in my underwear, waving a smoking revolver. I turned and went back into my room.

I looked under the beds to make sure that snake didn't have a brother that had sneaked in while I was outside. Then I reloaded the gun and put on some pants and a shirt. There is nothing more useless than an unloaded gun in a motel room.

I called the front desk and asked for the manager. When he came on the line, I said, "There was a water moccasin just outside my door, but it's okay because I shot it. Can you send housekeeping up to clean the patio?"

I expected him to thank me, but didn't. He went wild.

"You shot a gun in my hotel! Are you crazy? You are in big trouble, mister! You're going to jail! Don't you go anywhere. I'm calling the police!" Moments later, he appeared in my doorway, looking deranged and red in the face, shattering my tranquillity.

The sheriff's deputy came by in a few minutes. He was big, at least 250 pounds, with the mirrored sunglasses the police down South liked to wear. He didn't look too friendly, but I knew that was just for show. I had talked to him earlier when he'd stopped by the civic center to see the security arrangements for the show. He'd been in the service, in Vietnam, and we'd talked about the LAWS antitank rockets he'd used over there and how I wanted to use them in stage effects here. I had shown him some of the pyrotechnic devices we used in the shows. I was just beginning to work on rocket guitars.

"What happened here?" he said, in a slow drawl.

"I opened my door and that snake was there, waiting to bite me. So I shot him," I said. "Lucky for me I had a gun and I was alert. If I hadn't been paying attention, I could have been bit bad."

The deputy nodded his head. He observed that the first chunk was shot out of the concrete no more than two feet from my door, easy biting distance for a bad-tempered cottonmouth. He turned to the manager and said, "Goddamn, Fred, you're lucky this here boy was prepared. You'd a had a real mess on your hands if that snake woulda bit him or some kid."

The manager quivered a little and nodded. It was clear he didn't share the sheriff's point of view. I'm sure he would have preferred that the snake had slipped into someone's room, bit them, and left. Housekeeping would have found the body, dead and purple, and the undertaker would have hauled it away. Quietly. No gunshots. No disturbance. After all, dead people were a fact of life in Florida hotel rooms. Gunshots weren't, at least not in Lakeland.

Then the deputy turned to me and said, "What'd ya shoot him with, son?" So I showed him. He handed me back the gun and said, "That's a fine gun. If I couldn't kill a snake with that, I'd just drop it and back away slowly and wish that snake good day."

He had no comment at all about why a guy like me might have a big revolver in a gold briefcase. We all had guns. That was Florida in 1979. And with that, the deputy left.

I decamped for the Hilton, where I had no further reptile problems. But first I insisted on a credit for the room charge, as the place had clearly been unsatisfactory. The firm and positive manner in which I had dealt with the poisonous snake convinced the manager of the reasonableness of my argument.

The incident with the snake had been a welcome distraction, but I was still plenty worried about how my equipment would do at its first show. Tex and I set up both the guitars, and we checked and rechecked until it was time to go on. I went outside and walked in circles around the building until the show started, because I couldn't sit still. The crowd was getting bigger and by my third orbit there must have been ten thousand people in the parking lot.

I walked toward the main entrance, where fifty or more outlaw bikers had set up camp while they waited for the gates to open. I walked over to check out the bikes. One of the bikers saw my backstage pass, and he trotted over.

"Hey, man, can you get me and my buddies inside? We have some acid and other shit, too."

I was afraid to say I never touched acid. Two more bikers joined the first one. One had a heavy chain around his neck. They were considerably dirtier and smellier than I had ever been. They appeared to cultivate filth.

"You wanna beer?"

The police were eyeing them already, wondering if they should try to arrest them for having open bottles in public. The bikers were eyeing the law, wondering if they had the balls to try to arrest them for having open bottles in public. So far, it was a standoff.

A biker with no front teeth ambled over. He grinned. I was now surrounded.

"How many of us can you get in?"

"We got some great shit."

"You wanna bitch? We've got plenty if you want one. Ellie there is hot." She didn't have any front teeth, either.

I was reluctant to decline the female bikers, because the males looked dangerous. But I wasn't interested in a toothless, smelly, possibly diseased female. Unsure how to frame a polite response, I stood still for a few seconds. That gave them the wrong idea.

"You queer?"

"Okay, guys, I'll see what I can do," I said. I pulled out my pass and went to the front door and banged hard. When the security guy opened it, I waved my pass in his face, said, "Thanks," and headed back inside, out of sight, as quick as I could. I didn't go out front again. I was learning about mingling with the crowds.

Backstage, I couldn't stand still. The waiting was killing me. I kept talking to myself: *Is my stuff going to work? How many minutes till the show starts?* I walked to the back door, hoping the air would be fresher. It wasn't. There weren't any bikers out back, though, so I stepped out.

Now there was a crowd gathered by the back entrance to see the band drive in. I tucked my pass out of sight. There were people dressed up as KISS look-alikes, ten-year-old girls with their mothers, even a guy dressed like a medieval magician. As the parking lot filled, I found myself driven to the edge of the grass.

I walked back around to the front, keeping an eye out for reptiles, went back in, and made my way to the front of the stage. There was an aisle there, with a six-foot-high crowd barrier and security guys patrolling back and forth like guard dogs in a prison. We nodded to each other as we passed. Some of them had sticks, and I had a gun. We were ready. I watched the audience pour into the hall. Would my stuff work?

Finally, it was showtime. The band opened with "King of the Night Time World," and moved into "Radioactive." I was so wound up, I didn't even hear them Then it was time. Ace picked up the smoking guitar and began to play his solo. I didn't even breathe as I watched for his fingers to turn the knob that fired the bombs. When he cranked it, I heard the snap through the speakers, and the light glared from the front of the guitar while smoke poured out.

Still he kept playing, and the smoke kept getting thicker. Now the audience was on its feet. They were applauding! For my guitar! I was thrilled. I was so relieved, I almost collapsed as Ace's solo wound down and the song came to an end. The lights dimmed and he handed my guitar off for another one for the next song. But there was still one guitar to go . . .

A few songs later, Ace picked it up and stood facing away from the audience as he turned it on. The whole stage was dark. Everyone could see something flashing behind him, but no one knew what it was. He lit into the opening chords of "New York Groove," then turned around and the audience roared. I couldn't believe it. It was probably the proudest moment of my life, seeing the audience respond to my guitar like that. It was the hit of the show, and it was on the TV news that night. I was ecstatic. For once, everyone loved me.

Backstage after the show, Ace was all over me with questions about the guitars. "Ampie, can you make one that shoots rockets? Can you make one shoot nine-millimeter pistol ammunition? Can you make a laser guitar? Can we make the smoking guitar fly? Can we blow it up at the end of the song?"

"Sure, we can do all that." I sounded confident, even though my head was spinning. But I knew I could do it. And I was sure Jim and Little Bear would help. Ace had five brand-new Les Paul guitars for spares. I took one out and retreated into my corner to consider the next move.

When I got up the next day, I felt like a new person. My stuff had worked! I had proven myself. I had been so afraid it would all be a failure, and that I would head home in disgrace. All of a sudden, I was on top of the world. The tour was starting, and I had stuff to build. I realized I had not come to Florida with any fresh underwear or socks. I had one pair of pants, and two T-shirts. I needed clean clothes.

Two hours and five hundred dollars later, I was transformed. Gone was the old Ampie in ripped blue jeans and an outlaw biker shirt. Now I had a supply of respectable shorts and shirts with alligators and horses on them. If Orlando had only had a yacht club, I could have hung out and not been evicted. Still, I was on tour, and I'd be visiting other cities where children and salesclerks would no longer edge away slowly at my approach.

I considered getting a haircut but settled for a shower. Then it was time for lunch. The waitress smiled at me.

"I'll have two hamburgers, a bowl of the chowder, and four glasses of iced tea. And a brownie sundae in a few minutes." Silence. "Thanks." I was trying to remember to be polite, and still order efficiently. I wanted my food.

The Lincoln was starting to stink from the dirty clothes in the backseat. I packed them into a box and sent it home, using the band's FedEx account. (By the time I got back home, a few months later, the smell had dissipated. I washed them anyway, of course.) Then I went back to the civic center and talked with Ace about the guitars to come. Now I had a mission. I returned to the hotel and started making diagrams and plans.

I had figured to hand over that gallon of gin after the second show, but it didn't work out that way. While I was putting my gear away, I was startled by a commotion at the doors. It was the DEA. They came in and headed straight backstage. I shrank behind the equipment cases to render myself less visible and waited. They came out from backstage a moment later with two of our carpenters in handcuffs, and a sack full of something. Tex said, "They've got a pound of coke in the bag." They wouldn't need my gallon of gin where they were headed. I carried that gin around for a month before I found someone else to give it to.

I remained with the tour from Lakeland on. It was a hard life, but it was exciting, and I felt good seeing how people reacted to my creations. It was a wild life, too, something I had never experienced and didn't really know how to engage in. We played shows in south Florida where coke dealers came backstage with free samples.

"Here Ampie, take some." They had party trays with lines of coke, and punch bowls of the stuff on tables. Big bowls, like you mix cookies in at home. They also had pills. Anything you wanted, we had it.

And that wasn't all. We had madams come backstage with free samples, too. People would ask me, "Do you get lots of girls out there on tour?" People seemed to assume girls would throw themselves at me, and that I'd take them up on their offers. But it didn't happen that way. I was still shy about meeting people, so I never initiated conversations with girls, and I never really considered spending the night with someone I was going to have to say good-bye to the following day. The whole thing just seemed creepy to me.

And, of course, I had a girlfriend. "Who cares?" The guys would make fun of me. "When I leave home, it's open season on every girl I can catch!" they boasted. Somehow, I just couldn't embrace that concept. The idea of having to meet and befriend one person after another was just too scary to me.

Did any of the girls try to pick me up? I'll never know. My sensitivity to other people's actions was limited enough that any attempt to pick me up went unnoticed. I often felt lonely when I saw couples together, but I could not see any way I could change my own situation, so I just plodded along.

When people were drinking and doing coke around me, I often felt confused. I didn't like feeling out of control, and I had seen people do outrageous things while they were drunk and have no memory of it the next day. The mere thought that I might do things like that was enough to make me cringe. So I didn't know what to do.

"Relax, Ampie! Here, have a line! Here, have a drink!" An observer would have said temptation was all around me, but to me it wasn't tempting at all. I did a few lines and I drank a few drinks—just enough to feel like I was being polite. I never felt the desire to pack in all the beer I could drink or all the coke I could snort. I just did not like how it made me feel.

The few times I was drunk or on drugs, I would close my eyes and the world would spin, and I would say to myself, *When is this shit going to end? Why did I do this?* It didn't take me very long to outgrow it, if *outgrow* is the right word. I stopped doing drugs and liquor, and I didn't resume.

One of the high points of any tour is being the headline act at Madison Square Garden. We were scheduled to play several shows there midway through the tour. When the road crew was setting up Ace's guitars, a rocket went off, sending Tex to the emergency room with burned fingers. We had no spare for that guitar and I had to race to fix it. Showtime was coming, and people were starting to crowd around me in hopes I'd go faster.

"If you screw up and make us late, we're getting fined ten thousand bucks a minute. Get that stuff up there!" Fritz, our road manager, stood over me, urging speed.

I had not screwed up. I was saving his sorry ass. I was going as fast as I could.

"Go, go, go. Fines, Ampie, fines. Don't make us late!"

We carried it up there and started on time, and it all worked.

By 1980, my special-effects guitars were a regular part of the show. Each of the guys had a gimmick. Gene flew through the air and spat fire and blood. He also played a bass that was shaped like a bloody battle-ax. Paul had the eye, and a mirrored Ibanez guitar that reflected the spotlights. And Ace had my customized Les Paul guitars. Every show, he would start into Mick Jagger's "2000 Man" playing a stock black Les Paul guitar. Halfway through he would step to the edge of the stage and swap guitars for the black smoker. He'd begin playing his solo, and in the middle of it he'd twist the knob that set off the smoke bomb and the lights. Ace's projector lamp threw a square of light all the way to the back of the hall, and smoke poured from the hole. The guitar really looked like it had caught fire.

You could tell when Ace lit the smoking guitar just by listening to the audience. They loved it. We knew many KISS fans came for the spectacle, and I did my best not to disappoint them. Our pyrotechnics wizard said, "Ampie, we set off more fireworks every show than most towns shoot on the Fourth of July." I was inclined to believe him.

After a few shows, we improved the smoking guitar still more. A second twist of the knob would fire a second, larger, smoke bomb. Ace would almost vanish in the cloud, and the smoke would spread across the stage while the heat burned the strings right off the guitar as he continued to play. As each string burned through with a *ping,* the audience would roar.

At that point, we would drop an invisible cable down from the ceiling. We had rigged a track up there that allowed the cable to drop down, pick something up, then lift it and swing it around—all by remote control. The cable was rigged with a coupler and a powerful electromagnet, and one of us would be at the controls to run it. The guitar had a steel hook to grab the cable. Ace would begin to swing the guitar at the end of his solo, looking like he was chopping the air with his guitar. When he felt the cable grab the hook, he'd throw the guitar out toward the audience and it would start swinging around on the cable. One of the crew would be reeling the cable in slowly, so the guitar was swinging and rising into the air. Meanwhile, I'd be standing to the side with a radio-control rig that I'd scavenged from a model airplane. I'd start flashing the lights in the guitar off and on. It would look like a lighthouse beacon, swinging and flashing, as it rose fifty feet above the stage.

From that height, the flashes would shine all the way to the back of the hall, no matter how big a place we played. And some of those places were *big*. It seemed like a quarter mile from the stage to the last row of seats in huge arenas like Detroit's Pontiac Silverdome. While everyone watched the guitar, Ace was stepping over and grabbing the rocket guitar to play the next part.

The rocket guitar was another Les Paul, identical in appearance to the last two. It had a three-tube rocket launcher at the end of the neck. He'd start playing his solo again, and then he'd step to the front of the stage, stamp his foot, swing the guitar to the left, and fire the first rocket. The audience could hear a bang, and they saw the flash from the end of the guitar neck. We had hung a bag of flash powder and confetti from the roof above the audience— about a hundred feet back—and we'd blow it up when he fired. The audience would think we were shooting airburst shells over their heads. It was a great effect. The crowd loved it.

Then he'd swing to the right and fire again, and we'd blow another bag of flash powder. The flash powder bombs were filled with confetti that would rain down on the crowd for ten seconds or so. As the confetti from the first two bombs was falling, he'd point his guitar up and fire the finale—straight up at the burning smoker. We'd blow up the biggest charge of all, and I'd use the radio control to shut the smoker off. When everything went dark, the crowd assumed he'd blown it up.

It worked really well, too, until we played Olympic Stadium in Munich. At that show, the charge from the rocket guitar actually hit the smoker, and it fell seventy feet and shattered in the crowd barrier in front of the stage. There was a riot as mobs swarmed over the barrier to grab chunks of guitar. There was nothing left of it.

I jetted home so we could make a new smoker, and then I flew it back to Germany. I got two first-class tickets—one for the guitar, and one for me.

18

A Real Job

By the end of the 1970s, despite my success with KISS, I was barely making a living. I was working for the big bands as much as I could, but they only needed me to get ready for a tour. Then I went home, the money ran out, and I was flat broke.

In Texas, on tour, I dined at the Mansion on Turtle Creek and charged it to the band. I ate exquisite gourmet meals served by perfectly dressed waiters on fine china. In Atlanta, I dined at Trotters, beneath oil paintings of racehorses and jockeys. Limousines and private planes ferried me from place to place.

Back in Amherst, I had a Cadillac Eldorado convertible, but I couldn't afford the gas to drive it. I dined on Kraft macaroni and cheese. When I couldn't afford milk to mix it up properly, I made a slurry of water and macaroni and powdered cheese and ate it like that. I foraged for leftover slices at Bruno's Pizza and robbed the condiment bowls for dessert. Instead of the Plaza Hotel, with its beautiful wallpaper and marble bathrooms, I stayed at 288 Federal Street, with newspaper plastered on the walls and a plastic sink in a four-foot-square bathroom with a stand-up shower.

It wasn't too hard being broke. Any apartment was better than living in a lean-to under a tree, as I had for a time when I first left home. The hard part was living the contrast between being rich and being broke. It was like being smart, and waking up one day to find yourself dumb as a rock, but able to remember your former brains. What I needed was stability. I needed two hundred dollars a week for ten weeks, not three thousand dollars one day and nothing for three months.

"Ampie, you should move to L.A.! You could work on films with me."

"You should move to New York. You'd have more work than you could handle."

Everyone was full of well-meaning advice about where I should go and what I should do. I was constantly reminded of the bright future I'd have if I moved to the big city. But I had grown up in the country. My favorite places were the Georgia countryside and the woods in Shutesbury. I didn't like cities. They were full of people—people who made me feel anxious, people I didn't know how to relate to. I understood animals, and I understood the country. I felt safe in the woods. I never felt safe in a city or a crowd.

And I had someone else to think about. Little Bear was at UMass at Amherst, and we had just moved in together. She couldn't quit school, and I couldn't leave her.

It is scary, but what if I did move? I asked myself that question at least once every day. But I didn't have confidence that anyone would keep me around. Nothing else in my life had lasted. I had dropped out of school. My family had fallen apart. The thought of starting a new life two thousand miles away was overwhelming.

I was also afraid to leave my parents. As much as I disliked them, I didn't want to go away and find they had just crawled into holes and died. And there was my brother, too. So long as he was living with Dr. Finch, I felt as though I needed to remain in the vicinity, on standby. I wouldn't find out until years later exactly what he had gone through, but instinct told me I needed to stick around.

My father called every week.

"Son, I'm sorry I've been a burden to you. You won't have to worry about me anymore." His words were slurred, but it didn't matter; he always said the same thing. He'd call me, drunk, from the floor of his apartment, then drop the phone on the floor. I'd have to drive over there and see what he was doing. Was he dead or just passed out? Wine, cigarettes, and trash were everywhere. It was like taking care of a child.

"Get off the floor or I'm calling the cops. Get up! Now!"

"I'm sorry, John Elder, it's just so hard." He was drunk and wallowing, but he got off the floor. In just five years, he'd gone from beating me up to being a blubbering baby. I guess he had hit bottom. He was broke. His house was gone. His family was gone. He had a fifty-dollar car and he worked a second job as a security guard at Hampshire College to pay the bills.

Visiting my mother was worse. She had moved into an apartment in town and was still seeing women. She had a girlfriend who could have been my aunt. It just seemed unnatural. And some of the other females I saw over there were more like acolytes than girlfriends.

Sometimes it got even weirder than that. "This is my daughter, Anne. She's your new sister," she told me. Did she really believe some girl she took in was my sister? She was losing her marbles. Again. Soon enough she was back at Northampton State Hospital, and my new sister had thrown my mother's stuff in the backyard and taken over the house.

I was too ashamed ever to tell a stranger—or even a friend— what my parents were really like. "My parents teach at the university," I said. "My father is in philosophy," I would tell people. I made them sound clean, tweedy, and nice, not shackled to a wall, frothing like rabid dogs, behind four layers of locked doors, which was closer to the truth.

At least I had Little Bear. She knew what they were really like.

My friends had parents who sent them to college at places like Dartmouth and McGill. They had homes to return to, and they were in college. Not me. I rode my motorcycle back to Sunderland (a small town next to Amherst), to the three-room apartment I shared with Little Bear and her two roommates. I was on my own and I needed a job, now.

So I decided to do something about it. Jim Boughton and I started installing sound and light systems in local nightclubs. We started in the Amherst area and expanded south to Springfield. Then we went farther, to Boston and Hartford. The jobs didn't pay much, or we didn't know enough to charge much, but we had steady work.

Going into a discotheque at noon to install sound equipment is very different from entering the same place at midnight. It's completely quiet, and there is no natural light, because the windows and doors are painted flat black to keep people from looking in. Fluorescent work lights that are never on in the evening make the interior a uniform shade of gray. The place reeks of cigarette smoke and spilled liquor everywhere except the bathrooms. There, the stench of piss and vomit is stronger. A thin film of congealed smoke, sweat, and grease covers everything in the room. Wipe any surface with a white towel and it comes up the color of fresh iced tea.

That was our new workplace. We spent our days installing colored neon lights along the ceiling and subwoofers in corners that hadn't seen daylight in forty years. We put turntables and a mixer into a newly built DJ booth, looking down onto the dance floor.

It's enough to make a living, I told myself. *And it's still music.* We started returning at night to admire our creations. Little Bear seldom came with us to those places. It was usually just Boughton and me. We'd drive to one club, stay thirty minutes, and head to another. The VIP. The Viking. Infinity. The Arabian Nights. Marc Anthony's. The doormen all knew us, so we got in free. If we were lucky, the bartenders knew us, too, and we'd get free drinks. Not that I ever drank much anyway.

I'd watch the girls in dresses, girls in skirts, girls with hardly any clothes at all. They arrived alone and in groups. Sometimes they left the way they came. Sometimes they got lucky and left with a guy. At least, I assumed they were lucky.

I didn't leave with any girls, although I often wished I were as brave as some of the people I saw. I wished I could walk up to strangers and engage them in conversation. I don't know what I would have said or done. It would have felt good, though, having that confidence and making friends. I watched the people talking at the bar. I watched people dancing on the floor. I saw them in freeze-frame in the light of my strobes. They glowed red in the light of my lasers, and they glittered with the lights from the mirror ball. The DJs always used the mirror ball for the slow dances.

I knew everything there was to know about lighting the dance floor and lighting the people, but the people themselves remained a mystery to me. I could not figure them out.

I never set foot on the dance floor unless I was fixing or adjusting something. I couldn't dance. I was clumsy, and I was sure I would look incredibly stupid. I had learned by then not to put myself in situations where people would laugh at me. Anyway, I was too shy to ask anyone to dance, and too self-conscious to accept if anyone asked me. I watched people doing lines of coke and popping pills at tables, in plain sight of the sound booth. Sometimes I'd see people shooting up on the steps in the alleys out back.

Heroin was scary. I'd read how you could become addicted with a few pricks of the needle, and I saw how the addicts lived. In Dumpsters, and passed out in doorways. *No way am I going to do that,* I thought. That was even worse than my father's drinking.

I watched it all with the same detachment I had learned to feel when I was excluded from playing with kid packs when I was five. No one made fun of me, but I still could not integrate myself into the groups around me. I wanted to make friends, but I didn't want to engage in the activities I saw them doing. So I just watched. And I worked. And I stayed, convinced that it was better to be destitute in Amherst than in New York City.

The trouble was, the effects I wanted to design were getting more and more complex. I was starting to use microprocessors in my designs, and I couldn't afford the equipment to make and test my circuits at home. I needed a lab, but I was reluctant to go back to the university because they'd want to enroll me in some kind of organized school program, and I'd had enough of that. I needed the resources of some still-nameless corporation.

I realized it was time to get a real job. Everyone else had jobs, except the lowlifes sitting in doorways downtown. I didn't want to be one of them. I started reading the help wanted ads, looking under "Electrical Engineer." I wondered if anyone would hire me. Most of the ads were faceless, boring ads for boring companies. One ad caught my eye, so much so that I still remember it:

Money problems?
Woman trouble?
Running from the law?
You can find a home in the Foreign Legion.

I thought it was a joke, but it wasn't. The Foreign Legion was actually advertising for mercenaries. It was a shame I wasn't looking for what they had to offer: adventure, discipline, male companionship, and the chance to fight battles far from home.

I focused on local ads. Process Control. Jet Engine Testing. Quality Assurance Engineering. Field Service Rep. Sales Engineer. CNC Programming. But I could not imagine myself doing any of those things. I didn't even know what most of them were. Then, at the bottom of the last page in the Sunday paper, I saw it:

Electrical Engineers
Be part of the team designing next season's hottest
electronic games

That was the job for me. I called immediately, and was told to drop off a résumé. Résumé? I had never made one. So I started reading up on how to write one. By the next day, I had made up a fine-looking résumé, and the majority of the stuff on it—everything but my age and education—was actually true. I guess I did a good job, because Catherine from Personnel called the next day to schedule an interview. She also told me a little more about what they were looking for.

They were designing sound effects. They wanted to make games that talked and listened. They wanted people with experience in audio and digital design. "I can do those things," I said confidently.

My Aspergian ability to focus and learn fast saved me. Between Sunday, when I read the ad, and the interview eight days later, I became a passable expert in digital design. My head was spinning, but I had absorbed the contents of three engineering texts from the Graduate Research Center library.

When interview day arrived, I put on my suit and drove down. Actually, I was lucky I even had a suit. I had bought it the previous summer when KISS was interviewed for a TV show while touring in the South. It was light gray rough silk, from Christian Dior in Charleston. It was bought on the expense account, so I could thank KISS for my natty appearance at my first job interview.

It was a long day of questions and answers. I started with Paul, the manager of the R&D group. Then I met with Klaus, the senior engineer. Then I talked to Dave, the mathematician who was designing the speech synthesis system. Finally, I talked to Jim, the group vice president. It was an incredible piece of luck for me that the things they wanted were the things I knew the most about. And, even better for me, they had not found one single applicant with any knowledge of sound effects.

Of course, I made it sound like I designed my sound effects devices in a real lab, as they did—not on my kitchen table, or in a motel room, or on the floor in some civic center, the way it really happened. At the time, I was very worried by my lack of legitimacy, but now I realize it didn't matter where I created those things. What mattered was that I had done it. I had done it for KISS and I could do it for them.

"What do you know about digital filters?" they asked. *Nothing, but I learn fast,* I thought. "What do you know about sound effects?" I was on solid ground with that one. "I've designed filters to modify the sounds of musical instruments, and I've designed all manner of signal processors for sound reinforcement and recording. I've also designed circuits for monophonic and polyphonic synthesizers . . ." Once I got going on that topic, I didn't stop.

The letter arrived in the mail two days later. It began: "Milton Bradley's electronics division is pleased to offer you the position of Staff Engineer in our Advanced R&D Group. Your starting salary will be $25,000 per year."

I couldn't believe it at first. Then I felt proud, and also scared. Could I do it? I was about to find out. I called right away and agreed to start work the following Monday. I figured I'd better start quickly, before they had a chance to change their minds.

When I reported to work, I was pleased to find other geeks and misfits I could talk to. Most of the engineers were about my age. They had just spent four years in college; I had spent four years on the road. Since I had grown up around the university, I fit in fine. Several of the guys at work had even graduated from UMass and we knew some of the same professors.

We had a few senior engineers who were quite a bit older, and they were supposed to watch over the rest of us. I was assigned to Klaus, whom I had met during my interview. He was old and cranky but extremely sharp. We got along well.

I had never worked in an organization before, so I watched carefully to see how it worked and where I fit in. At the top of our organization, we had the senior VP, a blond German fellow who wore suits and did not speak to underlings like us. He had a large office at the other end of the building and a pair of secretaries guarding it.

The next level down was another VP, an ex-marine we called the Juice. He'd been given the name by Bob and Brad, two of my fellow engineers, and it stuck. He said, "What you assholes need is some military discipline!" That pretty much spelled out his attitude toward me and the other engineers.

The next level in the corporate food chain was occupied by Paul, the manager of our group. Paul believed he should smile and talk nicely to us, and he smiled all the time. If Juice had the stick, Paul had the carrot. I didn't trust him. I wasn't very good at reading people's expressions, but I knew people smiled when they were happy. Well, he couldn't be happy all the time. I wasn't happy all the time. I wasn't even happy *most* of the time. I certainly didn't smile all the time. Why did he? He didn't seem to be on drugs. Something was up with him.

And then there was us. The engineers. One of the first guys I made friends with was Bob Jeffway, who worked across the hall in product development. Bob was a prototypical geek: tall, thin, with signs of future baldness. He had a white dress shirt and a pocket protector filled with three pens and a small screwdriver. I quickly discovered that everything was a joke to Bob. I may have been the class clown in high school, but he was the company prankster here.

"So, I hear you're working for Little Ugly." Bob had nicknames for everyone I saw. The Juice. Mister Chips. Hooligan. The Snout. And Earth, Wind and Fire.

I smiled. *Little Ugly,* I thought. It did fit. But I learned an awful lot from Klaus. And I never called him Little Ugly, except in conversation with Bob.

Our group was designing the first talking toys, and Klaus assigned me to work on an analog-to-digital converter he had been developing. The converter would be used in the lab to study voice and sound patterns. It sounded right up my alley. Right from the beginning, people were impressed by my designs, and they worked. I was off and running.

I had been terribly afraid of what I'd find in a real job. But when I got there, it was easy. No one stood over me with a whip. I never once heard, "Come on, Ampie, move your ass. We need this stuff now!" They seemed willing to pay me to think up new designs at my own speed, in my own space. It was unbelievable.

The air was clean. There was no haze of sweat and cigarette smoke anywhere. The heat worked. No one carried a gun, at least not as far as I could see. There were no drunks passed out in our doorways, and our washroom sinks were never used as toilets. We didn't have any coke dealers or hookers in the parking lot, and it was always safe to walk to your car when work was done.

I realized that my coworkers had no idea how lucky they were. They took it all for granted. During that first week at work, I resolved that I would never again return to life in the gutter.

Within a year, I was responsible for projects on my own. I seemed to have made it into the normal world at last. If I was careful, I thought, no one would find out about my past.

19

A Visit from Management

Now that I had a real job, I figured the time had come to act like a grown-up. After all, I was almost twenty-three years old. I was a design engineer at a big manufacturing company. And I had a lab of my own, with state-of-the-art test gear even better than what I'd used at the university.

For the first time in my life, I put on a nice button-down shirt and a tie each morning. I was even on time, most of the time.

The strange thing was that I found myself reporting to work in a factory. The electronics division had sprung up overnight, it seemed, and there was nowhere else to put it. Eventually, we would work in a nice new wing of corporate headquarters, but at that time it was still under construction. So they gave me a photo ID that identified me as a member of management, and I trudged in through the factory entrance alongside fifteen hundred injection molders and printing press operators every morning. At least the salaried people like me didn't have to stand in line with the laborers and punch a time clock.

I don't know what I expected life as a professional to be like, but it wasn't walking through a factory, in between two-story-high plastic molding machines, jumping aside when one of the machines decided to spit fifty pounds of hot plastic into the path in front of me and spatter my new Bally loafers with little balls of molten plastic.

I collected some of the smaller plastic turds, five- and ten-pounders, and laid them in my backyard like products of some chemically treated cow. Yellows, reds, blues, and an occasional one in mixed colors. Visitors to the house looked at them, but no one had the courage to ask what they were.

"You'll be out of the factory soon," our boss, Paul, said. The Juice and the other higher-ups were already over at headquarters. But until the new wing was finished, we were stuck in the factory. And R&D, of which I was a new member, was located above the injection molding machines in an overheated garret in what used to be the attic of the factory.

Just imagine the scene—seventeen engineers, plus one secretary, a manager, and an intern, up in the attic, all designing as fast as we could. In the summer, it was brutal up there, because all the heat from the factory floor rose to the top floor and the sun roasted us from above, cooking the black tar roof. Black spots—bits of hot tar from the roof—began peeking through the nice hung ceiling that August. I retreated to our technicians' lab in a cooler part of the factory.

Vito was in charge of the technicians and, as a staff engineer, I was in charge of Vito. Sort of. Vito was really ungovernable. But he and I worked together well. Like a good sergeant in the Army, Vito showed us engineers how things really worked. For example, Vito showed us how to get rid of a pesky salesman with real flair.

The salesman gambit took two people. Vito always did the intro. Here's how it worked: When a salesman made a bad impression on Vito, he would say, "When you meet my boss, ask him about his sister. She just won the NCAA swimming championship at her college. He's really proud of her."

The salesman would meet me, and after a few minutes he would invariably say, "So, I hear your sister's some kind of champion swimmer" or some similar drivel. I would look shocked and say nothing.

After a moment, the salesman would say, "Did I say something wrong?"

To which I would reply, "I can't believe you would say such a thing. My sister had polio. She's been in a wheelchair since she was five."

Reactions to that statement varied, but they were always good. Sometimes I got an apology, other times shocked silence. It worked either way. After a few moments of silence, I would say, "I've got to be getting back to work." The salesman was all too glad to get out of there. By that time, Vito had discreetly vanished. I would escort the embarrassed sales rep to the door.

And that was it. No rep was a repeat visitor after that gambit.

The technicians worked among the printing presses that printed the artwork for puzzles onto big sheets of finished card-board. The sheets were carried over to another group of giant machines that cut each puzzle into hundreds or even thousands of pieces before it was boxed and packed and shipped to stores. The work area was a former supervisor's office, a room about ten feet wide and fifty feet long. Windows offered a panoramic view of the puzzle manufacturing operation on one side, and a plain Sheet-rock wall on the other. Everything was painted a sick pastel green, the color of fresh vomit, the kind you get from eating too many dandelions with your six-pack.

This far from the personnel office, the usual rules for office decor, dress, language, and behavior didn't apply. After all, we were in the factory, not the executive suite. Our technicians had gone native. There were girlie calendars on the walls, beer in the film cooler, and switchblades in the tool drawer.

Paul, the manager with the perpetual smile, came to visit one morning. "Guys, I need you to clean up your work area. We've got senior management coming to visit." Paul was very polite. He never swore or raised his voice. But we knew what he really meant: "Look, you assholes, this place is a disgrace. Get this shit off the walls and off the floors so we don't get our asses fired when the VPs come to check us out. *Now.*"

The techs started cleaning, slipping the calendars and porn into the backs of the cabinets, from whence they would pull them out again as soon as the tour passed through. Vito swept the floor, pushing the detritus over the railing. This was greeted with angry shouts from the factory floor ten feet below as the trash fluttered down onto the wet ink on a line of puzzles emerging from the press. Rolled flat and cut and boxed, Vito's cigarette butts and trash bits might make a novel addition to someone's Christmas present.

He didn't give a damn, and if they came up the stairs, he'd send them right back down at the end of a broom handle.

While the crew was cleaning up, I looked around for something to do. I wanted to be a good corporate droid. What could I do to help out? I couldn't sweep or wipe because I was management.

Then I found a piece of broken mirror in the corner. We certainly didn't want broken glass lying around. I picked it up. Eyeing the white Formica countertops, I had an idea. I asked Vito for a razor blade from the drawer and began scraping it across the countertop, shaving the Formica into a neat pile. An hour went by and the pile got bigger. The room was clean, but I was still working. The pile of fine white powder was starting to have the look of $2,000, maybe more.

Fine white crystals, with just a hint of sparkle.

I scraped the pile onto the mirror. Then I took a fresh razor blade and I cut some lines. Fat ones. I took a twenty from my wallet and rolled it up tight. I set it next to the lines. The tableau was complete. I slid the mirror discreetly under the corner of a workbench. Visible, but not too visible. Something anyone in a hurry to clean up could have missed.

I hoped no one would steal my twenty. I considered substituting a cut-off straw from the cafeteria, but the twenty just looked better.

Otherwise, the room was spotless. We were ready and, right on cue, management arrived. Our little area filled up with middle-aged men in suits, some of whom had visitors' tags. They asked polite questions, but it was evident they didn't understand what we were doing up there, and most didn't care. Two of them were brazenly discussing golf in low whispers, right in front of me. Standing in the corner by the door, I noticed more than one head swivel to look at my little mirror. As I expected, no one said a word about it. The tour filed out. Because I was the ranking management representative, they all shook my hand as they departed.

It was late, and we decided to wait till morning to redecorate the room. We talked about the mirror and the suits. How many noticed it? What would they say? We were kind of excited, thinking security was going to barge in, confiscate the mirror, cause a big scene, and send it out for testing so they could make an example of us. Frankly, we were surprised when by five o'clock nothing had happened. We headed home, careful to lock the door behind us.

Maybe the raid will happen tomorrow, I thought. I could just imagine it. Our own rent-a-cop force, pretending to be the DEA. And after all their testing and analysis, they would find that their confiscated drugs were . . . a pile of plastic dust. We anxiously awaited the vigorous enforcement of the company's antidrug policies. But security didn't show up.

"Is it possible they missed it?" I asked. None of us could figure it out.

In the morning, I checked in at my office—such as it was—in the attic, then headed for the lab. I stepped through the doorway and saw the lads had been busy. The calendars were back on the wall, and we had a new Penthouse Pet over the door. But there was a problem. Almost half my coke was missing. I showed it to Vito.

"Can't you be more careful? I spent a long time making that shit and now you've lost half of it!"

"None of us touched it. Look, your twenty is still there!" Vito insisted our techs had nothing to do with it. Maybe he was telling the truth, maybe not. We'd see. I got a fresh razor blade and made a new pile. Now I had $2,500 piled up. I put some in a plastic bag. I'd heard $35,000 bought a whole kilo, and I wasn't sure I could get that much off our bench tops, but I had a goal. The bag was half full by the time I knocked off for lunch.

The next day, my pile was down again. I showed Vito.

"Someone's fucking with us," I said.

Vito agreed. He had an answer. "Time for some video."

We had video cameras left over from our robot experiments the previous fall. We rigged one so that it sat on a table facing the workbench and the door, focused on the mirror. Then we disconnected the switch for the building's security system, and rewired the switch to the start button for the camera through a timer that we whipped together from a 555 timer chip and a few parts. Whenever someone opened the door, the camera would come on for five minutes. With all the other electronic equipment in the room, we were sure no one would notice.

Just in case, we left a radio and some idiot toys running all night so the noise of the camera wouldn't be noticed. The factory made the whole area noisy anyway. It was a simple system, but it would probably work.

We figured we'd catch one of our own crew messing with us. That's why we rigged the recorder after they all had left for the day.

The next morning, the bag was gone. Vito saw it first. "Someone's fucking robbed us again!" We played the tape and we were shocked. Watching that tape was like buying porn and finding your mother as the star. Right there in front of us, one of the VPs from the visit earlier in the week came in, did a line, and stole our bag of coke. He looked around furtively, pocketed my stuff, and walked out the door. Right before our eyes. On tape.

We were speechless. People like him were supposed to set the moral compass of a huge company. People like us were supposed to be the thieving coke fiends.

Vito thought we should confront him. I wasn't so sure. This

executive looting wasn't what I expected when I left the mirror lying on the bench. I was looking for some fun. I wanted to cause a ridiculous scandal—to be accused of illegal possession of plastic dust. I wasn't expecting to find a vice president coming into our office after hours and robbing us of drugs. And good drugs, too, stuff I had spent hours carefully preparing using only the cleanest and finest sections of countertop. If the stuff he stole was real, and we turned him in, he'd be looking at five to ten in state prison.

Maybe our coke problem was just the tip of the iceberg. I said to Vito, "Who knows what else this asshole is stealing from other people here." I was afraid that if he found out about our little scheme, he'd turn us in to Personnel, or even Security, and we'd be fired. Or worse. I thought we should toss the mirror and let the matter drop.

In the end, we decided to give it one more night. Maybe he'd have regrets. Maybe he'd return my coke.

That night, I laid out six nice fat lines. The next morning, four were gone. What was he thinking? I know what I was thinking: *This guy has been doing straight engineering lab Formica for five days, and he's coming back for more. Maybe we can sell it. Maybe we should investigate where this Formica came from.*

Vito looked at the new evidence, and we decided to confront him. Vito was better at that sort of thing, so we agreed he'd do the talking. He had an uncle who collected delinquent loans for a local bookie, and when Vito was little, he went with his uncle to collect money on days when there was no day care. He was a five-year-old bat boy turned electronics technician.

Vito called up to the executive offices and requested an appointment. The following afternoon he headed upstairs, entered the office, and discreetly shut the door. "I've got something I'd like you to see," he said. He had the tape and a portable player. He turned it on. Both days were on that tape. It wasn't pretty.

There was silence afterward, but Vito could see what he was thinking.

I can't believe they had fucking cameras.

"You know, you're goddamn lucky he didn't wire that bag to a hand grenade instead of a video switch," Vito said casually. "My boss is crazy." We both knew people who rigged Vietnam War surplus grenades and claymore mines to guard their pot fields in the woods. They sometimes blew up a deer, and occasionally a hiker would lose a leg. You saw it in the paper from time to time.

Vito continued. "My boss is very upset over what you've done. He'd like to be paid for what you've taken. He wanted to take matters into his own hands, turn it over to the Guinea beaters, but I said I'd come see you and see if we can work it out. Peacefully."

Vito was Italian, and he could say stuff like that.

The guy completely caved. He didn't even threaten us. No bravado at all. Vito settled for five hundred dollars. He gave the guy the tape. We could afford it. We had more.

Vito said, "You understand, you'll have to buy your shit somewhere else in the future." The guy nodded, grateful to have both legs and be off the hook so cheap.

Vito and I had a hell of a party for the crew that weekend. They had their own drugs. I took the twenty off the bench top and spent it. But not on coke. Its brief career as a straw was over.

From that day forward, any requests we sent to the executive offices were answered promptly, and never, ever rejected. But it didn't last. The economy changed and sales declined. Within a few years, some of us quit and others were laid off. I read that our former VP got arrested downtown, on the street with the pimps, whores, and crack dealers.

Why would he do that? I asked myself. I had left that life behind for good the second I got the chance, when I quit the disco sound booth for a real engineering lab. He had grown up in luxury and had a good job as a VP at a big company and had climbed into the gutter of his own volition.

Until then, I thought people who had been born to these upscale white-collar jobs must be inherently superior to a high school dropout like me. But I was wrong.

20

Logic vs. Small Talk

I'm a very logical guy. Psychologists say that's an Aspergian trait. This can lead to trouble in common social situations, because ordinary conversation doesn't always proceed logically. In an effort to improve my own interpersonal skills, I have studied computer programs that engage in conversation with people. The best programs follow logical pathways to arrive at suitable responses. The results, however, don't always sound natural, and I am not sure that I do much better than the machines.

For example, last week my friend Laurie said, "One of my girlfriends is having an affair. And the guy rides a motorcycle just like yours!"

Laurie's statement posed a problem. Unlike most interactions, ours had not started with a question. Should I respond with an opinion about the statement? Or should I ask a question myself? I considered what I had just heard:

Laurie has a girlfriend. *Yes, Laurie has lots of girlfriends. Which one is she talking about?*

The girlfriend's having an affair. *Why tell me? Do I know her? Do I know the guy? Is this a convoluted way of suggesting that I should have an affair, since I have a motorcycle?*

The boyfriend has a motorcycle. *Well, that narrows it down. Most potential boyfriends have cars, not bikes. So this boyfriend is one of the 5 percent, as opposed to the 95 percent of the motoring public. Do I know him?*

The motorcycle is just like mine. *How much does Laurie know about bikes? Does she mean he rides an Electra Glide Classic, or does she just mean his motorcycle is black?*

I was not able to deduce a suitable response to her statements. What did she mean by them? There was no logical connection between Laurie's sentences. I stared at the floor and pondered my next move. I knew I had to think fast. If I think too long, people say, "Did you hear me?" or "Are you paying attention?"

I knew she wanted a relevant response—something connected to what she had just said, more than just "Oh." I also knew from experience and observation that a statement like "I went to Newport to see the Jazz Festival last weekend" would not be an appropriate answer. It occurred to me that what I needed to do was to keep gathering information until I could frame an intelligent conversation. The successful conversational computer programs did that. So I asked a question.

"Which girlfriend is that?"

Laurie looked surprised. "Why would you want to know that?" she said.

I hadn't expected a challenge. She sounded suspicious. I wiggled my ears and wondered a little at that. The fact that she had responded that way told me she had been expecting some other response. *What did she expect me to say?*

Perhaps I should have answered with a made-up statement that echoed hers. I could have said, "My friend Spike is having an affair, too. And the girl he's involved with has a motorcycle like mine, too." But it would have been nonsense. And I never utter nonsense replies unless I'm playing a prank. I can't help thinking there must have been some purpose to Laurie's original statement, and a statement with a purpose calls for a meaningful response.

Perhaps I should have just played dumb. I have observed that a drawled "Wow!" accompanied by a smile can be an acceptable response to almost anything. But I can't smile on command, and I can't bring myself to act like a moron. Still, a "Wow!" would probably not have disturbed Laurie.

If I say, "One of the guys at work got into a car accident today," I am prepared for you to say, "Who was in the wreck?" If the identity of the person were a secret, why would I bring it up in the first place?

I could have focused on the motorcycle part of Laurie's statement. If so, I'd have said, "What kind of bike does he ride?" Once again, I'd expect some kind of answer other than "It's none of your business!"

When I asked Laurie why she was suspicious, she had a couple of questions for me: "Why do you need to know? Nothing good could come of me telling you. What if it got back to her husband?"

I figured out what I should have said by chance, observing two women talking at a restaurant a short while later:

"Jenny in accounting is having an affair, and the guy drives a Corvette!"

The opening line was strikingly similar, so I paid attention.

"How cool is that! Is he married?"

Listening to that exchange, it was obvious that this was the correct response. When I heard them talk, I suddenly understood that Laurie's statement had been meant to entertain or impress me, and that my response should have been an expression of admiration or excitement. However, that never occurred to me at the time. It's clear to me that regular people have conversational capabilities far beyond mine, and their responses often have nothing at all to do with logic. I suspect normal people are hardwired to develop the ability to read social cues in a way that I am not.

Small talk—or any kind of talk that goes beyond a simple exchange of information—has always been a challenge for me. When I was young, I learned that people would not like it when

I uttered the first thought that entered my mind when they approached. Since making that discovery, I have slowly taught myself how to succeed at conversation—most of the time. I have learned to begin conversations with a question, like "How are you?" I have learned a range of questions that are socially acceptable. But my inventory of questions is limited, and it seems other people are a lot more flexible.

I now know that my logically derived responses to statements like Laurie's sometimes come off as intrusive or prying. That makes no sense at all to me. I framed the first relevant question that came to mind after hearing her speak. My response was friendly. So why was she disturbed? After all, she brought the whole thing up. In my opinion, people should not make statements unless they are prepared to respond to questions about the words they utter. But the world doesn't always work that way.

Thinking about conversations like the one I had with Laurie makes me mad. People approach me, uninvited, and make unsolicited statements. When they don't get the response they expect, they become indignant. If I offer no response at all, they become indignant at *that*. So there is no way for me to win.

Given that line of reasoning, why talk to people at all? Well, many autistic people don't, possibly for that very reason. But, for some reason, I want the Lauries of the world to like me. To not think I am weird. I can be eccentric, but I don't want to be weird. So I persist. I try to say the things a "normal" person would say.

Normal people seem to learn certain stock questions and utter them to fill a conversational void. For example, when meeting someone they have not seen in a while, they say things like:

"How's your wife?"

"How's your son?"

"You're looking good—did you lose weight?"

Normal people will emit statements like this in the absence of any provocation, or any visual indication that there may have been a change in the wife or son or the weight. Some people I've observed appear to have many dozens of these stock questions at their command, and I have never been able to figure out how they choose a particular phrase for emission at any given moment.

When someone walks up to you, his appearance does not normally suggest a change in the status of his wife or son, and most people's appearance does not change enough from week to week, or even month to month, to provide a logical basis for the question about weight. Yet people say those things and the recipients of the words smile and answer with similar platitudes, such as:

"The wife is fine."

"The kid's up for parole next January."

"I had my stomach stapled and lost fifty pounds."

And then, surprisingly, they often say, "Thanks for asking."

How normal people know which of these questions to ask is a mystery to me. Do they have better memory than me, or is it just luck? It must be social conditioning, something that I am completely lacking.

I don't ask about "the wife" because when my friend walks up to me, I'm interested in talking to him, and the condition or status of his wife does not enter my mind. More specifically, his appearance does not give me reason to wonder about his wife's well-being. If he's a good friend, I assume (probably correctly) that any major change in his wife or son's status would precipitate some kind of notification to me and his other friends. So why ask?

As to the weight . . . if he looks bigger, I'd say, "You seem fatter than the last time I saw you." I've learned by life experience that people get fatter for any number of reasons, most of which are benign. I am aware that people may not like having their deficiencies—increased bulk, for instance—pointed out. But my mouth may spit out, "You look fatter!" before my brain concludes, *It would be rude to say he looks fatter!*

Losing weight is another matter. If someone looks a lot thinner, I might say, "You look a lot thinner . . . are you sick?" I know people go on diets. But people my age are just as likely to be thinner because there's something wrong with them. Maybe they have cancer or something even worse. So if they look a lot thinner, I might just cut to the chase and ask.

I've heard questions like "How's your son?" described as "ice-breakers." I don't think to say those things unless I have consciously prepared to engage in conversation prior to approaching someone. I am tongue-tied when approaching people unless they speak to me first. If I do speak up, I often say something that's taken as rude or surprising—especially when I've told people something true that they don't want to hear.

That's why I learned some years ago to utter a noncommittal "Woof!" if I need to begin a conversation or fill a silence. People hear that and are not sure what to say, but they don't usually perceive a woof as rude. I try to work with whatever response I get.

In the past, when people criticized me for asking unexpected questions, I felt ashamed. Now I realize that normal people are acting in a superficial and often false manner. So rather than let them make me feel bad, I express my annoyance. It's my way of trying to strike a blow for logic and rationality.

My conversational difficulties highlight a problem Aspergians face every day. A person with an obvious disability—for example, someone in a wheelchair—is treated compassionately because his handicap is obvious. No one turns to a guy in a wheelchair and says, "Quick! Let's run across the street!" And when he can't run across the street, no one says, "What's his problem?" They offer to help him across the street.

With me, though, there is no external sign that I am conversationally handicapped. So folks hear some conversational misstep and say, "What an arrogant jerk!" I look forward to the day when my handicap will afford me the same respect accorded to a guy in a wheelchair. And if the respect comes with a preferred parking space, I won't turn it down.

Woof!

21

Being Young Executives

When we started work at Milton Bradley, we were young and enthusiastic. My coconspirator, Bob, and I were convinced that our toys would change the world. Some nights, we worked till midnight as we raced to get the latest electronic gadget ready for production. And in this line of work, there was no need for any special skill making small talk. We were geeks before the age of personal computers. We were there to create new things and solve problems, not impress anyone with our suave social skills.

Still, it would have helped to know a little more about gaming the system in a big company. As it turned out, we had our first experience with corporate politics shortly after starting work. Dark Tower was one of our hot new games for the 1981 season. It was an electronic version of an older role-playing fantasy game. The centerpiece was a tower that rotated and stopped in front of each player. The trouble was, it was stopping in the wrong places. And as an engineer in the development group for Dark Tower, it was Bob's problem.

He scratched his head and pondered and guessed and experimented as he tried to figure out what to do. Now that I was on the inside, watching him, I was amazed to discover the technical sophistication in a thirty-nine-dollar electronic game. In many ways, such games were more sophisticated than the devices I'd worked with in the music business, some of which cost a thousand times more.

It seemed like a simple thing. You'd turn the motor on, and it would move. You'd turn the power off, and it would stop, right? Unfortunately, it wasn't that simple. Inertia caused the motor to keep moving for a little while before it stopped, just as a car rolls some distance after the engine stalls. The trouble was, there was no predicting exactly how far it would move.

"This would be easy if we had a fifty-dollar parts budget," Bob mused.

"Yeah," I said. "But it's a whole 'nother matter to figure out how to do it for twenty-five cents." And that was the crux of the problem. In the toy business, everything had to be done for pennies, and it took all our technical skill to devise solutions that worked with the fewest possible parts or the simplest possible assemblies. When we succeeded, we felt a certain pride in creating elegant and workable designs. But it didn't always work out.

After a month of sixty-hour workweeks, Bob had the answer. "A clamping circuit," he told me. "We'll use the transistors to clamp the motor so it stops as soon as we cut the power."

"That's just like the dynamic brakes on a locomotive," I said. I loved it. Who would ever guess that the same principles that held a freight train back on steep hills would stop the Dark Tower?

Bob's idea worked. The tower stopped where it was supposed to. The game was ready to sell.

But a month later, Bob got a rude shock. "Did you hear what happened?" he fumed. "Alan took credit for *my* design and they gave him an award! He stole my idea!" There wasn't much I could say. Our youthful exuberance was starting to wear off as our creative desires ran up against corporate politics.

Meanwhile, my group was racing to introduce the first talking game, and I had been given the task of designing a system to collect speech and turn it into digital data. I designed the analog parts of the system, and Klaus did the digital work. We used one of the first microcomputers—an IMSAI 8080—to collect and store the data. It was a Rube Goldberg kind of contraption, with hundreds of parts tied together with wire wrap and cables, spread across a bunch of breadboards on a workbench in my lab. And as soon as it was built and tested, we put it right to work. I sat in front of a computer monitor, with my finger on a keyboard. Operation was simple. G meant Go. The system would record whatever it heard for the next six seconds. S meant Save. We began collecting and digitizing speech.

"Hey, hey, hey! Pick your play!" One at a time, the entire staff passed through the lab, reading and recording the mindless phrases that would become our new game's vocabulary. "You pick three!" And the classic "It's my turn!" All the engineers and techs had a chance to try out as the voice of tomorrow's toy. In the end, though, the voice the public heard was that of Mike Meyers, one of the VPs.

It may have sounded idiotic, but I was proud of my design, and no one else stole the credit for my little part. The speech guys took the data my device collected and turned it into a tiny stream of bits that would feed our new talking integrated circuit. We had reduced the complexity of speech into a few crumbs, like the food left behind in my shirt pocket. Amazingly, it still sounded pretty good.

Today, it seems like every kid you see has a Game Boy or some similar electronic game. But in the late 1970s, there was no such thing. However, that was about to change. Not long after I started, we came out with the first handheld video game with changeable cartridges. They called it Microvision.

Microvision consisted of a console with snap-on game cartridges. All of a sudden, millions of kids had to have a Microvision, and the games that went with it—Blockbuster, Pinball, Bowling, Connect Four, and all the others. After its first Christmas, we could see that Microvision was going to be the next hot toy. Milton Bradley's Simon had been the hot game the year before, and it looked like we had another winner this season. The holidays had passed, and it still sold as fast as we could make it.

But in the early fall, news started filtering up from the plant. "Hey, did you hear about Microvision?" said Brad, one of the engineers who had worked on its release. "They're getting tons of dead ones returned. There was a crazed mom at the Federal Square plant yesterday, making a scene over her kid's broken Microvision. And now they're having trouble on the assembly line, too. Lots of defective units."

Brad didn't sound too concerned. After all, we were R&D, and that was a production matter.

They were very concerned in the factory. Just as they were ramping up production for Christmas, the defect rate on the production line skyrocketed. Defects went from 5 percent to 60 percent in a matter of weeks. Management was panicked. There were probably a million Microvision consoles on order, with no way to fill the orders. It was a toymaker's worst nightmare.

The company had never experienced anything like that in its hundred-year history. After all, puzzles and chess sets never broke down. Electronic toys were a new concept at Milton Bradley. The old-timers in the company thought longingly of the days when "new product" meant making blue checkers instead of the traditional red.

The first line of defense was our quality assurance and manufacturing engineering groups. But both departments were stumped. Management became desperate. There was desk pounding and foot stomping in the executive suite, until finally they decided to turn to "the weirdos in R&D." The R&D boss was accordingly summoned, and he said, "I have just the guy for you. He's an analog engineer. He'll have a fresh perspective on the situation."

Just like that, I had a new job assignment. I started reading books on manufacturing. Then I started in on quality. I read till one A.M. some nights. And I asked questions:

"What's changed in the manufacturing process?"

"Nothing."

"How about testing or shipping?"

"No change there, either."

"Are the parts different? Did we get a bad batch?"

"Nope. We bought two hundred and fifty thousand parts kits back in the spring, and we're still using that stock."

Bummer.

Back in the lab, I talked things over with my friend Bob, who worked in product development. We had started out wearing ties to work, and sport jackets. Supposedly, the engineers wore ties and the technicians didn't. We were expected to dress and act like young executives, though we had little concept of what that meant. Or rather, our concept differed sharply from what our bosses thought it meant.

We were there to design circuits, but more than that, we were there for fun. We were there to chase the girls in product testing and the art department. Our bosses, on the other hand, were there to work. Or more precisely, they were there to *make us work*. That was the definition of management—getting others to do your work for you. And we were the others.

This Microvision problem had the sound of serious work. I didn't like it.

"Maybe someone's sabotaging Microvision. Think that's possible?"

Bob was skeptical. He spent a lot more time in the plants than me, and he said the factory seemed pretty peaceful. "I don't ever see fights or blood on the floor when I go down there anymore. I don't think anyone's destroying them on purpose."

I pondered his words. *Anymore.* Did he mean there was once blood on the floor in the factory? I guessed he did. That's why I didn't go there.

I was getting a little worried. By now, hundreds of dead Microvision consoles were coming off the production line every day, and management had progressed from panic to outright frenzy.

But I knew I could figure it out. At least, I hoped I could. And if I couldn't, well, there were always other employers.

I needed help. I called Bob again. He suggested we have a meeting to talk things over. We agreed to get together a few hours later to discuss the situation.

At the appointed time, I stood waiting for Bob, tapping my watch and pacing back and forth. I had driven quickly to get to the meeting on time, but he was nowhere to be found.

I paced faster. I felt like the weight of the whole world was on my shoulders. We didn't have cell phones in those days, so there was nothing I could do but wait.

I became irritated. If I was left waiting at a senior management meeting, I could at least go hang around at the bar and get a drink or maybe a snack. Here, there was nothing but a parking lot. I had only been in a real job for a little over a year, but I was already getting a sense of corporate life. It wasn't what I had imagined, looking in from the outside.

Then I saw him. At least, I thought it was him.

I couldn't tell for sure—the boat was still a mile away, but it was approaching fast. As it got closer, I recognized Bob's Sea Ray, and within a few moments I could see Bob. I walked down the dock and jumped aboard as he pulled in close.

"Sorry I was late," he said, handing me a drink. "I had to get gas. And there was a line at Pizza Rama."

Bob backed away from the floating dock, swung the boat around, and headed into the river. I took a slice of pepperoni pizza and ate it while watching our wake roll out behind us. As Bob drove, I contemplated the future of Microvision. Back in the factory, 120 workers were building Microvision as fast as they could. Until we found an answer, six out of every ten machines were headed for the scrap heap. But there were no scrap Microvision boxes out here on the river. It was a fine fall day. The leaves were just starting to turn. This was the right place to contemplate our company's problems.

"So what do you make of it?" I asked Bob.

"Drinks are in the cooler" was his reply. Bob had also worked on another of the company's products, Big Trak. Big Trak was a programmable tank that crawled around on the floor and made noises. We in engineering were always seeking to expand our lowly tank's horizons.

"You know, Bob, I was thinking. We could put a stun gun on the arm of that Big Trak and make a serious ankle biter. Then it could defend itself. It'd be a rude shock for a smart-ass kid that kicked a Big Trak!" Bob smiled at the thought of some nine-year-old monster, knocked flat after going for our tank with a hammer.

We were ahead of our time with that idea. As I write this story, more than twenty-five years have passed, and today's toys still lack defensive capabilities. And kids still destroy them, much to the distress of their designers. But Bob and I thought of it, way back then.

In a subsequent meeting, management declined to add our enhancements to the popular tank.

As young executives, we had watched the big bosses conducting the truly important business of the company on the golf course. We knew that unimportant meetings took place in conference rooms. More important meetings took place in the boardroom. But the really important meetings—the ones that took all day and sometimes several days—took place at the country club. Bob and I had not yet been admitted to that inner sanctum, but we had it in our sights. We knew that we were following the example of our leaders, solving the tough problems for our factory out on the water.

"Do you think there's a problem with the chip design?" Bob wondered. We were both grasping at straws.

"I really don't know," I said.

"How about a power supply problem?" Bob wondered.

Perhaps the spray of water from a passing boat gave us the answer. I'll never know where or how it arrived. But that was what they paid us for. Design ideas that contained less than five parts, cost less than ten cents, and saved the world by lunchtime.

Once I saw the answer, it seemed obvious. As summer turned to fall, the air became drier. Lower humidity meant more static electricity. The same phenomenon that makes you crackle and spark when you pull on a sweater was killing the Microvision units.

"Static," I blurted out to Bob.

"Huh?"

"That's what's killing the Microvision. Static."

"Static." He repeated the word several times. Savoring it. "Yeah, maybe you're right."

My brain went into high gear as I considered how to prove my hypothesis that static was killing Microvision. And, assuming I was right, what would we do about it? Millions of dollars in faulty product was at stake, along with people's jobs. This was not some abstract R&D problem. This was production. And production was a rougher, tougher world. I had heard stories about how they motivated engineers down there when things got tough. Line up three and shoot two. The remaining one would work faster.

The whole concept of management was different down there. We had read books about manufacturing, labor relations, and the history of American industries like coal mining and steelmaking. We weren't sure how similar our factory was to a turn-of-the-century steel mill. And we didn't want to find out.

In our departments, managers motivated us with encouragement and inspiration. They smiled and had good manners. In the mill, manners and encouraging words were like a foreign language. Successful managers had bruised knuckles; some had brass knuckles. The bosses had worn and dented baseball bats leaned up against the insides of their doors.

The pizza was gone, but we had a plan. We returned to the dock as we pondered the next step. Would a better ground help? I had some adhesive-backed copper foil that I was using on another project. Perhaps I could use the foil to dissipate the static charge harmlessly. I stuck a piece to the front of a Microvision console. I attached the foil to the ground trace on the circuit board. Then I put a similar piece of foil on the cartridge door, and attached it to the cartridge's ground plane.

It worked. Whenever you plugged the cartridge into the console, the foil pieces touched before anything else, and the static charge was dissipated harmlessly. It was time to test the idea on some real games. I requested a box of new games, fresh from the production floor. They arrived moments later, reaffirming the importance management placed on our work.

I pulled my sweater off and on, and I shuffled across the floor in rubber-soled shoes. When I touched the light switch, a spark snapped from my finger to the wall. Satisfied with my static charge, I pulled the sweater off and on a few more times, then picked up an unmodified Microvision. It was dead in my hand. I then picked up my modified game, and it still worked.

I did this time and again, until I had filled the trash can with Microvision consoles. Not one of my modified units failed. I was elated. I knew then I would not be shot. I had found the answer.

In the end, it was such a simple thing. Paper clips are simple, too. Some of the finest engineering creations are in fact the simplest. At times, we are truly masters of the obvious.

From that moment on, the Microvision war was won. All the rest was just mopping up. I added some circuitry to toughen the circuits against static. The production engineers got antistatic materials to line the assembly areas. And the factory was fitted with a system that sprayed a fine mist of water into the air above the workstations to keep static from forming in the first place.

Bob and I had a better source of water mist: the Connecticut River. We continued to meet there, on that project and others to follow. I was hard at work on Milton, the next electronic marvel, and Bob was back to Super Simon. Milton was to be the world's first talking electronic game. Toys had spoken for years without electronics, using mechanical gramophone technology like the trumpet-horn record players of the 1900s. Dolls like Chatty Cathy would utter a phrase when a child pulled a string. But an interactive talking game would be a first. As it turned out, Milton did talk. Unfortunately, game buyers didn't seem to want to listen, and Milton vanished without a trace a year later.

I'm sure my solution to Microvision's static problem saved the company hundreds of thousand of dollars, maybe more. But, like Bob's experience with Dark Tower, the award never made it to my desk, and the bonus didn't reach *my* bank account. The bucks stopped a bit higher up the food chain.

We never did achieve that coveted country club membership, either. A decade later, Bob achieved renown as the designer and coinventor of Mattel's Diva Starz and Cabbage Patch Kids Kick 'n Splash and Milton Bradley's Whac-A-Mole electronic games. And that fall, I was offered a new job as director of R&D for a manufacturer of fire alarms and time clocks. I tramped off to climb the corporate ladder, leaving Bob in his world of toys. The trouble was, the higher I advanced in the corporate world, the more I had to rely on my people skills and the less my technical skills and creativity mattered. For someone like me, that was a formula for disaster.

I moved on to my new job at Simplex in Gardner, about an hour's drive away. At Simplex, I wore a suit to work. I had an office with a door, and my own secretary to guard it. And after a year, I managed a staff of twenty people. But it proved to be a mistake. I wasn't happy. I felt I was surrounded by mediocrity, both in my own work and in my choice of employment. I had gone from designing toys (a fun thing) to overseeing the design of time clocks to keep track of America's factory workers (not a fun thing).

Unfortunately, there was no going back. Things had gone bad at Milton Bradley Electronics shortly after I left. The company wrote off a $30 million investment in computer games, and Bob and most of my friends lost their jobs. A short while later, the company was sold. I was beginning to realize that *executive job* did not equal *job security*.

In the midst of my struggles to become part of corporate America, I got married. Little Bear and I tied the knot in the summer of 1982. I was twenty-five years old. We were happy at first, but as things worsened at work, I brought my problems home. I was upset about work, and Little Bear was wrapped up in the world of the Science Fiction Society, a club at the university. She was once again a college student after having taken the previous few years off. After seeing Bob lose his job, I was laid off from Simplex in 1984. They, too, were experiencing financial troubles. It was a scary time for Little Bear and me, since I was the sole breadwinner while she was in school. And to make things worse, while I was out of work, her brother Paul died in a car crash. With the stress of all those things, we began to grow apart. It was not a happy time for us.

Luckily, I found a new job fairly quickly. I started work at Isoreg, a small company that manufactured power transformers. Unfortunately, I now had a one-and-a-half-hour commute. Life as an executive was not turning out the way they portrayed it on TV.

By 1988, I had moved through two more jobs, and I had swallowed all I could take of the corporate world. I had come to accept what my annual performance reviews said. I was not a team player. I had trouble communicating with people. I was inconsiderate. I was rude. I was smart and creative, yes, but I was a misfit.

I was thoroughly sick of all the criticism. I was sick of life. Literally. I had come down with asthma, and attacks were sending me to the emergency room every few months. I hated to get up and face another day at work. I knew what I needed to do. I needed to stop forcing myself to fit into something I could never be a part of. A big company. A group. A team.

When I was five, I had wanted more than anything to be part of the team. When I was a little older, I had tried out for Little League, but no one had picked me. I never tried out for a team after that. Maybe those rejections were still with me, twenty years later.

"You need to be part of the team," I heard over and over.

What, be one more idiot in a suit? Not me.

"You need to be a little more diplomatic when you point out problems in other people's designs."

Well, the design is just junk. It will never work. I did better work than that when I was fifteen.

"You may think your circuit is the greatest thing ever, but it's not the direction we want to go in."

So you want to use the other group's design—the one that costs twice as much and is half as efficient—just because Dan sucks up to you in meetings and doesn't call you a jerk the way I do. Do I have that right?

It took me four jobs and ten years to realize the folly of my efforts.

And by the way, years later, in 1998, I was admitted to the country club. But I had no need for it by then. I wasn't a part of management anymore. And I couldn't play golf.

22

Becoming Normal

I've thought a lot about how I made the transition from being an Aspergian misfit to seeming almost normal. It's been a gradual process.

I believe there is a continuum from autism to Asperger's to normal. At one extreme, you have children who are turned completely inward from birth. They go through life thinking their own thoughts, and parents and other outsiders can barely connect with them at all. At the other end of the spectrum, you have kids who are turned completely outward. They have scarcely any ability to be introspective or to perform difficult mental calculations. People like that might not make good engineers, but they often go far in life because interpersonal skill is one of the most important predictors of success.

And in the middle you have people like me—some more functional, some less. We can focus our minds inward, and we also have some ability to relate to people and the outside world.

Some Aspergians can focus their minds extremely sharply, and those of us who cultivate this gift are sometimes called savants. Being a savant is a mixed blessing, because that laserlike focus often comes at a cost: very limited abilities in nonsavant areas. I don't think I'm a savant, just a highly intelligent Aspergian. But I suspect

I was on the edge of becoming a savant when I was a small child, and my later ability to visualize mathematical functions and the operation of circuits was savantlike.

Until recently, there were no widely available sources of knowledge about how savants or Aspergians actually think or see things. But recent books and studies have started to shed light on this. When I read Daniel Tammet's book, *Born on a Blue Day,* I was amazed by the similarities between thought processes he describes and my own thinking. I've seen similar parallels between my thought process and Temple Grandin's descriptions of thinking in pictures. As more firsthand accounts of lives like ours emerge, I sense we are on the brink of many exciting discoveries about autism and Asperger's.

When we are young, our brains are constantly developing, making new connections and changing the way we think. As I recall my own development, I can see how I went through periods where my ability to focus inward and do complex calculations in my mind developed rapidly. When that happened, my ability to solve complex technical or mathematical problems increased, but I withdrew from other people. Later, there were periods where my ability to turn toward other people and the world increased by leaps and bounds. At those times, my intense powers of focused reasoning seemed to diminish.

I believe that some kids who are in the middle to more high-functioning range of the autism continuum, like me, do not receive the proper stimulation and end up turning inward to such an extent that they can't function in society, even though they may be incredibly brilliant in some narrowly defined field, like abstract mathematics.

Scientists have studied "brain plasticity," the ability of the brain to reorganize neural pathways based on new experiences. It appears that different types of plasticity are dominant at different ages. Looking back on my childhood, I think the ages of four to seven were critical for my social development. That was when I cried and hurt because I could not make friends. At those times, I could have withdrawn further from people so that I would not get hurt, but I didn't. Fortunately, I had enough satisfactory exchanges with intelligent grown-ups—my family and their friends at college—to keep me wanting to interact.

I can easily imagine a child who did not have any satisfying exchanges withdrawing from people entirely. And a kid who withdrew at age five might be very hard to coax out later.

I also believe considerable rewiring took place in my own brain in my thirties and even later. I believe this because I can compare my thought process today to my processes as expressed in writing and circuit designs from twenty-five years ago.

Papers I wrote back then are flat and devoid of inflection or emotion. I didn't write about my feelings because I didn't understand them. Today, my greater insight into my emotional life has allowed me to express it, both verbally and on paper. But there was a trade-off for that increased emotional intelligence. I look at circuits I designed twenty years ago and it's as if someone else did them.

Some of my designs were true masterpieces of economy and functionality. Many people told me they were expressions of a creative genius. And today I don't understand them at all. When I look at those old drawings, I am reminded of a book I read as a teenager, *Flowers for Algernon*. Scientists took a retarded janitor and made him a genius, but it didn't last. His brilliance faded away before his eyes. That's how I feel sometimes, looking back at the creative engineering I've done. Those designs were the fruit of a part of my mind that is no longer with me. I will never invent circuits like that again. I may conceive of something like Ace Frehley's light guitar, but someone else will have to design it.

My story isn't sad, though, because my mind didn't fade or die. It just rewired itself. I'm sure my mind has the same power it always did, but in a more broadly focused configuration. No one would have looked at me thirty years ago and foreseen that I'd have the social skills I have today, or the ability to express the emotions, thoughts, and feelings you read in this book. I would never have predicted it, either.

It's been a good trade. Creative genius never helped me make friends, and it certainly didn't make me happy. My life today is immeasurably happier, richer, and fuller as a result of my brain's continuing development.

I suspect that grown-ups drew me out enough as a child to keep me engaged and on a path that led to being functional in society. Adults were able to deal with my conversational limitations better than children. They could follow my disconnected responses, and they were more likely to show interest in anything I said, no matter how bizarre. Had I not been drawn out by interested grown-ups, I might well have drifted farther into the world of autism. I might have ceased to communicate.

Even at sixteen years of age, it would have been easy for me to retreat from dealing with humans and move into the world within my own mind. Looking back, I can see a path that might have led somewhere far away, perhaps to autism, perhaps to the place where the savants who can multiply ten-digit numbers in their minds live. After all, I got along well with my circuits, and they never ridiculed me. They presented me with tough problems to solve but they were never mean. Around the time I dropped out of school, it was almost as though I stood in front of Door Number One and Door Number Two, as perplexed as any game-show contestant and with much more at stake, and was forced to make a choice.

My crazy family situation and my need to run away from home and join the working world in order to survive kept me from making that choice. So I chose Door Number One, and in doing so moved farther away from the world of machines and circuits—a comfortable world of muted colors, soft light, and mechanical perfection—and closer to the anxiety-filled, bright, and disorderly world of people. As I consider that choice thirty years later, I think the kids who choose Door Number Two may not end up able to function in society.

As a functional Aspergian adult, one thing troubles me deeply about those kids who end up behind the second door. Many descriptions of autism and Asperger's describe people like me as "not wanting contact with others" or "preferring to play alone." I can't speak for other kids, but I'd like to be very clear about my own feelings: *I did not ever* want *to be alone.* And all those child psychologists who said "John prefers to play by himself" were dead wrong. I played by myself because I was a failure at playing with others. I was alone as a result of my own limitations, and being alone was one of the bitterest disappointments of my young life. The sting of those early failures followed me long into adulthood, even after I learned about Asperger's.

As a young adult, I was lucky to discover and join the world of musicians and soundmen and special-effects people. People in those lines of work expect to deal with eccentric people. I was smart, I was capable, and I was creative, and for them that was good enough.

In some ways, it was a mistake for me to have left that world, because I was accepted and made to feel welcome there, something I seldom felt in corporate life. But I could not afford to keep moving ahead with my work in electronics with my nonexistent resources. I had to get a job.

In the corporate world, I had started out as an engineer, making $25,000 a year. Back in the 1970s, that was pretty good money. As I moved up, the pay increased. Staff Engineer, Manager of Advanced Development, Assistant Director of Planning, Director of Engineering. And, finally, General Manager of Power Systems. After ten years, I was making $100,000 a year. I was the envy of all the people below me in the food chain, but it was a vicious trap.

In the beginning, I created circuit designs. That was something I loved to do, and did well. Ten years later, my job was managing people and projects. I enjoyed the status and respect, but I wasn't good at management, and I didn't like it. The problem was that if I

wanted to be an engineer, I'd be looking at a 50 percent cut in pay
and a job in some other company. The message was clear: Managers are more valuable than engineers. That made me mad. I
wasn't going to consider going down the ladder and down the pay
scale just to be creative. I wanted it all—good pay, independence,
and creativity.

"You should really be working on your own," I was told by my
bosses.

Was that a precursor to "You're fired"? I had already been laid
off—rejected—twice. In 1983, I went from a seemingly secure
$60,000 salary to a $197 weekly unemployment check. And I had
to stand in line for an hour and fill out two forms to get even that.
I resolved in 1983 that I would never again collect unemployment.

I realized the comments were right. I was not a team player, so
I needed to work on my own. But what could I do that might
make money? I thought long and hard about how I could control
my own destiny. I could design electronic circuits, and I could fix
cars. Those were the two great loves I had grown up with. Either
might offer a career. Could I exchange my suit for overalls and start
fixing automobiles instead of supervising engineers?

I had always loved cars. I had continued to buy old cars, tinker
with them, drive them, and sell them as long as I'd been on my
own. I began to seriously consider the idea of abandoning electronics to become a mechanic or car dealer. I broached the subject
to some of my friends and colleagues at work.

"I just can't do this anymore. I can't stand the bullshit, being in
a company like this. It's just no fun anymore."

They either didn't believe me or thought I was just depressed.
"You're going to quit electronics to become a car mechanic?
You've got one of the top jobs in the company! Don't you know
how many people would give their right arm for a job like yours?"

Or they would say, "You're full of shit. You can be straight with
me. I'm your friend. If you've got a good job at a competitor, tell
me. Maybe I can go, too!"

Everyone thought there was some angle, some trick. But there wasn't.

"If you leave the industry it's going to be very hard to get a job again in a few years. Look at Tom." Tom was one of our technicians. He had been an engineer until he quit work in order to build houses with his brother-in-law. When he wanted to return to engineering, the only job he could find was as a technician, a big step down from where he had been.

But my mind was made up.

"I got into this business because I wanted to be creative. I wanted to design things. Now, I'm just an administrator."

Everyone I talked to at work seemed to think I was nuts, but in the end it didn't matter what other people thought about my job. What mattered was what I thought about my job. And I didn't like it.

It was time to take my chances on my own. In 1989, I quit my job and became a car dealer. That meant taking out a second mortgage against my house. That $30,000 was my seed money, and it was all I had, so it would have to last. I started to buy secondhand European cars, fix them, and sell them. In addition, I serviced what I sold. My first acquisition was a five-year-old Mercedes 300SD, which I cleaned up, serviced, and sold for a profit of $1,500. It seemed I was off to a great start.

I knew fixing up cars and selling them was not creative like designing sound effects, but it had much to recommend it. There was no long commute to work. I could be myself. I would no longer live in fear for my job. There would be no one to fire me. I would no longer feel like a fraud. Selling cars and doing car repairs would be whatever I could make of it. No one would question my qualifications or ability.

If only it were that simple. By the time I realized there was more to it, the $30,000 was lost, and I was an additional $50,000 in debt. Somehow, the $1,500 profit I'd made on each of my first cars had turned into $2,000 and $3,000 losses on later ones, as the economy slid into recession and I made bad decisions. But there was no turning back. I had to succeed. I still remembered mixing my thirty-cent macaroni dinner with water because I couldn't afford milk, and I had vowed never to return to that state.

The thing that saved me was my technical skill, fueled by my Aspergian need to know all about topics that grabbed my attention. And cars certainly had my attention. I may not have made money selling them, but I had the knowledge to fix them when no one else could, and people paid me for that. Even more, their praise made me feel good about myself and gave me the courage to go on in the face of my financial losses. And the electrical problems that had other mechanics scratching their heads proved trivially simple for me.

For ten years, I had listened to my bosses tell me that I could not communicate or work with other people. Now the stakes were higher. And I seemed to be communicating successfully. How could I tell? Because people were coming back. And some of them were even visiting with me while work was done.

I had found a niche where many of my Aspergian traits actually benefited me. My compulsion to know everything about cars made me a great service person. My precise speech gave me the ability to explain complex problems in simple terms. My directness meant that I told people what they needed to hear about their cars, which was good most of the time. And my inability to read body language or appearance meant—in an industry rife with discrimination—that I treated everyone the same.

I lost money at first because I had to learn the business, which was to some extent a lesson in humility. Before going into the business of fixing cars, I had always looked at car repair as fundamentally simpler than, say, engineering. Having now done both, I know that isn't true. If anything, running an automotive repair business is harder for me because it uses a different kind of brainpower—a kind that I had never developed during my engineering days. I had to acquire a broad range of new skills, and fast. Chief among them was the ability to deal with people in a friendly way that would make them want to return. In the past, I had not done very well with that, but circumstances were different now. Perhaps in my new setting, I could learn to succeed in dealing with people and leaving them feeling happy, or at least reasonably satisfied.

My choice of car made a difference, as it turned out. I chose to work on high-end cars like Rolls-Royces and Land Rovers because I loved the way they were put together. I appreciated the way a Rolls-Royce interior was made: like a piece of fine furniture. Each Rolls-Royce is a unique work of art, something a machine aficionado like me can really appreciate. And I loved the rugged simplicity of the Land Rover Defenders. From the first time I saw a Land Rover—in the pages of *National Geographic*—I had been drawn to them. *One day,* I told myself, *I will own one of my own.*

The cars I worked on tended to belong to affluent and better-educated people. Such people were better able to connect with an eccentric Aspergian like me, and they had an incentive to do so. There were not many people willing to fix a Rolls-Royce or a Land Rover in my area. In many cases, the only service alternatives were in Boston or Hartford—an hour's drive away. So an owner of one of those cars had an incentive to make a relationship with me work, whereas a Chevrolet or Toyota owner had service alternatives everywhere he turned.

At first, I did everything—repairs, billing, scheduling, and planning. As the business grew over its first few years, I added a technician to work on cars with me, then another, and another. After almost twenty years in business, Robison Service now employs a dozen people.

When I worked as an administrator for a big company, I was in the position of bending my staff to the whims of my employer. Yet I often felt my employer's desires and wishes were ill-conceived or just plain wrong, which made it very hard for me to feel good about imposing those wishes on others. As an owner, I imposed only my own wishes on my staff. And I only did what I believed in. I felt a lot better about that.

Before opening my business, I had only interacted with a few people at one time: other engineers, people from marketing, family, and a small circle of friends. They were almost all people who knew me, or knew of me. All of a sudden, my new line of work put me in front of the general public. Anyone with a car and a problem might call, and I had to talk to them. I had never been exposed to such a variety of humanity.

This was beneficial to me in a number of ways. First, my ability to interact with people improved tremendously over the first few years I was in business. People who watched me during that time noticed a change. My friends remarked on how "polite and nice" I had become.

I also learned a lot about how to succeed in life from the people who patronized my business. My clients taught me about real estate management, banking, investing, and general business principles. That education has been priceless, and I could never have gotten it from any school.

For the next fifteen years, I built myself a world of machines, a world in which I was securely positioned in the center. We worked on better and better cars, and we solved tougher and tougher problems. We became the repair shop of last resort—the place people went when no one else could figure it out. My Aspergian understanding of machines made our company unique in the auto service world. People began shipping Rolls-Royce, Land Rover, and Mercedes cars hundreds and even thousands of miles to our service department. I had finally made myself a place where I could feel safe and secure.

And then I got the call. I was driving back from lunch when my phone rang. "Hello, Mr. Robison? This is Teri at Chicopee Savings Bank. Can you hold a minute for Mr. Wagner?" Bill Wagner is the president of the bank I do business with.

I pondered what might be wrong for ten long seconds. Then Bill came on the line. "What's wrong?" I asked. "Nothing," Bill said.

"John," he said, "I was hoping you would be willing to join the Board of Corporators of the Bank." I was stunned. Me? On the board of the bank?

"I would be honored" was all I could think to say. And I realized that for the first time I had become legitimate, a part of the local community and not just an outcast.

23

I Get a Bear Cub

In the spring of 1990, in the midst of starting my company and losing all my money, I acquired a son. His mother was Little Bear, so of course I called him Bear Cub. Cubby for short. The name on his birth certificate was Jack, in honor of my grandfather, and his mom used that name, but for me he's always been Cubby, right to this day.

Although I was excited and looking forward to his arrival, Cubby came along during a stressful time in my life. After living together for a few years, Little Bear and I had gotten married in 1982. But things started going bad between us four years later, after her older brother Paul died in a car crash. I was hoping things would improve with Cubby's arrival. In the months before he was born, I was anxious. Little Bear was sick all the time while she was pregnant, and I was afraid Cubby would be born sick, too.

I was also afraid he'd be born with two heads or three arms.

He was born in the Hatchery at the Cooley Dickinson Hospital in Northampton. I drove Little Bear to the hospital on the evening of April 11 in an old gray Jaguar. We parked and checked in at 11:45, and he was born at 12:15. I was in the delivery room for the event. I had read a number of books on the topic and I pretty much knew what to expect. Everything seemed normal. I was surprised at how little he was, though.

I'd been timing him since we learned of his mom's pregnancy, eight months back. According to what the doctors had told us, Cubby was hatching a week early. I'd done a lot of reading, and I knew hatchlings put on quite a bit of weight in the three weeks before being born, so I was expecting him to come out somewhat small, but he was even littler then I expected.

He weighed only six pounds and six tenths of an ounce.

"He's little but he'll be fine," the doctor said. "No need for the incubator for him."

Of course, they had no idea if he would be fine. They were just saying that to reassure us. They had not done any tests. They had, at that moment, done nothing more than a cursory external inspection. But I had studied the infant mortality statistics and I knew this hospital gave us better than average odds.

If all went well, we wouldn't be there long. One night in the hatchery and they'd be sending mom and Cubby home. That first day, I discreetly measured him on my forearm and noted his size and appearance. He didn't really do anything at that point, but I looked at him closely to try and remember what he looked like so I could tell if I had the right kid the next time I saw him. I was afraid I'd fail to recognize him the next day, which would be both embarrassing and humiliating.

His mom was pretty excited, and so were our parents.

I made sure he was tagged with a nylon serial number plate on a ring around his leg before I allowed him to be released into the general population of hatchlings. They had a big room where all the babies lay behind glass and grew under heat lamps, just like the baby chick display at the State Fair. Some were in incubators but most were just on trays. I was glad he was tagged, because despite what they say about moms knowing their kids, you could not tell the one-day-old babies apart except in the most general way, like whether you had a boy or girl. And I suppose if yours had an extra arm or missed a leg he'd be recognizable, but most of the babies in there looked whole and virtually identical.

The next morning, my parents came to see him, separately, since they had been divorced for many years, and my father had remarried. My mother came in first, followed by my father and stepmother. Little Bear's father and stepmother came, too. Her mother and second husband lived in Florida, and they weren't there. But they called. We had a regular parade of visitors that first day.

"Oooooh, just look at him. He's so sweet."

"Hey there, baby boy!" This with a jab in his belly.

"Ooooooh, he looks just like you."

Standard baby drivel, I figured, especially the part about how much he looked like me. How could a six-pound baby with misshapen features and a head the size of an apple look "just like me"?

I was glad I'd noted the numbers stamped on the bracelet. I didn't really think someone would intentionally swap him for another child, but mistakes do happen. I had also tagged him with a waterproof felt-tipped marker in case the bracelet went missing.

That second day, my recognition fears from the previous night proved to be unfounded. When I arrived, Cubby and mom were together in her bed. And just to be sure, I checked his tags and marks. They matched. After going home that day, Cubby never returned to any hospital overnight. So, as a result of my initial marking and caution, I have a very high level of confidence that the baby that emerged from his mother seventeen years ago is the same kid living in my house today.

We brought him home that second afternoon. I had bought a basket that doubled as a car seat to transport him. Little Bear wrapped him up and strapped him in. She carried the baby basket in her lap as they rolled her out of the hospital in a wheelchair. As we were leaving, I realized the hospital hadn't given us very much for the $4,400 hatchery fee. No accessories. No clothes. No toys. Just the kid.

I never did figure out why they insisted on rolling Little Bear out the door in a wheelchair. After all, she came in on her own two feet, walking and talking. She wasn't sick, and she was twenty pounds lighter. Their insistence on rolling her out made me think of an auto repair shop where the cars drive in under their own power and get towed home on wreckers a few days later. Sort of backward.

Cubby was so small he could stretch nose to tail and not reach the length of my forearm. When we got him home, we lined a small laundry hamper with soft fabric and nestled him inside. Within a few weeks, he'd outgrown the little hamper. We moved him into one of Little Bear's big hampers, where he lived for most of the next year.

When he was three days old, I took him to work and carried him around the neighborhood to show him off. Everyone praised and admired him. He didn't say much, but I'm sure he was taking it all in.

We continued to carry him around wherever we went, thinking he would be better socialized the more he was around people. I had not yet learned about Asperger's when Cubby was born, but I knew I had a hard time with people, and I wanted Cubby to get along better than I had. I thought long and hard about how to accomplish that, and one of my ideas was to show him as many interesting people as I could. He was easy to carry around when he was small, and he looked closely at everyone and everything. I'd zip my windbreaker halfway, and drop him in the opening. With his little arms sticking out and the zipper holding tight, he was securely wedged in place. But just to be sure, I always tied the string at the base of my windbreaker, so he couldn't fall out the bottom. I often saw people staring at Cubby, zipped up like that, but they seldom said anything.

"This is Cubby," I would say, while pointing at my jacket, from which he gazed serenely. I was very proud of him. I couldn't wait for him to get bigger and do more tricks. I even daydreamed of a time when he could actually be put to work—mowing the lawn and washing the car. Sadly, that day never came. He was destined to get bigger, but it proved extremely difficult—virtually impossible, in fact—to get useful work out of him. But I'm getting ahead of myself.

When Cubby was little, I tried to show him all the things grown-ups did. When I worked on a car, I took him out with me and set him in the shade, under the hood. He never said much in those early days, so I don't know what he made of it all.

In the beginning, he wasn't very interesting because he didn't do anything, but then he began to yell. I took him out of the hamper and let him sleep on my chest. I had read that hearing a parent's heartbeat calmed a baby. If he continued to yell, I held him tightly against me.

I had a mantra for him: "Calm and docile animal. Calm and docile animal. Calm and docile animal. Caaaaaaaaaaaaaaaalmmmmmmmmmm and dooooooocilllllle animal." Eventually, if I squashed him hard enough and murmured to him long enough, he would stop struggling and go to sleep.

I liked it when he slept on my chest, except when he drooled, peed, or threw up on me. But I always worried about him, too. I was afraid I'd roll over and suffocate him, but I guess parents have instincts about those things, and I never did.

When he got bigger, he started to crawl. Cubby's laundry hamper proved its worth, as I turned it over to form a storage enclosure within which he could crawl to his heart's content. He grew fast, and in no time at all he could upend the hamper. At that point, we got a crib.

Then he started talking. He would come up to me and say, "Baby Toss, Baby Toss," until he got my attention. He stuck his arms up, too, to make sure I understood. I would pick him up and toss him in the air and catch him time and time and time again. He never tired of Baby Toss. He had the most remarkable confidence in my ability to catch him. If I were him, I'd never have done Baby Toss. I'd have been afraid the tosser would miss and I'd go splat on the floor.

We began reading books together. He loved Dr. Seuss. I read those books so often I could turn the pages and say the words from memory. I became bored with repetition, and I began to make subtle alterations. The story turned into:

> *One fish*
> *Two fish*
> *Black fish*
> *Blue fish*
> *I eat you fish.*

And

> *See them all*
> *See them run*
> *The man in back.*
> *He has a gun.*

I liked my improvisations. They broke up the monotony of reading the same thing, time and time again. But despite the smoothness with which I worked these modifications into the good Doctor's stories, Cubby would notice. He would get mad.

"Read it right, Dad!" he would yell.

Eventually, I started making up stories. That worked better because he didn't have a routine to expect, but it was harder because I had to make the stories up as fast as I could recite them. His favorites were about Gorko, Uuudu, and Wuudu. They were flying lizards, and they had lived in Flying Lizard Land, but now they were here. I wove his children's books into the Gorko stories, and he liked that. He especially loved hearing how Thomas the Tank Engine—his favorite train—was picked up and carried off to Flying Lizard Land by the cargo lizards, big lizards with nets.

We spent many enjoyable hours riding around, looking out the windows of our cars at distant flying lizards drifting on the breezes.

I also told him stories of where he came from. It seems like all kids wonder that. I told him about the Kid Store, and how he was on a tray, stuck in the window, when we picked him out. He felt proud when I told him he had been the most expensive kid in the store, the top model. Later on, when he went to school, he heard alternate explanations for where he came from. But he was happy and content until then.

We built stuff together, too. Cubby loved Legos. But he always insisted on building the kits exactly as they told you in the instructions. Little Bear encouraged that. I couldn't stand it. I wanted to modify them.

Cubby especially disliked my attempts to fit two heads or three arms to the Lego action figures. "Build 'em right, Dad!" he squawked indignantly at my two-headed spacemen.

I worked a lot while Cubby was small, and I left many of the kid management decisions up to Little Bear. She stayed home with him, and she deserves all the credit for his basic training. It was probably better that way—I'm not all that well trained myself, so I'm not always the best of role models. But when he became fully self-propelled I started taking him on expeditions, and I felt good at that. Sunday was our special day. Every Sunday he would wake up and say, "Adventure day, Dad!"

I took him to all the places little boys love. Train yards. Junkyards. Shipyards. Airports. Museums. Restaurants and bars. Many weekends we went to the Conrail yard in West Springfield to watch the trains. Once, when Cubby was five, he got to drive a switching engine as it moved cars from Westside to East Springfield. Another time we rode a freight train over the Berkshires to the big marshaling yards in Selkirk, New York.

Cubby was always fascinated by penguins. We would go see the penguins at the aquariums in Boston and Mystic. Sometimes, when it was quiet, he would talk to them. When he was seven, we went to the New England Aquarium but arrived late. The Aquarium was closed, but snappily dressed people were entering through a door under a sign for some kind of reception. Cubby and I slipped inside when the attendants weren't looking.

All the people were seated at folding tables looking into the aquarium itself. The penguin area below was dark, lit only by night lights. That's where we went. Cubby began talking softly to the penguins.

"Hoooooot. Hoooooooooot. Hoooo."

And they began to hoot back. It was the most remarkable thing. He talked to those penguins for an hour that night. Then we slipped out the back door and went home.

I cherished these times together. We roamed all over New England in those years. Cubby was a good traveler.

One day we headed to the Port of Boston. We liked all kinds of machinery, especially big ships. I told Cubby that we were going to the shipyard to watch container ships, and that maybe we would see some tugs or a tanker, too.

"Neat," he said. He wiggled his ears a little, thinking about ships. He was only five, so he almost always wanted to do anything his Dad wanted to do. It was great. I knew he'd turn on me later, but at five he liked anything I liked.

We were driving along, and I said, "Did you know Santa works in a shipyard like this?"

"He does not!" Cubby said. Cubby was always troubled when I told him strange things about childhood heroes like Santa. But I could never accept the cookie-cutter feel of standard children's stories. I had to liven them up.

"What do you think Santa does all the time it's not Christmas?" I asked him.

Cubby looked puzzled. Clearly, he never considered that Santa had to *do* something for the rest of the year. Like most kids, he forgot about Santa from December 26 until the following November.

"He has a job, just like all the other grown-ups."

"What does he do?" Cubby looked a little dubious, to the extent that a five-year-old can look that way.

"Santa runs a container crane at Europoort, in Rotterdam. He works all day unloading ships. We're going to see container cranes just like the ones Santa works on. Santa has a lot of friends that work the ships and the trucks. Maybe some of them will be here today."

After a moment, Cubby asked, "What's a container crane?"

Now I had his interest. I told him, "The container cranes are machines that pick the containers off the ships and set them onto trucks so they can be delivered to stores and warehouses and factories. We're going to go see one today, unloading a ship."

A minute or two passed while Cubby pondered the idea of Santa working in a shipyard. He asked, "Will we see elves in the shipyard?"

"Maybe," I said. "Look closely at the people on the ship. Most container ships have crews made up of elves and sailors from the Philippines. The look similar but if you look carefully you can tell them apart because the elves are smaller. The elves are hard to see because they stay out of sight when the ship is near shore, so they don't get kidnapped by bad people."

Cubby didn't ask why bad people would want to kidnap shipboard elves, but I could see he was thinking hard.

By and by, we arrived at the port. We threaded our way through the gates and warehouse buildings to come out on a wharf directly opposite a big yellow container crane unloading a ship. The crane looked like a huge daddy longlegs, with four huge legs anchoring it to the dock. It had an arm with a hook that dropped down to grab containers on the ship. The arm moved back and forth and in and out on tracks, so the crane could lift a container and move it hundreds of feet to set it in stacks on shore. We looked at the ship, with the name *MSC Fugu Island* in rusty letters. I read the name to Cubby and he asked, "What's Fugu Island?"

"It's an elf island in the Pacific. It's on the way to Flying Lizard Land." At the mention of Flying Lizard Land, Cubby looked overhead to see if any of the great lizards were visible, circling high above the harbor. We saw them out west, usually at a great distance. There were no lizards visible that day. Just seagulls.

"That ship has to have elves aboard."

We watched as the crane lifted containers off the ship and I read the names to Cubby. Hyundai. Hanjin. Cosco. APL.

I said, "Those are all names of shipping companies. They own the containers. People who want to ship things call a freight line and get a container, and they fill it with their stuff." Cubby was beginning to understand. "Container transport," I said.

"Hard word," said Cubby.

"They are hard words," I agreed. "Just like *helicopter.*"

"Yeah," he said. "*Helicopter.*" Cubby liked that word.

"Most of your toys came here from China in a container. Your shoes came here in a container. And so did Mom's computer." Cubby was impressed. He had no idea his clothes and toys had traveled the world.

After a while, the operator seemed to get tired of unloading. He started picking containers off piles on the dock and putting them on the ship. We watched the crane moving back and forth. Some people would have found it boring, but not us.

"Watch him carefully, Cubby. Sometimes they drop a container into the harbor and smugglers drag it away and loot it."

The *Fugu Island* was at least 750 feet long, the biggest ship Cubby had ever seen. A passing tug looked like a bathtub toy in comparison. I pointed to a speck just visible between two container rows toward the middle of the ship.

"Elves! Right there!"

"Yeah!" he said excitedly. "Elves!" As soon as we saw them, they vanished. They seemed to have a sixth sense for when we were watching. Every now and then, we'd see an elf out of the corner of our eye, but then it would disappear.

Cubby said, "I wish we had a net." Then he had a Christmas thought out of the blue. "What about the reindeer, Dad? Where do they go in summer?"

"Well," I began, "reindeer are mostly for show nowadays. Think about all the kids in the world. The population of the world has gotten so much bigger since Santa first opened for business a hundred years ago. There's no way he could deliver all those presents riding a herd of deer. Today, Christmas presents are moved by container ship and truck. So they use the reindeer to take pictures for Christmas cards and stuff. The rest of the time they live on a reindeer ranch in Finland. Maybe we can see them one day."

Over on the pier, a bunch of trucks were getting ready to pull out with loads of cargo from the ship. "Look," I said. "There's Santa's friend Butch, driving that truck!"

Cubby waved at him. Butch waved back as he pulled his truck out of the yard.

Across the pier, they seemed to be done loading the container ship. We saw smoke coming from the stacks and water was pumped overboard from holes in the side of the ship. Cubby asked if they were getting ready to leave.

"Probably so," I said. "But it could be a while yet. We don't see any tugs yet. I doubt they'll be leaving before dark. You know, Cubby, Santa and his friends all go to the Sailor's Rest after work. They've got a Sailor's Rest right here. Want to go there and get a hamburger?"

"Yeah!" Cubby was hungry now.

We drove back out through the piers and across the street, where there was a scrap iron dealer and a run-down-looking bar with a sign hanging on a board and lights in the window. I pointed it out to Cubby.

"Michelob," he said, looking at the sign in the window. He was already learning to read.

We went inside and sat at the bar directly under a NO MINORS sign. Cubby did not notice it, or if he did, he didn't say anything. A bearded bartender in a leather vest came over, and I ordered two Cokes, a hamburger, and a hot dog.

The bartender snorted and moved off. Cubby looked around.

"Are Santa's friends here?" I saw some bikers, some truckers, some dock workers, a pimp, and two hookers. At a table in the corner, five rough-looking guys were playing cards. Quite a bit of money was visible on the table.

"I don't know," I said. "Santa's pretty old. You've seen that white beard he's got. He's been working shipyards all over the world since before I was born. Santa's father worked the docks right here in Boston, unloading sailing ships over there near the Black Falcon Terminal. That's how Santa ended up in the shipping trade. He learned about it from his dad. And his dad passed on the Christmas racket to his son, just as his own father had passed it on to him."

"Why is Christmas a racket?" Cubby asked.

"Because Santa skims some of the toys he's supposed to give away, selling them on the black market in Russia and Mongolia, places where they don't have Christmas. Toymakers donate stuff to Santa on the condition that he gives them all away, and he's not supposed to sell toys. But he's got a drinking problem and he can't help himself."

Cubby frowned. The image of a drunken, crooked Santa was disturbing.

"And you see that building over there?" I said. He looked at a large building across the harbor with *Boston Edison* written on the side.

"That's a power plant. They burn oil and coal to make electricity. And around here, a company called Boston Edison owns all the power plants. They give Santa the coal he leaves in stockings when kids are bad." Cubby and I had watched trains carrying hundreds of cars of coal to power plants like this near home.

"Sometimes the kids are so bad the power company has to get him a whole train load of coal."

That image troubled Cubby. Luckily, he'd only gotten coal in his stocking once. And even then, Santa left him presents, too. We figured the coal was just a warning.

"Why isn't Santa here in Boston like his dad?" he asked. "Why is he in Rotterdam?"

Cubby was only five at the time, and I didn't want to shock him with talk of the scandals, so I just said, "Santa had some trouble with the law, and he had to leave town."

Cubby was fascinated, hearing all this Christmas history. I could tell he was anxious to go home and tell his mom and his friends what he'd learned.

"See that thing like a spear over the bar?" I pointed to a huge lance hanging over the top shelf of whiskies. Cubby looked up. Like most boys his age, he loved weaponry. "It's called a harpoon. That's from Santa's great-great-grandfather. He hunted whales with it. He might have used it to fend off polar bears when they had to walk out across the ice."

Cubby's eyes were wide. He was imagining holding a giant polar bear at bay, snapping at the harpoon. Even in the dark barroom, I could see he was very impressed. Our food arrived. He drank two more Cokes and ate half his hot dog. It was really tough to get him to eat all his food, even with harpoons on the walls.

It was late afternoon when we left the Sailor's Rest and headed for home. Cubby was tired, but he'd had a good day. He got up off his barstool, staggered to the door, and climbed into his car seat. I strapped him in, and he fell asleep.

It would be a few more years before Cubby stopped believing my stories. Until then, he scanned the skies for flying lizards and watched for elves whenever we saw a ship.

There's quite a bit of evidence that suggests Asperger's can be inherited. When I learned about my own Asperger's, Cubby was six, and I was immediately concerned that Cubby might be that way, too. And he is, but to a much lesser extent than me. As he grew up, I watched him carefully and remembered the times I had struggled as a child. Sometimes I'd watch him make the same mistakes I did, and I would cringe. I tried explaining what was happening to him, and it seemed to work. Cubby began making friends, and he grew up without the worst of my Aspergian traits.

Now that he's a teenager, the difference between Cubby and me is staggering. On Friday nights, he'll invite six or seven friends over, and they'll talk and laugh and watch TV and eat pizza till midnight. He's the life of the party—something I dreamed about but never attained.

In other ways, we are very much alike. He's blessed with my gifts for mathematics and imagination. At sixteen, he got Cs in school because he was bored, but his knowledge of calculus exceeded that of his teachers. And he shares my fascination with pyrotechnics. He figured out how to make his own flash powder, and he detonates homemade fireworks in the meadow behind our house. It's quite impressive.

I am quite sure Cubby will accomplish another of my child-hood dreams: to graduate from high school and go on to finish college.

Cubby has gotten bigger and smarter over the seventeen-plus years that I've had him. He has his own ideas and thoughts now, and he has little use for me anymore. At about age nine, he became very hard to trick. By thirteen, it was almost impossible to trick him. Now he tries to trick us, and he successfully tricks other kids.

Last summer, when he thought I wasn't looking, I observed Cubby telling one of the neighborhood six-year-olds that there were dragons living in the storm drains, under our street.

"We feed them meat," he said while dropping bits of hot dog through the grate, "and then they don't get hungry and blow fire and roast us."

Little James listened closely, with a very serious expression on his face. Then he ran home to get some hot dogs from his mother.

I was very proud of Cubby.

24

A Diagnosis at Forty

By the time I was forty, I had managed to make and keep a few friends, one of whom is an insightful therapist, TR Rosenberg. He had called me wanting to buy a Land Rover. I had a red one that I was looking to sell, and I drove to his house in Leyden, up in the Berkshires, to show it to him.

We decided to go for a ride on some trails near his home. He owned a Suzuki Samurai and he wanted to see if the Land Rover would outperform it off-road. So we drove the Land Rover all the way to the edge of the Green River, deep into the woods by the Vermont border. At that point, the trail dropped into the river, at a spot where ox teams used to pull wagons across the shallow ford to the other side. Descending to the river, the road had been worn deeply into the ground so that we were driving at the bottom of a V with high dirt banks to either side. There was no room to maneuver. The only choices were straight ahead or straight back. TR stopped at the edge of the river and got out.

"You better back this thing up. I'm not comfortable backing it all the way up the hill."

I looked back at the rough and rocky trail leading up the hill, and out at the river. I wasn't eager to back the Land Rover all that distance up a steep hill, either. The oxcart road emerged from the river on the other side, about one hundred feet away. Water swirled around rocks in midstream. Maybe I didn't have to back it out.

It can't be that deep if they drove ox teams across, I said to myself. *I'm sure I can drive out there.* I walked to the edge. I could see bottom under the swirling water. I got back in the Rover.

"Let's go," I said. And I drove over the edge, into the river. Water surged back over the hood, and TR recoiled in alarm. *Deeper than I thought,* I said to myself. I gunned the motor and the Rover moved into shallower water in midstream. The water at the edge must have been about three feet deep.

I could hear the water bubbling at the back, where my exhaust pipe was now submerged, and water was beginning to come up through the floor seams. I cut the wheel, did a three point turn in midstream, gunned the motor, and headed for the bank. The wheels spun a bit and we scrambled onto shore, pointing back uphill.

"You can drive again," I said, climbing back out of the driver's seat.

"Wow!" TR didn't have anything else to say for a long moment as we listened to water pour out of the Rover as it drained. It never missed a beat. "Damn! My Suzuki couldn't do that!" Having gotten over his shock, TR bought the Land Rover.

When I delivered it a few days later, we decided to take another ride. This time, we drove far into the woods, just over the Vermont border. I drove a long way down a woods trail, and when I went to turn around, I hit an old tree stump that was hidden under the leaves. We were stuck.

We got out to see what was wrong, and TR said, "The wheels seem to be pointing in two different directions."

It was true. The stump had bent the front end so that the left wheel was turning left and the right wheel was turning right. TR's new Rover wasn't going to drive home without a new tie rod.

We decided to walk back to the road and find a phone. "I'll have to get some parts and come back to rescue the car," I said.

TR was remarkably calm, given that I'd just impaled his new rig on a tree stump.

As we started up the trail, darkness fell and it began sleeting. My asthma was aggravated by stress in those days, and it started acting up. I could hardly walk. *Son of a bitch,* I thought. *First I wrecked his truck, and now I'm going to freeze to death in the woods.* But I didn't drop dead. I kept going. TR was remarkably patient, and we made it to a phone. His wife came and picked us up, my asthma settled back down, and I rescued the Rover the next day.

From that beginning, we became good friends. For someone as mechanical and robotic as I can be, he's an unlikely companion. He's warm and friendly—sort of chubby and jolly and teddy bear–like. I've also learned that he's a very perceptive fellow. For a number of years, he was director of counseling for the Academy at Swift River, a well-known school for troubled teens in the Berkshires. He then went on to found a company that helps teenagers in difficulty make the transition into functional adulthood.

Over the years, TR had noticed certain odd things about me, but he never said anything. One day, having known me about ten years, he decided to tell me about his observations. He deliberated about telling me for quite a while, though. He was worried about how I'd react. After all, I looked pretty normal most of the time. I had founded a successful business. I was able to talk to people, and people got along with me, although some found me odd. I had a wife and a son. I wasn't in trouble with the law, I didn't drink, and I didn't do drugs.

TR had taken to coming down to visit me at lunchtime every now and then. One day he said, "Therapists learn not to analyze their friends if they want to have friends. But there is a condition in this book that fits you to a T. I'd like you to read this and see what you think." And he handed me a book: *Asperger's Syndrome,* by Tony Attwood.

I picked it up. Warily. "What the hell is this?"

I thought, *Ten seconds ago, I was telling him what I had just read about Caterpillar's newest D10 bulldozers and how they plan to compete with Komatsu in Asia, and now he hands me this?*

Seeing my wariness, he quickly continued, "I'm sorry to spring this on you like this. I've thought about it a lot. This book describes you exactly. You could be the poster boy for this condition. Your fascination with trains and bulldozers . . . it's in here. The way you talk. The way you look at people, and how hard it is for you to make eye contact. The way you think."

"So is there a cure?" I asked.

"It's not a disease," he explained. "It doesn't need curing. It's just how you are."

Sitting at the table, I began scanning the book. I always read when I am eating alone, though I have learned that it's rude to do so when eating with other people. But this moment appeared to be an exception. One of the first things I read was this:

Diagnostic Criteria for 299.80 Asperger's Disorder

A. Qualitative impairment in social interaction, as manifested by at least two of the following:

> *Marked impairments in the use of multiple nonverbal behaviors such as eye-to-eye gaze, facial expression, body postures, and gestures to regulate social interaction.*

Well, I thought, that certainly describes me. Not looking at people, making the wrong expressions, and gesturing when I should be still . . . that was me all right, and it wasn't good. I kept reading.

> *Failure to develop peer relationships appropriate to developmental level.*

That fit me exactly. When I was younger, I had never been able to connect with kids my own age.

> *A lack of spontaneous seeking to share enjoyment, interests, or achievements with other people (e.g., by a lack of showing, bringing, or pointing out objects of interest to other people).*

Well, sure. If I can't connect with people, how can I be expected to show them stuff? That was me, too.

> *Lack of social or emotional reciprocity.*

I've certainly heard that one before.

I immediately realized he was right. It did fit me. Completely. It was like a revelation. I realized that all the psychologists and psychiatrists and mental heath workers I had been sent to as a child had completely missed what TR had seen.

As a child, I had been told I was smart but I was lazy. Reading the pages, I realized I wasn't lazy, just different.

I knew that I did not look at people when I talked to them. Hell, I had been beaten up and criticized for that all through my childhood. But until I read that book I had never realized my behavior was unusual. I had never understood why people treated me the way they did. It had always seemed so mean, so unfair. It had never occurred to me that other people might find what I did (or did not do) naturally disconcerting. The answer to "Why won't you look me in the eye, young man?" was right there in the book.

The realization was staggering. *There are other people like me. So many, in fact, that they have a name for us.*

I kept reading, willing my eyes to pick up the pace. My head spun.

I had spent most of my life listening to people tell me how I was arrogant, aloof, or unfriendly. Now I read that people with

Asperger's *display inappropriate facial expressions.* Well, I certainly knew about that. When I was a child, I was told my aunt had died, and I grinned even though I was sad. And I got smacked.

Just reading those pages was a tremendous relief. All my life, I had felt like I didn't fit in. I had always felt like a fraud or, even worse, a sociopath waiting to be found out. But the book told a very different story. I was not a heartless killer waiting to harvest my first victim. I was normal, for what I am.

How could all those so-called professionals have missed that? How could they have been so completely wrong?

To be fair, Asperger's syndrome was not recognized as a distinct condition in the *Diagnostic and Statistical Manual of Mental Disorders,* the bible of mental health professionals, until fairly recently, when I was in my thirties. The upshot was that I spent many years adapting to a condition I didn't know I had. Learning about Asperger's was truly a life-transforming experience.

One of the most surprising things I learned was that Asperger's is an *autistic spectrum disorder.* That is, it's a *form of autism.* If someone had suggested I had an autistic disorder as a child, I'd have said, "You're nuts!" To me, an autistic person was someone like Tommy, the autistic kid on the TV show *St. Elsewhere.* He never said anything, and he didn't do much at all. Autism, to people of my generation, was something we imagined as almost a living death. I had no idea of the continuum that really exists, with profoundly impaired people like Tommy at one end and people like me at the other.

I guess it's possible that even if I had been diagnosed at six, no one would have believed it. Perhaps our culture needed to evolve a bit more for subtler conditions like mine to stand out from the background noise of society.

If my parents had known what caused me to be the way I was, and acted on the knowledge, life might have turned out very differently for me. My life has been filled with lost chances because I didn't fit in.

I left school in the tenth grade despite intelligence tests showing me to be smarter than most college graduates. A number of
professors had encouraged me to start at UMass even though I had
dropped out of high school, but I couldn't bring myself to do it. I
was too jarred by my failure. I did not want to let another school
try and fit me into their mold so I could fail there, too. Starting at
about six years of age, I learned not to submit myself to repeated
humiliation from people or institutions.

I left Fat, the first band I was with, because I could not cope
with the close personal interactions living in a house with ten
roommates. And many of my earlier relationships fell apart because of my unusual style of communicating.

There were also missed career opportunities. At one point, I
was asked to interview for an R&D job at Lucasfilm, which would
have been ideal for my creative skills, but I was too afraid of going
there, getting the job, and being found out as a fraud and fired
once I had moved across the country. So I faded out of the music
scene despite the fact that I was happier there than anywhere I
have worked since.

Once I studied the book, I began to understand the differences
between how I acted and how "normal" people acted in different
situations. I started making a conscious effort to look people in the
eye, and even when I looked at the floor while framing a response,
I learned to glance at the person occasionally.

I learned to pause before responding when people approach me
and begin speaking. I trained myself to respond in a manner that is
only slightly eccentric, rather than out-and-out weird. When someone says, "Hey, John, how's it going? How have you been?" I can
answer, "I'm doing okay, Bob, how about you?" instead of "I have
just been reading about the new MTU diesel engines that American President Lines is installing in their newest container ships. The
new electronic engine management system is fascinating."

I have taught myself to remember what's happening with
people close to my friends. When I see someone I have not seen in

a while, I sometimes remember to say things like "How's Mallory doing at college?" or "Is your mother out of the hospital yet?" That has proven hard to do, but I am making headway with it.

Changes like these have made a huge difference in how people perceive me. I have moved from being weird to being eccentric. And let me tell you, it's a lot better to be eccentric.

Learning about my Asperger's has benefited me in other ways, too. I've talked about feeling like a fraud, waiting to be found out and thrown on the rubbish pile of humanity. I felt like a fraud because I could not do anything in the normal way. I couldn't complete school. I couldn't "advance through the ranks." I couldn't "do it by the book." And I always ignored the rules.

Because of that, I never felt legitimate. Now, with my understanding of my Asperger's, those negative feelings are in large measure gone.

I now realize that the knowledge I have is genuine. When I worked as an engineer, my ability to create beautiful-sounding amplifiers and sound equipment was real. My ability to think up striking special effects was real, too. And now that I am older, I understand how rare those abilities are.

There are plenty of people in the world whose lives are governed by rote and routine. Such people will never be happy dealing with me, because I don't conform. Luckily, the world is also full of people who care about results, and those people are usually very happy with me, because my Asperger's compels me to be the ultimate expert in whatever field of interest I choose. And with substantial knowledge, I can obtain good results.

So I'm not defective. In fact, in recent years I have started to see that we Aspergians are *better* than normal! And now it seems as though scientists agree: Recent articles suggest that a touch of Asperger's is an essential part of much creative genius.

25

Montagoonians

Names have been a source of difficulty for me as long as I can remember because the names I use are often not the ones other people expect. In some cases, people object to my use of names, and they occasionally get angry. Complaints like "I'm not Chubster! I'm Martha!" are all too familiar to me. But familiar or not, Martha will always be the Chubster, unless I adopt a different name for some reason, like her order of appearance among her sisters.

Why is she Chubster? Because at the time I named her, she had an obsession with being fit and thin. And what else could you name someone obsessed with fitness and weight? So Chubster it is, unless you want to use the diminutive form, which is Chubbykin.

To be considerate, I have tried on many occasions to use a name other than one I've chosen. I just can't do it. When I try to call the Chubster Martha, I choke on it. Martha does not work for me. But *you* can call her Martha if you want. I won't mind. I don't impose my name usage on others.

I refer to my current house as The House. If, in the future, I acquire additional houses I might refer to them as Dwelling 1 and Dwelling 2, but until now The House has been an adequate, functional name for whatever house I have lived in.

The only exceptions to the rule of calling my dwelling The

House have been the brief periods when I occupied The Apartment or The Tent or The Cabin or The Shed. Those times were considerably less pleasant than times spent in The House, so I don't think about them very much. The least pleasant—and, luckily, very temporary—domiciling arrangements for me were The Dumpster, The Box Pile, and The Jail, but I don't think of them at all.

My names for nonhumans are clear and descriptive. They are never tricky. For example, consider Dog and Poodle. There is no mistaking what they are. These are good, true, functional names.

My brother, who does not have Asperger's, got a dog and named it Kitty Kitty. I would never do that. One day, my brother came to visit and we took Kitty Kitty for a walk in the Berkshires. He fell into a pool of road-repair tar. It served them both right for a name like that. I would never name a dog Kitty Kitty or Cat, and my dogs would never fall in road tar.

My brother persists in this deviant naming of animals. He currently has two dogs. One he has named Bentley. I believe he did that because I have a Bentley and he liked it. However, my Bentley is a car. An old one. Naming a dog Bentley is just wrong. The other one is worse. He calls it Cow. It's a mystery to me why he would do that, since he presumably has the same genetic material as me. Sometimes I think he did it just to annoy me.

I think people who choose names like that must not be very logical thinkers. Perhaps they are people I've heard described as "Oh! So dramatic and emotional!" Or perhaps they just suffer from some kind of arrested development. I believe that anyone who interviewed my brother and me, and viewed examples of our naming practices, would reach that conclusion. My brother, of course, would disagree.

Another example of arrested development is the person who names a pet something like Molson. A dog is not a bottle of beer, no matter how much an alcoholic owner may wish him to be. Confusing a dog with a beer bottle is a sign of deep-seated mental confusion.

Unlike most people, my brother actually chose his own name. He was born as Christopher Richter Robison, but he didn't like our parents, so he changed his name to Augusten Xon Burroughs when he was eighteen. I have never called him Augusten, nor do I call him Chris. And he outgrew both Snort and Varmint. Our cousin Little Bob called him Xon, with the X pronounced as a Z, but that doesn't work for me, either. In the absence of a workable name, I just refer to him as "my brother" without actually using a name.

To his partner, Dennis, I say, "Where's my brother?"

To my son, I say, "Where's your uncle?"

To my brother, I say, "Hey!"

Sometimes I have alternate names, and my names reflect function or position as opposed to type. For example, my wife has two sisters, and of course she had a mother and father, too, until they died. Sometimes several of them would be together, and I would have to introduce a stranger to them as a group.

In such a situation, I might point to a parent and say, "This is Unit Zero." If Annie, the youngest child, were present, I would say "This is Annie, Unit Three." If Ellen were there, I would say, "This is Ellen, Unit One." If my own mate were there, I would say, "This is Martha, Unit Two."

My descriptions make the relative position of each Unit clear in the greater scheme of things, which seems to me perfectly reasonable. Once again, we have an example of functional naming that is perceived as strange by the general public.

When I was little, grown-ups told me the names for everything and everyone. The hot thing was a stove. The dog was a poodle. The kid was Little Robbie, or Jeff. I had no power over the names, and I didn't like it. Who were they, intruding into my innermost thoughts in that manner? But as I got bigger, I got my own naming rights. I began to acquire things that I could name. I was given a tractor, and I named him Chippy. But nobody respected my names. My father called my tractor "your tractor," not Chippy.

Sometimes people actually laughed at my names, which hurt my feelings or made me mad.

But I persisted. As I got older, I carefully evaluated each name I was handed for any new person or thing and decided on a case by case basis whether I'd accept it. If I didn't accept the proffered name, I supplied one of my own. This sometimes presented problems, as when other kids didn't understand their names were being offered to me on a take it or leave it basis. Looking back, I can understand how a kid might not have liked my naming him Blob, no matter how good a match that name was, or how repulsive he was.

There can be disadvantages to my naming habits. For example, when Little Bear and I divorced and I remarried, she lost her name. She's antagonized by being called Little Bear, because it reminds her of happier times when we were together, and I don't have anything left to call her except "Hey!"

The closer people are to me the less likely I am to call them by the names they were given. Bobby or Paul at work will always be Bobby or Paul when I refer to them. But my mother is never Margaret or Mom, only "my mother." (I ceased calling my parents Slave and Stupid when I moved out, at age sixteen.)

Sometimes I recognize existing naming conventions and use them, to people's surprise. We take for granted that people who live in America are Americans. People who live in Canada are Canadians. So what are people who live in the town of Montague? I was introducing a lawyer friend and his wife to some other people and I said, "This is George and his wife, Barbara. They're Montagoonian attorneys." To me, that was perfectly sensible, but George looked like he'd just been mortally insulted.

I had observed that people—when meeting someone for the first time—will invariably ask two questions within a few minutes of engaging in conversation: "Where do you live?" and "What do you do?" My statement addressed both questions with a fine economy of words, and no waiting or delay. Why were they offended?

It was a puzzle to me. What else could someone from Montague be but a Montagoonian?

I guess it's the idea of being a Montagoonian that's tough to take. Perhaps he was insecure about exactly what a Montagoonian was and whether it was good. Or maybe people only like to "be" things on a big scale. It's not insulting to say, "Bob's an American," nor is it insulting to say, "Bob's very tall." But saying, "Bob's a Montagoonian," elicits about the same response as "Bob's a Jew" or "He's queer."

That last statement highlights a difficulty I have in conversation. In some cases, introducing a person by saying, "He's a Jew," or "He's a queer" would be offensive, on a par with saying, "He's a car thief." But in other cases, it appears to be complimentary or even funny. Figuring out the difference can be a challenge for me.

If you can't identify with where you live, there is only one good answer: Move somewhere else. I'll bet George would have nodded smugly if I had said, "This is George, he's a New York attorney." After all, everyone knows everything is better in the big city—the food, the Broadway shows, the lawyers, the girls. But he's not a New Yorker. He's a Montagoonian. And he should face that fact with a smile, or move. He has no right to get annoyed with me over it. I didn't put him there.

After the reaction I got from the Montagoonian attorneys, I gave some thought to what it means to be something. If you say you're an American, people will draw some predictable conclusions about you based upon their knowledge of Americans. But what if you say you're something people don't recognize? Outside of Montague, most people would not know what a Montagoonian was. I tried to conjure a mental image of what one might be. I even asked people on the street.

Try it yourself—what do you think of when you hear "Montagoonian"? Is your Montagoonian a short, stocky guy with a sloped forehead? Does he hunch over when he walks, his shoulders bunched together, with a club like a baseball bat in his right hand? Is his back covered with hair? Does he look like he could lift your pickup truck with his left hand? Or is your Montagoonian tall, thin, and distinguished looking? Neat as a pin, with wire frame glasses, a rumpled sport coat, and a dress shirt? Maybe a book and a pipe in his hand?

If you're like me, your idea of a Montagoonian is the first example, not the second. I guess I wouldn't like to be thought of that way, either, but then again, I didn't choose to live in Montague. And there's no two ways about it. Living in Montague makes one a Montagoonian.

I lived among Montagoonians myself for many years, so I know. I was a Chicopean from Chicopee—a town famous throughout western Massachusetts as the gateway to Montague. I moved away, and like magic the club vanished from my hand and my brow straightened.

So despite my increased adaptation to polite society I still occasionally have trouble with the names I give people and things. And I'm sure many other people with Asperger's would say their experience is similar.

What is a person with Asperger's? We are Aspergians.

26

Units One Through Three

My skill at choosing people with whom I might form relationships was always less than my skill at choosing mechanical or electronic things. You can set me loose in a parking lot with an order to find the one car that's never had any bodywork, and I can do it every time. Need help picking a farm tractor or stereo amplifier? I'm your man.

It's too bad my skill with respect to people is impaired. Even worse, people have to choose me back to form a relationship, and my own choosability may be limited. Although people tell me I'm perfectly presentable now, I have at various earlier times been unkempt, fat, slovenly, foul smelling, and rough looking. At those times, it's possible that many highly desirable people passed me by. There's no way to know.

When choosing a potential mate, I have always been very fearful of rejection. So I was always very careful to display little sign of interest lest the girl ridicule me. Memories of girls pointing and snickering at the few high school dances I attended are never far from my mind. I chose Little Bear when we were very young, and she chose me back. We were very happy for a few years, but it didn't last. As we grew older, we seemed to grow in different directions, and our relationship fell apart. I had to return to the choosing stage, or allow myself to be chosen yet again, to find lasting happiness.

Martha, my next mate, had to choose me, at least to a sufficient extent that I knew she would not ridicule my own expression of choice. Even before we had heard about Asperger's, I noticed that she watched me very carefully. She found that I would calm down if she stroked my arm or rubbed my neck. She also scratched my head and rubbed my ears. Those things soothed me and made me less fidgety.

I liked the fact that she paid close attention to me and was always kind. She never seemed to get tired of me. It seemed like a good match. With the passage of time, I began to feel good about my choice. I think she did, too, because she stuck around.

Now that she's here, life is the best it's ever been for me. There is a joy and tranquillity that I never experienced before. I don't dread coming home, as I did at the end of my first marriage. I have a home where I feel comfortable, and I like being there. I haven't had that feeling since I was a child in Georgia.

But there has always been a question, one that many guys must face. Was she really the best choice for me? There are millions of girls in the world, so it's reasonably certain that other good matches for me exist. They could even be better matches. But is what I have good enough to justify a cessation of searching? I think so. But what about the sisters?

Martha is one in a set of three sisters. She's the middle Unit, Unit Two. Since Units One, Two, and Three share the same genetic source material, differing only in training and conditioning, it begs the question—did I get the best one? I'm sure anyone else would agree that when there are three of something, only a fool would not want to pick the best of the three for himself. As it happens, all three sisters are reasonably similar in appearance, clean and well kept. They look like a matched set, except for Unit One being somewhat smaller than Units Two and Three. Outside of the normal variations from youngest to oldest, there is no visible basis for decision. The younger Unit has the advantage of youth, the older Unit the advantage of greater experience. The middle Unit, the one I've ended up with, may represent the happy medium.

Unfortunately, when picking a mate from a set of three sisters, it is usually necessary to establish a relationship with one in order to meet the other two. That usually precludes a person from selecting a different sister once an initial choice has been made. That was certainly the case for me. It's a tough problem, one with no good answer. Unless you blindly believe the one you picked first is the best, you are bound for trouble.

Since I have a hard time blindly believing anything, I try and reassure myself by asking Unit Two questions.

"Do you think I got the best sister?"

Often her answers are disturbingly vague.

"Depends on what you want her for," or "Depends on who you ask."

I would have thought that she'd want to reassure her mate, saying something like "Of course I'm the best sister." It troubles me that she doesn't. Even after all this time, I cannot tell if she is being nice to Units One and Three, if she lacks self-confidence, or if she really does not know. Two of the three possibilities are unsettling, to say the least. I wish I could be sure.

The most troubling part is this: If one or both of the other Units also has a mate, he might also believe he has the best Unit. Would that mean one of us is wrong? That's a scary prospect for a logical thinker like me.

The situation with sisters may be similar to what happens at a car dealership. For example, say three of us walk into the Mini dealership intent on buying cars. One of us chooses the red Cooper with leather seats. One takes the yellow Cooper convertible. One of us takes the Cooper S coupe. If there is no squabbling among us, an observer might conclude that each of us felt he'd acquired the best Mini, depending on what he wanted it for, as Unit Two would say. After all, there are buyers of sports cars and buyers of trucks.

However, it is equally possible that two of us made wrong choices, and one of us chose a Mini that is or will be far superior to the others. A revisiting of the situation in fifty thousand miles might reveal the true winner.

And so it is with sisters, but with an important difference. I alone can select a Mini. It's a one-sided choosing. But a successful sister selection requires that my chosen sister also choose me. That's a major complication. In fact, it complicates the whole process so much that it's beyond my level of social skill to manage it. And that's why I allowed myself to be chosen—as opposed to being the chooser—by a sister, and I've lived reasonably happily with the choice.

I'm actually more than reasonably happy. I'm the happiest I've ever been. But I wonder sometimes . . . *could I be happier still?* There is no way to find out short of starting over, and then I could end up with no mate at all, which would be much worse. So I don't pursue that line of thinking.

The business of choosing a sister highlights two common Aspergian traits I exhibit: logicality and directness. Every guy who marries a girl who is one of a set of two, three, or four wonders if he got the best sister. But most of them won't admit it. Some guys in that situation are so hypocritical as to deny wondering. Others will shrink away and say nothing, hoping such thoughts will go away. But I lack those inhibitions, so I ask the question out loud. And sometimes people seem offended, but why?

After all, it's acceptable to wonder whether we got the best car. People openly debate which brand of chain saw is best. We all want to live in the best neighborhoods. So, given a choice, why wouldn't we want the best sister?

Some people will consider that argument and respond, "I don't care about the best sister. I want the best girl for me, period!" That presents a completely different question. Choosing a sister is like saying, "I want a chain saw, and I've decided on a Stihl. Should I get the five-horse farm model, or the four-horse home model?" Choosing the "best girl, period" expands that field of choice from one make, all models to all makes, all models. The decision becomes a lot tougher.

We are choosing a family, as it were.

At that point, a wise girl-chooser would look at the Units Zero—both parents, if available. The behavior, condition, and appearance of the source material of any girl under consideration will tell you a lot about what you will have twenty-five years hence. I attribute much of today's sky-high divorce rate to people's failure to choose wisely among families, and within families, among brothers or sisters.

It surprises me that others don't approach questions like this in an analytic manner, since people commonly subject car or dishwasher selections to extensive analysis, and indeed public analyses are available for many of those products in magazines. But nothing of the sort is offered for people, and when I suggest it, folks act offended. I guess that's the directness of Asperger's that people have trouble with.

Somehow, people often interpret my thoughts to mean that I don't much like my mate, or anything else. People say, "You're just skeptical of everything." That's not true. I do like my mate, more than I can say. And to a lesser extent, I like my car and I like my chain saw. But I also like to feel that I came to be associated with each as a result of intelligent consideration and choice, and not just chance.

It must be my logical consideration of a decision many see as purely intuitive or emotional that throws other people for a loop.

27

Married Life

The first time I heard about a person "turning" was when I was ten, and my grandmother told me that my uncle Bob was getting divorced. "Your aunt Marsha got on the Pill, and she just turned!" said Carolyn, in a whisper, as if she were scared.

Great-grandpa Dandy had told me how wild animals and dogs could turn, but I had never thought of Aunt Marsha that way. Dandy had an old double-barrel shotgun under his seat in case he ran across a turned animal. *Will she come around here, and would Dandy shoot her?* I was embarrassed to ask, because I was sure everyone except me knew what to do when a person turned. And from the knowing nod my grandfather gave, they all seemed to know about the Pill, too. I resolved not to take any more pills myself.

I didn't see Marsha again for a long time. By the time I did, she must have calmed down, because she didn't attack. She must have turned back. Dogs do that. One minute they snap at you, and ten minutes later they come up and wag their tails as if nothing happened.

A few years later, Uncle Bob decided to get married again. At the wedding, I said the first thing that came to mind, in typical Aspergian fashion: "Uncle Bob, how many times do you have to get married before you stay married?" I don't remember what he said, but I remember the result: I wasn't invited to his next wedding. That was to my aunt Relda, and that was the one that finally took.

When my father got married the second time, he didn't invite me, either. Maybe he was afraid of what I'd say, too. In any case, he thrived for over twenty years with his second wife. That marriage lasted until he got a skin infection, at which point the liver damage from years of drinking and experimental medication caught up to him, and he died.

Myself, I've had to get married twice for it to stick. I've pondered the reasons the second marriage has been more successful than the first, and for the sake of other Aspergians with relationship troubles, I will share the things she does that have kept us together:

First, she watches me very carefully. She has learned to tell if I am sad, or anxious, or worried. Some people say I never smile and I don't have many facial expressions, but somehow she can get me to smile, and she can read what little expressions I may have. And she usually knows what to say or do to make me feel better. Or make me feel worse, which happens occasionally, when she's turned.

She always shows interest in me, and she seems to believe in me without reservation. When I tell her I'm going to do something, she always thinks I will succeed. I am sure that her confidence in me increases the odds for my success. When I succeed at something, I come home and tell her.

"I always knew you could do it," she will say. "That's why I married you."

I really don't know how she could possibly "always know" I could do something I never did before unless it was so trivial anyone could do it, but that's what she says.

I never had a mate who thought I was going to fail, but I have pondered the possibility that such mates may exist. And I am sure my present situation is better.

Second, she watches what people say and do around me, and explains things I miss. Even today, I miss conversational nuances that are a typical component of conversation between "normal" people. Humor and sarcasm often go right over my head. There are times when a person says something they expect me to laugh at and I just stand there. There are times when people say things that are meant to be nasty, and I completely miss their meaning. She points those things out, gently, and I try to learn from what I missed. I miss less and less with every passing year.

Third, she is patient when I ask the same questions over and over. For example, at noon most days I phone her and say, "Woof! Do you like your mate?"

"Yes, I like you," she reassures me.

An hour later, I must have forgotten the last call because I call again and say, "Woof! Do you like your mate?"

"Yes, I still like you," she says.

This may go on four or five times in the course of a day. By the fifth time, she might say, "No, I don't like you anymore," but by then I know she is just teasing. She really does like me. So I feel safe.

I have no idea why I ask the same thing over and over, but I do. If I am made to stop, I often become very anxious.

Fourth, she pets me. My childhood experience petting Chuckie didn't work out too well, and that one bad memory pretty much cured me of petting other people later on. Luckily, Martha did not have an experience like that earlier in life. So, even though things did not work out for me being a pettor (one who pets), I thrive as a pettee (one who gets petted).

When Martha first met me, I was anxious and jumpy. I was always tapping my foot, rocking, or exhibiting some other behavioral aberration. Of course, now we know that's just normal Aspergian behavior, but back then other people thought it was weird, so of course I did, too.

One day, for some reason, she decided to try petting my arm, and I immediately stopped rocking and fidgeting. The result was so dramatic, she never stopped. It didn't take long for me to realize the calming effect, too. I like being petted and scratched.

"Can you pet me?" I say when I sit next to her.

I also say, while tilting my head, "Scratch my fur." I have observed dogs tilting their heads like this, and it often works for them. She will scratch my head or rub my ears. Sometimes she rubs my forehead or my shoulders. And she scratches my back.

"Scratch lightly, with claw tips," I say. Light scratching with somewhat sharp nails is best. For a while, I worried that the fur scratching would cause all my hair to fall out, and that the ear rubbing would give me floppy ears, like a beagle. But that didn't happen. I just got calmer. I believe it calms her, too. Psychologists have done studies of people petting animals. They've proven it has a calming effect on the people, lowering their heart rate and blood pressure. I wonder why they haven't done studies of people petting people. Normal people haven't caught on to the benefits.

While I went through life as a pettee, I watched the dogs and cats around me, and I realized something: The pets that get petted the most have the thickest fur. Petting does not make your fur fall out. I am now sure of that. And you will never see a well-petted cat with floppy ears, either. The dogs with floppy ears all started out that way.

And the final thing is, we sleep in piles.

When I was little, I used to like hiding in small spaces. I don't do that so much anymore, but I can still become unsettled lying down by myself on a bed. If I lie down by myself, I will pile pillows on top of me, but the best situation by far is to have my mate lie down, too, and pile herself up against me.

Every night, when we go to bed, she puts an arm or a leg on me, or lies up against me until I fall asleep.

If she doesn't, I complain.

"Come on," I say. "Put a paw on your mate!"

"Can you pet me?"

"Can you scratch my fur?"

I am always calmer and more relaxed in a pile, being petted. Nowadays, for the first time, I fall asleep quickly and I seldom have bad dreams.

If I wake up, she puts a paw on me and I go back to sleep. I put a paw on her, too. Sometimes I wake in the night, and find we have rolled apart. We'll be sleeping on our sides, facing in opposite directions. I'll slide over until our backs are touching, and I'll slide my bent legs back toward her. She'll awaken enough to reach her own foot over, and our feet will touch. I fall back asleep, content and warm.

I feel safe sleeping in a pile. I'm not sure why that would be, since I am the bigger and stronger one, but it's true. Ever since I was a child, I knew that lying under a pile of pillows was a lot better than just lying on top of the bed. Sleeping in a pile is a lot better than that, though. It's the best of all.

I like married life a lot.

28

Winning at Basketball

I never did well at sports as a kid, and I was never a sports fan. A childhood of being the last one picked and the first one tossed hadn't left me with very fond feelings about school sports. I came to be a fan rather late in life, and in a somewhat circuitous fashion.

In 2003, my son was about to enter high school. Since Little Bear and I had gotten divorced, and I had gotten remarried, Cubby had lived half the time with us in Chicopee, and half the time with his mom in South Hadley. We always chose one school for him to attend, and until then he'd been in South Hadley. But the school there wasn't very good, and we began searching for alternatives. We looked at private schools, but they were very expensive. There were Internet sites that ranked school districts, and the top ones in our area were Longmeadow, Wilbraham, and . . . Amherst. South Hadley and Chicopee were right next to one another, at the bottom.

With some trepidation, Unit Two and I decided to look at Amherst, where I had grown up thirty years before. Although my family had lived in the tiny town of Shutesbury, it was part of the Amherst school district, and Amherst was where I had gone to school, where I'd hung out, and where I had met Cubby's mother.

I called Jim Lumley, an Amherst Realtor who'd helped my parents years ago. He drove a Land Rover, and I saw him whenever it broke. He brought a list of Amherst homes down to my office right away, and we set out that afternoon to check them out.

As we drove around Amherst looking at houses, I began to feel that it was where I belonged.

It's true that Amherst was the setting for some of the worst times of my life. Other kids hassled me. The school system wanted me gone. The police wanted me in jail. And my parents had fallen completely to pieces. All right there, in Amherst.

Even in my most Aspergian days, I knew I had many of the qualities needed to be popular. I was smart. I was gentle. I was funny. I even looked pretty normal, in a geeky sort of way. But my behavioral oddities had hidden those qualities from others, and had caused me to hide myself in shame. Everywhere I'd lived, until now, I had carried the burden of Asperger's with me.

When Unit Two, Cubby, and I moved out of Chicopee, I left that burden behind.

So why would I return? Because I'd finally have the chance to turn a failure into a success. Moving to Amherst with my new knowledge of Asperger's would give me a chance to start my life over again. A new me, in a new house, in a new town.

Jack would start high school in Amherst, just as I had. But unlike me, he was going to pass.

The move was a smashing success. The bad people from my youth had all vanished. The teachers who wanted me gone had long since retired. Most of today's police force hadn't even been born when I had moved away in the 1970s.

More important, people I had hardly seen in thirty years welcomed me with open arms. *Why are they doing this?* I wondered. Then I understood. They welcomed me because I didn't do anything to drive them away. I had learned how to be friendly.

It was remarkably simple, but it had taken so, so long to figure out.

My friend Paul Zahradnik had dropped out of school the same year I had, and now lived just half a mile away. Thirty years later, he was an accomplished metal sculptor and real estate developer living at the end of a quarter-mile driveway. Gordy, the long-haired kid who had worked in the junkyard, lived in a beautiful home across the road. He still worked in the junkyard, but the yard had grown by twenty acres, and now he *owned* it. What a long way we had all come.

Like me, my brother had left home as soon as he could. He had stayed far away, working at advertising jobs in Boston, New York, Chicago, and San Francisco. I hardly ever saw him in those years. When he wrote his first book, *Sellevision,* he decided to get back in touch with his family up here. I helped him find a small house in Northampton, and he started coming up here on weekends. He stopped drinking and doing drugs, and he met Dennis. His life started to turn around.

As soon as he heard I was moving to Amherst, my brother said, "Is there another building lot over there? Dennis and I can build a house next to you!" And they did. We built new homes next to each other, on a little cul-de-sac. His is gay and frilly, and mine is Aspergian and functional. I am sure mine is better engineered, but he doesn't care. His is prettier. Even though the plumbing fell apart and left him ankle deep in water right before Christmas that first year.

When he walks his weirdly misnamed French bulldogs past my house, Cubby sets off a homemade bomb in the yard, and the roar and smoke tell him he's finally home. In the winter, when it snows, I clear the street with our father's farm tractor. And when his house floods, I rescue his furniture with my Land Rover and trailer and dry it in my garage.

Who would have guessed? After all those years, the success of my brother's book *Running with Scissors* made me feel good about my condition and proud of who I was. And it brought us back together, in the town where we'd started, so long ago.

Appearing as a character in my brother's books taught me something about myself. For most of my life, my history as an

abused child with what I saw as a personality defect was shameful
and embarrassing. Being a failure and a high school dropout was
humiliating, no matter how well I subsequently did. I lied about my
age, my education, and my upbringing for years because the truth
was just too horrible to reveal. His book, and people's remarkable
acceptance of us as we are, changed all that. I was finally free.

When I returned to Amherst, everywhere I went it seemed I
recognized someone. And I recognized the places. But the bad
associations from my childhood were gone.

"You have to come to a UMass basketball game," Paul and
Gordy said one day. I had never been to a college basketball game
in my life, but I somewhat reluctantly tagged along.

"Before the game, there's a reception upstairs. Come up with
us," Paul said.

There were probably a hundred people in the room when I
walked in. Thirty years earlier, that crowd would have terrified
me, and I would not have known what to say. I would have hidden
in the corner like a trapped animal, waiting to escape.

But now, with my knowledge of Asperger's and my new confidence, nothing bad happened. I wasn't scared and I didn't hide.
And something remarkable occurred: People liked me. People
came up to me, shook my hand, and made me feel welcome. Just a
little bit of knowledge of what to say and how to act made all the
difference in the world.

It was incredible! I found myself making friends everywhere I
went, and to my amazement, they looked out for me. For
example, my friend Dave said, "Let's get seats together!" A perfectly ordinary suggestion, but it was something I had never done
before. I would hear the referee's whistle, and Dave would lean
over from his seat next to me to explain what had happened. Even
if I was ignorant, the games were fun. And so were the people.
They all knew more about basketball than me, but no one cared.

Not only did I make friends everywhere I went, but nothing
bad seemed to happen. No one called me a Monkey Face. No one

threatened me. No one threw me out. The last time I had been here, no one wanted me on their team. Now, it seemed everyone did.

Even my lifelong feeling that I was a fraud began to vanish. At a party at the coach's house, one of the athletic department staffers sat down with me.

"You know, I dropped out of school, too," he said.

I didn't know what to say. I wondered how he knew I had dropped out of school. I realized he must have taken the time to ask someone else about me.

"You're as much a part of this school as any other alumnus," he continued. "You're always welcome here."

I almost cried.

I began attending all the games. Even though I was never a "real" student, I had acquired most of my education in those buildings. And it felt good to be back, among friends, in a place that felt like home.

I didn't have to know everything. Other people could tell me the answers. I didn't have to notice everything. My friends would look out for me. Suddenly, I had a revelation: *This is what life is like for normal people.*

I joined the UMass Athletic Association, and began supporting the school. *My* school. The team picked up speed. With me on board, the team hired a new coach, and headed to the play-offs for the first time in years. My past was finally behind me. Whatever happened with our basketball team, I knew that I had won.

29

My Life as a Train

I have always liked trains.

One day when he was about six, Cubby and I drove to the Conrail freight yard in West Springfield. The tires crunched with a pop-popping sound as we rolled over the gray stone that covered the yard and filled the space between the train tracks. My father had taken me to see the trains when I was little, and thirty years later here I was, doing the same thing with my own son. My father let me drive a train when I was five, at the museum in Philadelphia. I would soon do the same with Cubby.

I guess a fascination with trains runs in my family. When my father was little, his grandfather took him to watch the steam engines passing his drugstore, back in Chickamauga, Georgia. And here we were, over fifty years later, doing the same thing up here in Massachusetts.

Cubby looked out the window, scanning the lines of boxcars. He was a fifty-pound kid, bouncy, with a blue striped train conductor's cap on his head. If he were a dog, he would have been wagging his tail.

We had driven forty-five minutes to see trains, and we were ready for action. We clumped across a few lines of track and parked next to the yardmaster's shack, an old wood building that had faded to the same shade of gray as the stone ballast on the ground. The train dispatcher was watching us through the dirty plate-glass windows, and we waved. Oily smoke curled from a rusty pipe chimney. Everything was drab and dirty because it was dusted with years of soot from the diesel engines in the locomotives, which at that time ran twenty-four hours a day, 365 days a year.

This train yard has been there since the days of steam engines, fifty years ago, so even before the soot from the diesel engines there was a pretty thick layer of coal dust. Cubby likes being clean, so it's good he didn't know any of that. When he got bigger, he would develop the same compulsive hand-washing habit as his grandfather and his uncle, but even then he hated getting grease on his clothes or on himself. I tried to keep him out of the worst of the dirt.

"Look, Dad—F types!" Cubby shouted as he pointed to two long silver FP40 locomotives on the far side of the yard. He'd picked out an Amtrak passenger train that stood out among the freight cars filling the yard. It's unusual to see Amtrak trains idling among the trash and squalor of a freight yard.

We walked over to check it out. As I was about to cross a few lines of tracks where fifty old boxcars were quietly rusting away, Cubby shouted, "Stop!" At six years of age, Cubby already knew to stop and look carefully before crossing the tracks. After watching the parked train cars for the slightest sign of movement, we quickly jumped over the tracks. We stepped over some crack vials left by last night's visitors.

"Look Cubby, do drugs, lose your mind, and get run over by a train," I said.

"How come there aren't any pieces of people on the tracks?" he asked.

"Maybe they got dragged farther into the yard."

Cubby lost interest in drug addicts as we approached the FP40 locomotives, which rumbled at idle and hissed occasionally as excess air popped the safety valves.

Why were we there? Because Aspergians are driven to learn all they can about subjects that interest them, and one of my favorite subjects has always been transportation machinery. When I was learning to read, my favorite topics in the encyclopedia were trains, ships, and airplanes. And my favorite books for a time were *High Iron: A Book of Trains* and *Automotive Technology.*

As we walked around the engines, Cubby spotted a little pile of beach sand in front of the wheels on the front locomotive. He asked what it was. "It's sand from the train engine's sandbox," I said. Cubby was skeptical. He was used to being tricked. He had a sandbox at home, one that he and I had built. But trains should not need sandboxes. His ears twitched.

We moved closer.

"Look Cubby, that's the sand pipe, and that's the box where the sand is stored on the engine. The train engineer pushes a button to dump sand on the wheels when his wheels are slipping. Trains shovel sand in front of their wheels to get traction."

I felt comforted knowing this exposure to the practical application of technology at an early age would benefit Cubby for the rest of his life. Especially with respect to understanding traction issues. As I pointed out, "Cars use sanders, too." Cubby would nod sagely at tidbits of knowledge like that. Later, when he thought I wasn't looking, I would catch him explaining traction to the other little animals at his school.

I felt very proud of him at times like that. A little engineer.

As Cubby grew bigger, so did the engines. Conrail was making a change from the older General Motors locomotives with DC traction motors to the newest GE units with AC traction. On later visits, I would explain the advantages of AC traction motors to Cubby, and I even showed him the inside of one of the new cabs with its sophisticated control panels. The big new engines were impressive to watch, especially pulling heavy loads. After watching the trains in the yard, we decided to go out and see them on the road. And I knew just the place.

One spring day, we drove to Middlefield, where the railroad crosses a pass in the Berkshires on the way to Albany, New York. We turned off the highway and followed a country road up into the mountains until we passed over the railroad. Shortly after, we turned in to a wooded road that ran about a mile to the tracks.

Up there, the air was fresh and clear. The sky was a brilliant blue, a shade you never saw in the city. Water was running in a little waterfall down the rock face where the railroad line had been blasted through the mountainside. The tracks hugged the side of the mountain, with a drop of at least a hundred feet into the Westfield River on the other side. There were two tracks side by side, with a service road next to them. We walked up the service road and waited for a train.

"Look, Dad!" Cubby threw rocks and watched them hit the water far below. He looked around for wildlife. "Think we'll see any bears?" Cubby sounded hopeful. "You can get a gun and I'll shoot it. Mom will skin it and we'll eat it. Let's find a bear, Dad." Cubby was bouncing up and down at the thought of catching a bear for dinner.

But we didn't see any bears.

Pretty soon we heard the rumble of an approaching train. Over the next few minutes, the noise got louder until the ground began to shake. Cubby and I moved closer to the edge, away from the tracks. The tracks began to sing and we saw the headlights come around the bend. Even from a few hundred feet, we could feel the engines as they struggled to pull the train up the hill. By the time they reached us, they were moving at a brisk walk, which was all the speed 15,000 horsepower could muster going up that hill. They struggled past us as we stood on the gravel road and watched.

"Sanders, Dad!" Cubby shouted as the second of five engines went past. Sure enough, the sand pipes were pouring sand in front of the wheels to help the train get a grip. Cubby was proud of himself for picking up that detail. Cubby waved and the engineer tooted his horn.

Five engines passed us, then 133 cars. Cubby counted them all. And all of a sudden it was quiet again. After a moment, we turned and walked back down the hill.

"How can anyone get run over by a train out here?" Cubby asked. "We could hear him coming for a long time. You'd have to be deaf to miss that."

And then, without any warning, a train appeared behind us. Rolling fast, down the hill. Going the other way, on the other set of tracks. Silently. It came up on us so quickly that the startled engineer didn't even have time to blow the horn till he was fifty feet beyond us. As the engines passed, we jumped a little farther out of the way, and I pointed to the air shimmering in waves over the engines.

"Those are his dynamic brakes," I explained. "They use the electric motors on the wheels as generators, and the generators are feeding huge heating grids on top of the engines. So they are using the motors as brakes, converting the energy of the train into heat. The locomotives don't make any noise, because their engines are idling."

Cubby bobbed his head a bit as he soaked up that idea. The train continued to roll past in near silence, picking up speed as it went.

Cubby didn't ask how people got run over by trains again.

As we walked back to our Land Rover, we picked up two old railroad spikes to add to our considerable collection of railroad memorabilia. I'd been picking up pieces beside train tracks since finding those telegraph insulators with Little Bear, fifteen years before, and now Cubby was continuing the tradition.

Don't all the dads take their kids to see trains? I wondered. I guess not, judging from the crazy looks I've gotten from other parents. Mothers would say things like "How can you take a child into a train yard? He could get killed!" Well, nothing killed us. Nothing even came close. Cubby and I were well aware of the enormous weight of these trains. I showed Cubby how objects can trail from the sides of moving trains, and we made sure to stay ten feet back whenever a train went by so we didn't get hit by any loose steel strapping.

All those visits to train yards with Cubby probably had at least something to do with my favorite book as a child, *The Little Engine That Could*. The book had a yellow cover, with a bright blue loco-motive driving across the page, and when I was two, I couldn't hear it often enough.

"Choo choo!" was what I said when I wanted to hear the story.

My mother read it to me, over and over. I would huff and puff and imagine myself as a little steam engine. The harder I puffed, the more convinced I became. (A few years later, I became lost in the fantasy that I was a pair of windshield wipers. But at the time, I was in my steam engine phase.)

In the book, it was only a steep hill the train had to climb. But in my two-year-old brain, it was a giant mountain—bigger than anything I had ever seen. The engines chanted to themselves as they slowly climbed the hill.

"I-think-I-can! I-think-I-can! I-think-I-can! I-think-I-can!"

And I would chant along with them. I would bounce, too, with the effort of pulling that train. Today, I know that head bobbing and rocking back and forth and bouncing up and down—things I still do today—are characteristic of people with autism or As-perger's. But that's where it started, with me believing I was a steam engine, pulling those cars up the mountain. Bobbing up and down. And bouncing.

Eventually, we got to the top, that train and me. As we coasted down the other side, I grinned happily and bounced and said, *"I-thought-I-could! I-thought-I-could! I-thought-I-could! I-thought-I-could!"*

Somehow, I always remembered that refrain as I grew older. It was very reassuring. But while I kept telling myself I was going to make it, I would also hear competing voices, at times quite loud and forceful. They were hard to ignore.

You're no good.
You failed at school, and you'll fail at this.
You're just a fuckup.
It will never work.
You can't do that.
You belong in prison!

I'm sure many kids hear voices like that as they struggle to grow up and make it on their own. And some kids give in and quit. I know that because I see those children every day. You can see them, too, sleeping in cardboard boxes in any city. I tried sleeping in boxes and Dumpsters, back when I was seventeen. I didn't like it. And I resolved never to do it again.

All the bad things that have happened to me in my life have simply increased my resolve to overcome the obstacles that are thrown in my path. And I've done that with reasonable success so far.

But those voices were still there. And as I got older, they began to emanate from other people, too. The message was the same.

"You're so anxious and worried! You should try antidepressants!"

"John, you need to relax. Sit down and have a drink!"

"You know, smoking pot calms you down. You should try it. You might not be so hyper all the time."

I don't know why, but I never gave in to the voices. Many times, quitting would have been easier than going on, but I never did. And I never turned to antidepressants or liquor or pot or anything else. I just worked harder. I always figured I'd be better off solving a problem as opposed to taking medication to forget I had a problem.

I am sure antidepressants, drugs, and liquor have their place. But so far, that place is in others, not me.

When I heard the voices as a child, I would say to myself, *I think I can! I think I can! I think I can!* As an adult, my vocabulary and my world have expanded. Now *I think I can* is reinforced by *I did it before.* But the negative voices are smoother and more sophisticated, too. Now, when I hear those voices, I tell myself:

All the other guitars worked; this one will, too.

The other jobs came out fine; this one will, too.

I am sure I can walk up this mountain.

I think I can drive across that river.

And so far, with some notable exceptions, I have.

Epilogue

When KISS was on tour, we'd always come out and do one last song, an encore. This is the encore for *Look Me in the Eye*—the story of how I made peace with my parents during the writing of this book.

My father had been in precarious health for years, with psoriasis, arthritis, diabetes, and a weak heart. But in the late summer of 2004, a spider tipped the balance. A brown recluse spider. Brown recluses live in woodpiles, sheds, and attics—sometimes even in shoes—and seldom bite unless cornered. We think my father was chopping wood when he was bitten. In any case, a few days after he was bitten, his finger swelled up and began to hurt terribly and my stepmother, Judy, drove him to the emergency room.

I had never heard of a brown recluse until then so I went home and researched them. They are only the size of a quarter, and most people don't even notice when they're bitten. Still, the bite of the brown recluse can be worse than the bite of a rattlesnake. The skin around my father's bite turned black and a hole appeared, right down to the bone.

Brown recluse bites are rare in New England. Of the four hundred bites logged in one database, only nine were in Massachusetts.

Most were in the South. It was my father's bad luck to be one of those nine in his weakened state.

His finger looked awful where he'd been bitten, and you could smell the sweet odor of gangrene. I thought they should cut his finger off right away to save him, but the doctor insisted the finger was still alive, so they held off. My father seemed to hold his own with the IV antibiotics, but he remained in a lot of pain. I wondered how long he'd be in the hospital.

When he wasn't in the hospital, my father and Judy lived in a 1970s contemporary house that they'd added on to and made their own over the twenty years they had lived there. The main room had a cathedral ceiling and a woodstove in the corner. The stove burned wood my father and Judy cut together on the property. Bears and raccoons came up onto the deck, and the snow drifted higher than my head in a cold winter.

They'd moved there after getting married, each for the second time. My father had never been especially sociable—he may have even had a bit of Asperger's himself—so a home in the woods suited him. He spent his days outdoors, puttering around the property. He had grown up on a farm in Georgia and he'd always wanted a tractor of his own. That summer, he had taken delivery of a brand-new John Deere 4510 with a cab and a front-end loader. Now, he was too sick to drive it, but he'd be able to look at it through the window while he waited to get stronger.

I lived about an hour away, but my father seldom called me. The only days I could count on his calling were my birthday and Christmas. And after my son was born, I'd hear from my father on Cubby's birthday, too. Any other time I wanted to talk to him, I had to make the call. And even then he only came to the phone about half the time. Yet he always enjoyed seeing us whenever we went there. I never figured it out. Why didn't he call?

By November, my father was back home, still weak but hoping to get better. Although he was pretty much bedridden, my stepmother got him into the car and brought him to our house for

Thanksgiving dinner. We were all together—me, my mate, Cubby, my father and Judy, and my brother and his partner, Dennis. We even had Martha's sister, Unit Three, and her mate, Three-B. Everyone looks happy in the photos I took that day.

At nine o'clock on New Year's Eve, I got another call. "Your father was wandering around and he fell down the stairs to the garage. The ambulance is coming for him now," Judy said. This time she sounded scared.

It turned out to be a pretty bad fall. He'd broken his back and his hip. He was lucky he hadn't been paralyzed. He survived an operation to repair the break and was put in a cast to keep him still. Once again he was in a lot of pain. After a couple of weeks in the hospital, he went to a nursing home to recover. They told him he had to be able to climb two flights of stairs and walk two hundred feet before they would let him out. He was determined to succeed. But it was hard. We went to see him in late January and he looked as if he had a basketball in his stomach. Judy said he was retaining fluids because of trouble with his liver. Martha felt sick, because her mother had died of cancer the year before and that's how her stomach had looked. It was not right, not right at all.

They let him go home on February 25. He was able to walk up the stairs and get around with the help of his walker. It was going to be a long road, but it seemed as if he was going to get better.

A week later, we went to see him. He could barely sit up. His stomach was swollen up like a beach ball, and his scrotum was like a grapefruit. He did not belong at home. While I was there, he had to go to the bathroom. Judy and I helped him stand, and he moved the five feet in his walker at a glacial pace. He said, "John Elder, don't let me fall. I'm so scared of falling." At that moment, he was once again a small terrified child. My confidence in his recovery was shaken to the core.

A few days passed. The swelling in his stomach worsened. His liver had been damaged by years of drinking, then by all the medicine he'd taken for his psoriasis and his arthritis.

On Monday evening, Judy called and said my father was being taken to the hospital again. Somehow, I knew this was going to be different from all the other trips to the hospital. I realized he was dying. I rounded up Martha and Cubby and headed for the hospital. On the way there, I was angry because I could not remember a single good time we had shared when I was young.

When we arrived, he was very weak but lucid. He seemed glad to see us. I sat there for quite a while thinking that asking him for better memories would be an admission of his impending death. Finally, I did it.

"Can you tell me about any fun times we had when I was small?" I asked.

I waited for the answer, terrified by the prospect that there might not have been any fun times. What would I do then?

But he began to speak. "When you were five," he said, "I'd take you to the museum in Philadelphia. They had a big model train layout, and you loved to watch it." And he turned to my son and said, "One day your dad asked the man in the booth if he could drive the train. And the man said yes. Your dad climbed into the booth with him and he drove those trains all over the board with a big smile on his face."

I had forgotten about those trains, but when my father told Cubby, I remembered it like it was yesterday. I said, "After I drove the model trains, your grandpa took me to another part of the museum where they had two real locomotives."

"Baldwins," my father piped up. "The locomotives were made by Baldwin Locomotive Works in Philadelphia." I was shocked that he remembered. A few years before, I had read a history of the Baldwin Works but I had no idea my father knew about it.

As he told his stories, things I had forgotten for almost fifty years suddenly came into focus, clear as day. I remembered the spring I learned to ride a two-wheel bike on the paved walkways outside the Cathedral of Learning in Pittsburgh. I never used training wheels. I went straight from a toy fire engine and a trike to a big kid's two-wheeler, and I didn't crash or fall off. I was really proud of myself.

My father said, "I got you a Rollfast bike, just like I had as a kid. Yours was a Space Racer, with a red gas tank and a coaster brake." My father had a black Raleigh, an English Racer, with three speeds. We rode them together. When I outgrew the Rollfast, he gave me the Raleigh. He'd sort of given up riding bicycles by then.

I could not help sobbing as he talked.

"Do you remember Valley Forge?" he said.

I remembered running across the fields of Valley Forge national park, chasing the kite he made me. I remembered both of us running in the sun, my mother watching from the shade, until I fell and tangled the string around my ankle. To this day, I have a scar there.

There had been fun times, after all. When we left that day, he could see I was sad. He smiled and patted me on the head and said not to worry about him. He said he would be okay, but inside I knew he wouldn't. I wished I were small again.

From that time until the end, I visited him almost every day. He got weaker and weaker, until one day he said, "John Elder, I'm dying."

"I know. It's sad," I said. "Where do you think you're going to go?"

"It's a mystery," he said. "No one knows."

"Are you scared?"

"No, not really."

Judy made plans to move him back to Buckland the following Tuesday so he could die at home.

My father said, "Will you be okay?" I said I'd be sad but I'd be okay. He said, "Will you look after Judy? She's been really good to me." I said I would. He asked if I'd help Judy with the house. I said I would. He asked about his tractor. I asked if he'd like me to get his tractor out for him to see one last time. He said he'd like that.

Then I sat for a couple hours and talked with him, my mother, and Judy. He became tired and I left for home, promising to return that night. I was very sad. I stopped at my brother's and told him the end was near.

Afterward, I cried, and I wondered why dying people asked me to look after what was left. My great-grandfather Dandy had asked me to take care of the farm. My grandfather Jack had asked me to take care of Carolyn and to take care of the fields and the trees his father, Dandy, had planted. Well, it's been more than twenty years, and those things are all gone now. Carolyn died, and the house burned, and the trees and fields are all gone. But I guess I did what I could. I returned just about every month to Lawrenceville, from the time my grandfather died until my grandmother moved away. Judy said it's hard, being the oldest child. She's an oldest child, too.

Monday, I went to work. A few hours later, Judy called. "They're going to bring your dad home today. He's getting weaker. We can't wait till Tuesday."

It was time to move the tractor. I gathered up my tools, my shovels, and my winch cables. There was no telling how deep it would be buried after the winter snows. I went by the school and picked up Cubby. We would move the tractor together.

It was spring in Amherst, but it was still winter in Buckland. The snow was waist deep in the field, and the tractor was sitting a hundred feet up the hill next to the shed. The bucket on the front of it was not even visible. Neither were the front tires. Still, the sun was shining and the tractor started right up. I put it in gear, and it shook but didn't move. I tried to lift the bucket but it was frozen to the ground. I rocked it and twisted it, and all of a sudden it came off the ground with a bang, filled with a foot of ice.

"Let's dig it out, Dad!"

Cubby and I dug around the wheels until the tractor emerged from the snow. We dug the snow away from the front and the back to give it room to move. I rocked the gears but it didn't move.

We dug some more. We were sweating even though it was thirty-five degrees outside. As we shoveled around the back, the drawbars emerged from the snow. The arms were frozen right into the ground. Kicking them didn't do anything, but a pull on the hydraulic lever in the tractor broke them free. Now the tractor moved. A whole foot!

"Dad, look! The front tire is flat!" Cubby was right.

"Damn, Cubby, how are we going to get a three-wheel tractor over a seven-foot snowbank and into the driveway?"

Cubby said, "Let's winch it."

Our Land Rover had a good winch on the front. Cubby waded through the snow to get to the Rover. He angled it in the driveway so it was pointing out into the field.

"Here's the cable, Dad." Cubby had dragged the line through the snow so I could hook it to the tractor.

Cubby waded back to the Land Rover and started the winch. I got in the tractor, put it in four-wheel drive, and locked the differential. That tractor rolled right through the enormous snowbank and into the driveway.

When the tractor came out of the snow, Cubbie saw it first. "Dad, look! The front tire is gone!" There was nothing but a bare steel rim. The struggle to get out had torn the tire right off the rim.

We fished the tire out of the snow and levered it back onto the rim with two big bars. We installed a tube and got that tractor back on all four feet within thirty minutes. Then we set to work moving the snow to make room for all the cars and the ambulance. That tractor could really dig, and I was sorry my father would never get the chance to see it run.

The sound of the diesel engine, the smell, and the activity were a good distraction for us. I showed Cubby how to run the loader and he shared the snow moving with me. A picture I took that day shows him with a big grin, lifting a huge bucket of snow and dropping it down the hillside. We got the snow moved, and when we were done we parked the tractor right by the stairs and sat down to wait.

The ambulance arrived and the two attendants pulled my father out the back. He smiled when he saw me, and he looked at the tractor. He couldn't talk much. I asked if he wanted to go over to it and he said no, he was cold. But he smiled again. Cubby and I helped carry my father into the house and then onto the bed. Finally, he was home. I stood for a while and held his hand.

My brother came up and he got some old photo albums and showed them to my father. But my father couldn't concentrate. He said he'd have to look at them later.

I gave him a hug, and I said I loved him. Very faintly, he said, "I love you, too." And that was the last time I saw him. He died quietly at 2:30 in the afternoon the next day, while I was at work. It was a sunny late winter day. I got up and went home. It was over. The tire went flat on the tractor the next day.

In place of my father, I have my memories. For so many years, I could not recall anything about him except the bad and the ugly. Now stories and memories that were lost to me for thirty years have taken on life. I hope they stay.

Other memories began to stir, too. Today, at fifty, I can feel my bare feet sting on the sharp white pebbles in the dirt driveway of my grandparents' house, and I can hear the crickets. I can smell that Georgia clay and my great-grandfather's pipe. I can hear the *twang* as I reach up to open the screen door on the front of the house, and I can feel the cold floor as I step onto the black-and-white checkered tiles.

It is these memories—a last gift from my father—that have made this book possible.

Although some memories were as vivid and real as today, others were spotty. So, in an attempt to get more answers, I spoke to my mother. I had been estranged from her for some time, but we began talking as I wrote this book.

At first, my mother had a hard time accepting that my memories could be different from her own and still be valid. She'd say, "You weren't in the back of that VW that trip!" And I'd say, "I was, too. I remember the sky!" We both learned something from that. My mother was troubled by some of what I'd written about her.

After we talked, I understood that I had made one or two errors in my portrayal of her, and I corrected them. In other cases, she and I have different memories, or we interpreted things differently, and she came to accept my version. I believe the process of writing this memoir gave me a better understanding of who she is and how mental illness affected her, and I know she gained a better understanding of me.

For much of her life, my mother dreamed of being a well-known author. She published a few works of poetry, but the larger work of memoir always eluded her. She had the skills and the stories, but her life got in the way. The mental illness that gave her experiences to write about also prevented her from capturing them on paper. Her stroke and partial paralysis made it hard for her to write, and hard to think. But she hasn't given up, and I am confident that her story will appear in bookstores one day soon, alongside her postcards and poetry.

There is no doubt that the storytelling skills people see in my brother and me were inherited from our mother. Whatever flaws our parents had, they were exceptionally intelligent, articulate, and creative.

It's a shame that my father died before my book was written. I hope he'd be proud if he read it now. I think he would, and so does his brother, my uncle Bob. I'm afraid my portrayal of him may be less forgiving than it might have been because he was not here to offer explanations that may have moderated some of my harshest descriptions.

With the insight gained from writing the book, I now believe my parents did the best they could under tough circumstances. They were both damaged as children, and my brother and I grew up damaged as a result. But damage is not always permanent, nor is it always passed down from one generation to the next. I'm okay today, and so is my brother. Cubby has never been whipped, and he has never known the rougher things my brother and I experienced. Hopefully, he will avoid those dark corners of life.

I've already heard Cubby tell little James about the dragons. He makes his own fireworks, and the math and computer programming he does is already beyond me. So as much as he'd deny it, Cubby is a lot like his dad.

It will take a few more years (I hope!), but I'm looking forward to the day when I can watch Cubby take his own son to the train yard to watch the locomotives.

Acknowledgments

I would like to thank all the people who made this book possible.

First are all the people that appear in my stories: my family, my friends, and even folks like Rug, who bought the porn for my high school teacher. Without them, there would be no book. Jim Boughton deserves special attention for being most unique.

I will always be grateful to my friend TR Rosenberg for telling me about my Asperger's. TR lives near me in Amherst, Massachusetts. He has a thriving practice working with troubled young adults, and you can visit his website at www.strongbridgeassociates.com.

I also particularly thank my brother and Cubby for encouraging me to write this book, and my wife, Martha, for supporting me. The Robison Service staff deserves recognition for holding the company together while I focused my energy on writing. I also appreciate the support of my other family members: Judy, Little Bear (Mary), Big Bob, Little Bob, Leigh, and Relda Robison, Unit One (Ellen) and Unit Three (Annie), Three-B (Magnus), and Dennis. I also mustn't forget Uncle Bubba (Wyman) Richter, his wife, Ann, and their kids, Leigh and Meredith. I thank the people who offered early encouragement and advice: my old friends Neil Fennessey and Leeann Every; my first listeners and then readers: Lois Hayes and her daughter Bekah, Alison Ozer, Claudia Hepner, and Jan Anderson; my friends who encouraged me: Bob Jeffway and his wife, Celeste, who spent hours reliving old times with me; Jim Lumley, Gordon Palley, Paul Zahradnik, David Rifken, Chris Cava, Charles Burke, Matt Dufresne, and Gene Cassidy; my friend Rick Colson, who took the author photos; my literary agent, Christopher Schelling; and Steve Ross, Rachel Klayman, and the team at Crown that worked so hard to make the book a reality. For the British edition of *Look Me in the Eye*, I want to extend my thanks to Charlotte Cole and the staff at Ebury for publishing my book in my ancestral home.

Reading and Resources

I ENCOURAGE READERS who want to know more about some of the companies, bands, and individuals in this book to read about them online. Fat, my first band, has a small online presence at www.mainstrecords.com/fat. If you'd like to learn about the first big sound company I worked for, check out the history of Pink Floyd and their sound company, which was called Britannia Row, or Britro, at www.pinkfloyd-co.com. The equipment I worked on was built for Pink Floyd's sound company, and other sound companies, but used on many tours, including Roxy Music, Sha Na Na, Blondie, Talking Heads, April Wine, Black Sabbath, Phoebe Snow, Dan Hill, Meat Loaf, Iron Maiden, Toby Beau, Nantucket, Cheap Trick, and others.

There is a wealth of information online on KISS and what it was like on tour. In particular, I'd suggest reading about the Alive II, Return of KISS, Dynasty, and Unmasked shows. Some of the websites I like are www.kissfanshop.de, www.kissasylum.com, www.kissfaq.com/tours/tours.html, and en.wikipedia.org/wiki/Kiss_timeline. There are other articles elsewhere in Wikipedia, and each of the band members is in the www.imdb.com database. There are also many books about KISS, including works by band members, crew, and fans. If you look closely, you can find me in the group photos that appear in books from that period. One that I particularly like is *KISS and Sell,* by Chris Lendt, our business manager in those years.

KISS was a very big deal for many people, and some of them gather annually for a KISS convention—usually in New York or New Jersey—where they swap stories and trade memorabilia. For 2007, the convention site is online at www.starzcentral.com/kissexpo. After leaving KISS, guitarist Ace Frehley continued to play my instruments in his own band, Frehley's Comet. My light guitar and smoking guitar were key parts of his act for many years.

Milton Bradley was a pioneer in electronic games in the late 1970s. The products I worked on were Microvision, Super Simon, Big Trak, Milton, Omni, and the stillborn Game Computer. I also worked on speech recognition and sound effects for several games that never made it to market. In fact, that was one of my biggest frustrations: I'd work hard on something, only to have management cancel it at the last minute. I'll bet 90 percent of our R&D group's work ended up on the scrap heap. As an interesting aside, the computer we used to develop speech chips was a VAX, from Digital Equipment Corporation. The VAX was Data General's competition in Tracy Kidder's wonderful book *The Soul of a New Machine.* I worked on the design of custom integrated circuits in conjunction with General Instrument and Texas Instruments, both of whom supplied chips to MB.

Bob Jeffway, the engineer who appears in some of my stories, is online at www.jeffway.com. He went on to be a highly success-ful inventor of toys and games for many different companies. As a Milton Bradley staffer, he worked on many of the same games I was assigned to, and he also played a role in Dark Tower, Simon, and the Star Trek Phaser Guns. Later, as an independent game inventor, he helped create Mattel's Diva Starz and Cabbage Patch Kids Kick 'n Splash toys, and Milton Bradley's Whac-A-Mole electronic games. All the games we worked on can be researched online, and they still pop up for sale on eBay. But they're not cheap anymore! Collectors are paying upwards of ten times the original price for working editions of these old games, and it looks like prices will keep on rising.

My automobile business, JE Robison Service, has been in business in Springfield, Massachusetts, for almost twenty years. We specialize in BMW, Bentley, Jaguar, Land Rover, Mercedes-Benz, and Rolls-Royce vehicles. The company started out fixing cars in a two-bay garage, but we've expanded into a multibuilding complex where we do major repair, overhaul, customization, and restoration work. The company has grown from two to twelve employees in that time, and we now take in work from all over the eastern United States. We're online at www.robisonservice.com.

Our car projects often appear in enthusiast magazines. Sometimes—as in the February 2007 edition of *Land Rover Monthly*—we even make their covers. My pictures and articles appear in *Land Rover Lifestyle, Rover News,* and other car magazines.

I have been very fortunate to have achieved my childhood career goals not just once, but three times. I guess that means three things: I picked attainable goals, I persevered, and I was lucky. If I had decided to become president of GE, get elected to the Senate, and then become an astronaut, that might not have happened. Perhaps there's a life lesson in there somewhere.

There are many Asperger's and autism resources available now, and more appear every day. As a starting point, I recommend checking out OASIS, the Online Asperger Syndrome Information and Support site at www.udel.edu/bkirby/asperger/. OASIS founder Barb Kirby cowrote a book that I found helpful, *The OASIS Guide to Asperger Syndrome* (Crown, 2001).

Local Asperger support groups can be an important resource for parents of children with Asperger's and adults who grapple with it. In my area, there's the Asperger's Association of New England, with a website at aane.autistics.org. There are similar organizations in many big cities throughout the United States. Keep in mind, though, that many Aspergians are still "in the closet," so you may not see as many people as you'd expect at such groups. Until my brother publicized my condition in *Running with Scissors* (St. Martin's Press, 2002), I would never have participated in such a group. It was only the positive feedback from his book that gave me the courage to do so.

Psychologist Tony Attwood has written a number of excellent books that describe Asperger's from a mental health professional's point of view, and he's online at www.tonyattwood.com.au. It was his book *Asperger's Syndrome* (Jessica Kingsley, 1998) that introduced me to my condition. His latest work is *The Complete Guide to Asperger's Syndrome* (Jessica Kingsley, 2007).

Temple Grandin's stories about her life with autism should not be missed. I particularly like *Animals in Translation* (Scribner, 2005) and *Thinking in Pictures* (Vintage, 2006). She's also got a website, www.templegrandin.com. I also enjoyed autistic savant Daniel Tammet's book, *Born on a Blue Day* (Free Press, 2007). He's online at www.optimnem.co.uk.

Dawn Prince-Hughes has written several interesting books. *Songs of the Gorilla Nation* (Harmony, 2004) came out a few years ago, and her new book, *Passing as Human,* will be published by Harmony in 2008.

Although it's a work of fiction, *The Curious Incident of the Dog in the Night-Time* (Doubleday, 2003) contains many fascinating insights from author Mark Haddon's work with autistic kids.

Finally, my brother is online at www.augusten.com, and I'm at www.johnrobison.com.

About the Author

JOHN ROBISON lives with his wife and son in Amherst, Massachusetts. His company, JE Robison Service, repairs and restores fine European automobiles. Visit his business website at www.robisonservice.com and his author website at www.johnrobison.com.